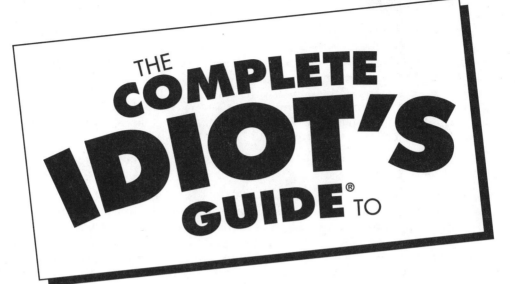

THE COMPLETE IDIOT'S GUIDE® TO

Awakening Your Spirituality

by Jonathan Robinson

alpha books

Macmillan USA, Inc.
201 West 103rd Street
Indianapolis, IN 46290

A Pearson Education Company

THE COMPLETE IDIOT'S GUIDE TO and Design are registered trademarks of Macmillan USA, Inc.

International Standard Book Number: 0-02-863826-3
Library of Congress Catalog Card Number: Available from the Library of Congress.

02 01 00   8 7 6 5 4 3 2 1

Interpretation of the printing code: The rightmost number of the first series of numbers is the year of the book's printing; the rightmost number of the second series of numbers is the number of the book's printing. For example, a printing code of 00-1 shows that the first printing occurred in 2000.

Printed in the United States of America

Note: This publication contains the opinions and ideas of its author. It is intended to provide helpful and informative material on the subject matter covered. It is sold with the understanding that the author and publisher are not engaged in rendering professional services in the book. If the reader requires personal assistance or advice, a competent professional should be consulted.

Publisher
Marie Butler-Knight

Product Manager
Phil Kitchel

Managing Editor
Cari Luna

Acquisitions Editors
Mike Sanders
Susan Zingraf

Development Editor
Michael Thomas

Production Editor
Christy Wagner

Copy Editor
Faren Bachelis

Illustrator
Jody Schaeffer

Cover Designers
Mike Freeland
Kevin Spear

Book Designers
Scott Cook and Amy Adams of DesignLab

Indexer
Angie Bess

Layout/Proofreading
John Etchison
Ayanna Lacey
Stacey Richwine-DeRome

Contents at a Glance

Part 1: What Do You Seek?   1

  1 Defining the Target   3
*What is spirituality? It's a way to quiet your mind, open
your heart, and connect with something beyond your ego.*

  2 Keys to the Kingdom   13
*All spiritual traditions emphasize certain traits helpful to
seekers. Learn eight of the most important and how to develop them.*

  3 Diving into Now   23
*Now is all there is. By becoming fully present to your life
and listening to your intuitive guidance, you can avoid a
lot of trouble.*

  4 The World According to Awareness   35
*Learn how to grow your innate pure awareness and break
free of the prison of thoughts you normally live in.
This is a line about Chapter 14 that is a little bit lomger.*

Part 2: Different Shades of Light   43

  5 The Way of the West   45
*A little background on the unique and helpful aspects of
the three main Western religions: Judaism, Christianity,
and Islam.*

  6 The Way of the East   57
*A little background on the unique wisdom of three of the
main Eastern religions: Hinduism, Buddhism, and
Taoism.*

  7 Twelve Steps to Transformation   69
*From Alcoholics Anonymous to every other twelve-step
program, what is it that keeps this spiritual process alive
and well?*

  8 The Way of Devotion   79
*Devotion is a great way to open up the heart and let God
slip in. Fortunately, various traditions have developed a
science of devotion that can be helpful to you.*

Part 3: Spiritual Disciplines   89

  9 The Wonderful World of Prayer   91
*There are many ways to pray. Learn why this method is
found in every tradition, and how to revitalize your prayer
life.*

10 The Significance of Service   103
Service is natural, but our minds get in the way. Learn to overcome such obstacles and make service a joyous part of your path.

11 The Art of Meditation   113
There are many ways to meditate. Choose from the many methods offered here and begin the process of quieting that chatterbox you live with (your mind).

12 Body-Centered Practices   125
From yoga to breathing methods to whirling dervishes, your body can be a valuable assistant in connecting to Spirit.

Part 4: Using Negativity to Develop   135

13 Using Negativity as Rocket Fuel   137
You can use negative feelings as a way to alert yourself to your shortcomings as well as help awaken yourself out of blame, denial, and other inner obstacles.

14 The Yoga of Relationships   147
Relationships are like the yoga of the West. Learning how to use honesty and vulnerability in relationships can help to accelerate your growth.

15 Selves of Lead   157
Certain parts of you may be blocking your peace of mind. Learn how to watch these parts, identify them, and lessen their power over you.

16 Turning Lead into Gold   167
You can use ordinary life to turn negative feelings into greater presence. You can also grow qualities that will serve you spiritually.

Part 5: Experiencing the Sacred in Daily Life   177

17 The Alchemy of Money   179
Money can be a great aid in spiritual awakening—if you use it properly. Learn about money traps to avoid and smart ways to invest in your soul.

18 Work as a Spiritual Path   189
If you do what you love, you don't have to work for a living! Find out how to follow your intuition into finding your right livelihood.

19 Aligning with the Divine 199
Spirituality can be joyous. Learn how to use gratitude and the appreciation of art, music, and beauty as a way to feel closer to God.

20 From Fear to Magic 207
By facing small fears, pursuing meaningful goals, and opening up to your inner child, you can move toward a more expanded life.

Part 6: Spiritual Accelerators 215

21 Retreats and Workshops 217
When you need a lift, it's important to know where to go. Here's helpful advice on what's out there and how to choose what's right for you.

22 Back to School: Students, Teachers, and Groups 227
Once you become serious about your growth, finding a teacher and/or group of like-minded souls is imperative. Here's what to keep in mind on your search.

23 Enjoying Sacred Space 237
From power spots to pilgrimages, it's helpful to know how to find both an external and internal space to tap into the reservoir of peace within.

24 Going Beyond the Body 247
Pain, sickness, and death can be great motivators and methods of spiritual awakening—if you know how to make use of them.

Part 7: Spiritual Inspiration 255

25 Inspiring Movies and Books 257
In an often cynical world, consistent inspiration is a must. Here are a bunch of great suggestions, including how to best make use of them.

26 The Creative Spirit 267
God is not the only one who can create. So can you! Learn how to use your creative spark to bring you in closer connection to your spirit.

27 Sex, Drugs, and Rock 'n' Roll 277
You can use these powerful "methods" to simply feel better, or as spiritual methods of great power. Here's how to use them for your growth.

28 Final Words of Wisdom   287
    Whenever possible, learn what works from the experts.
    Many wise spiritual people offer their best piece of advice
    for those seeking Spirit.

Appendixes

    A From Allah to Zen: Glossary   299

    B Surfing to Enlightenment   305

    C Everything Explained in 800 Words   311

       Index   313

Table of Contents

Part 1: What Do You Seek?   1

1 Defining the Target   3

Show Me the Spirit 4
  Knowing Your Target *4*
  Asking Questions, Finding Answers *4*
Spiritual Without Spirit 6
Wayward Hope...7
The Cosmic Carrot and Stick..............................8
What to Expect When You're Expecting...............9
  How to Be a Spiritual Jerk *9*
  Out of Control *10*
Being a Spiritual Scientist 11

2 Keys to the Kingdom   13

Honesty Will Set You Free 14
The Power of Humility 15
Use Humor to Become More Fully *You* 16
Ya Gotta Have Courage 17
Catch 'Em with Kindness 18
The Fervent and the Urgent 19
The One in Wonder...20

3 Diving into Now   23

The Present of the Present................................23
Into Inner Presence 24
  Into Intuition *25*
  Is It Intuition? *26*
  Listening for Intuition *27*
Going out of Your Mind 28
  Staying Awake *28*
  Getting Lost *29*
Know About Flow 29
  Going with the Flow...................................*29*
  Feeling the Flow *31*
Creating a More Perfect Union 31

4 The World According to Awareness   35

The Parade of Selves 36
Taking Off the Tinted Glasses 37
How to Be Nobody 38
Waking Up in Jail 39
Breaking Out of Jail 40

Part 2: Different Shades of Light   43

5 The Way of the West   45

One Family..46
Judaism: The Ultimate Legal Contract 47
  God Makes a Deal 47
  Law Leads to Love 48
Christianity: Love Fulfills the Law 49
  Love Fulfills the Law 50
  The Cry of Christianity 51
  Opening to Spirit 51
Islam: The Way of Surrender 52
  The People of the Book 53
  The Is of Islam..54
  The Five Pillars 54
  Sufism, the Mystical Branch....................55

6 The Way of the East   57

The Here of Hinduism 58
  The Many Faces of God 59
  The Final Goal of Liberation 60
The Science of Buddhism 61
  Buddha's Teachings 62
  Is Buddhism a True Religion? 64
  Buddhism Today 64
The Now of Taoism...65
  The Contribution of Chuang Tzu 66
  The Importance of Yin-Yang...................67

7   Twelve Steps to Transformation   69

A Framework for Recovery 70
  The Twelve Steps Approach *71*
  Step by Step *71*
Using the Steps 73
Caring for Others..74
Seeing It as It Is 75
The Flip Side 76
What Is Addiction? 76
Fixing What Is Broken..77

8   The Way of Devotion   79

The Hindu Science of Devotion 80
  The Devoted..*80*
  The One in the Many *80*
Emotional Buddhism...81
Devoted to the Guru in You 82
The Devotional Christian 84
The Technology of Devotion...86
  Cleansing Rituals *86*
  Chanting *87*

Part 3: Spiritual Disciplines   89

9   The Wonderful World of Prayer   91

Questions Are the Answer 91
Prayer as a Cosmic Proposal 93
The Many Faces of Prayer 94
  How Hindus Pray..*94*
  How Jews Pray..*95*
  The Prayer Life of Muslims *96*
  Christians and Prayer..*97*
Let Thy Will Be Done 97
Making Space for Quiet Time 98
How Do I Pray? 99

10 The Significance of Service   103

What Is Service?..103
Service Comes Naturally 105
Obstacles to Service 107
How Can I Serve?..109
Service and the Path 111

11 The Art of Meditation   113

Meditation and Your Mind 114
Transcendental Meditation 115
   Meditating the TM Way......................................*116*
   Consistency: The Key *117*
Contemplating Your Navel 117
Visualization Meditations 118
   The Pure Love Meditation....................................*119*
   Pure Love Variations *119*
Meditation for People Who Can't Sit Still 120
   Questions and Answers *120*
   Staying Active *121*
Initiation Meditations 122

12 Body-Centered Practices   125

Yoga for Beginners...126
Qigong and the Body Electric 127
Martial Arts 129
Is T'ai Chi for Me? 130
The Bridge of Breath 131
The Wonders of Whirling 133

Part 4: Using Negativity to Develop   135

13 Using Negativity as Rocket Fuel   137

How to Not Learn from Life 138
What You Resist Tends to Persist............................139
   Holes in the Balloon...*140*
   The Signposts..*141*

What's the Point? 142
Getting a Wake-Up Call 144
   Negative Alarm Clocks 144
   The Alarm Clock in Action 145

14 The Yoga of Relationships 147

Making Shadows Visible 148
The Path of Radical Honesty 149
Being Right vs. Being Loved 150
Overcoming Separateness 151
Expanding Love Through Awareness 153
Overcoming Judgment 154

15 Selves of Lead 157

The Hurried Task Completer 158
The Blaming Excuse Creator 159
The Anxious Stimulation Filler 160
The Looking Stupid Avoider 161
The Idle Worrier 162
The Righteous Winner 163
The Know-It-All Judger 164

16 Turning Lead into Gold 167

Lightening the Lead Through Disidentification 168
Inoculating Yourself from a Self's Effect 169
Watching a Self Until It Disappears 170
Work on Small Things 171
Do Sweat the Small Stuff 172
Feeding Selves Deliberately 173
Relax into the Gold 174

Part 5: Experiencing the Sacred in Daily Life 177

17 The Alchemy of Money 179

The Mission of Money 180
Money Traps 181
   Not Enough 182
   Attachment 182

Selfishness and Arrogance..*182*

Laziness..*183*

Money Miracles 183

The Road Less Traveled—to Riches 184

Tithing and Other Experiments 185

18 Work as a Spiritual Path 189

Right Livelihood 190

Working on Your Self...191

Learning on the Job—About Yourself *191*

Facing Your Fears...*192*

Making Your Vocation Your Vacation..............................194

Getting Hotter, Getting Colder *194*

The Moses Model *194*

God Is My Boss 195

Giving to God *196*

Letting Go *197*

19 Aligning with the Divine 199

Thank God for Gratitude...200

Thanking, Not Asking *200*

Thank-You Prayer *201*

Flowers Through the Concrete 202

Beauty Is Soul Deep 203

Everything's Perfect 204

20 From Fear to Magic 207

The Way of the Easiest Thing 208

Risking Your Way into Life 209

Facing Your Fears...*209*

Getting Stronger *209*

Living Your Dreams 210

Scheduling Your Spontaneity 211

The Inspiration of Conversation......................................212

Ask Big Questions *212*

Exploring the Depths *213*

Part 6: Spiritual Accelerators   215

21 Retreats and Workshops   217

The What and Why of Retreats and Workshops 217
Spiritual Retreats 218
So Many Choices *220*
Finding a Retreat *222*
Spiritual Workshops...223
Choosing a Workshop *223*
Don't Become Addicted *224*
Finding a Workshop *224*
Go for It! *225*

22 Back to School: Students, Teachers, and Groups   227

Why Be a Student? 228
The Challenge of Dependence *229*
Being a Student of Life *230*
Who and Where Are Teachers? 230
Looking for a Teacher *231*
Recognizing a Teacher *232*
How Teachers Can Help *233*
Spiritual Groups..234

23 Enjoying Sacred Space   237

Altars 237
Your Own Sacred Space *238*
Community Altars *239*
Tuning in to Sacred Space Outdoors...........................239
Spiritual Monuments...240
Ley Lines and Power Spots 241
Alfred Watkins..*241*
Dowsing and Mapping *242*
Energy Vortexes 242
Pilgrimages: Travel with a Special Purpose 243
The Pilgrimage in History....................................*243*
A Few of My Favorite Pilgrimage Destinations *244*

24 Going Beyond the Body   247

Death: The Cosmic Shake-Up of Old Routines.............247
The Miracle of Life...............................248
Death as a Part of Life..........................248
Studying Death While Alive 249
The Hospice Example..............................250
"Little Deaths" 251
Losing Control.....................................251
We Are Not Our Pain................................253

Part 7: Spiritual Inspiration   255

25 Inspiring Movies and Books   257

Inspiring Movies 258
Movies to Tickle Your Funny Bone 258
Spiritual "Drama" Movies 260
Movies of Hope and Joy 262
Reading Your Way to Spirit 264

26 The Creative Spirit   267

The Magic of Creativity............................268
The Artistic Calling 268
The Product vs. the Process......................269
Opening to Creation 270
The Inner Critic 270
Liberating Ourselves 271
Creating Our Lives.................................271
Inviting Creativity into Your Life 272
Overcoming Resistance 273
Art and Healing 273
Extraordinary Forces.............................274
The Shadow Side 275

27 Sex, Drugs, and Rock 'n' Roll   277

Tantra: The Spirituality of Ecstasy................278
Sacred Sexuality 279
Circular Breathing 280
Slow-Motion Love.................................281

From Acid to Zinc 281
The Muse in Music 283
The Romance of Dance 284

28 Final Words of Wisdom 287

Lynn Andrews 288
Pat Boone...289
Joan Borysenko 289
Levar Burton 290
Mantak Chia 290
Deepak Chopra, M.D. 290
Alan Cohen 291
Ram Dass 291
Bruce Davis 292
Wayne Dyer 292
Wayne Farrell 293
Louise Hay 293
The Dalai Lama 293
Kenny Loggins 294
Dan Millman 294
Bernie Siegel, M.D. 294
Marsha Sinetar 295
Charles Tart 295
Mother Teresa 296
Marianne Williamson 296
Jonathan Robinson 297

Appendixes

A From Allah to Zen: Glossary 299

B Surfing to Enlightenment 305

C Everything Explained in 800 Words 311

Index 313

Foreword

What does the term "spirituality" bring to mind? To one person, spirituality may imply actions such as meditation, yoga, chanting, or prayer. To another, spirituality may mean listening to an inner voice, or getting in touch with one's honest feelings. To many, spirituality is synonymous with "religion." As a result, their opinion about spirituality is colored by positive or negative experiences with a church, temple, or synagogue. Spirituality, depending upon your perspective and beliefs, may conjure images of angels, Jesus, menorahs, crosses, crystals, and other symbols of the Divine.

Regardless of your religious or spiritual background or beliefs, we can all probably agree that it is a vast and vital topic. Vast because it touches all aspects of life, impacting our family, career, and community. And vital because of the many studies showing that people with a spiritual foundation often live healthier, happier, and longer lives.

Because spirituality is such a broad and important topic, it's easy to feel overwhelmed by the many avenues for spiritual exploration. One look at the many spiritual books, workshops, and tapes currently available, and you're likely to throw up your hands and say "Where do I start?"

Such questions, even when rhetorically posed, are always answered by heaven. In fact, you may be holding this book in your hands as an answer to your prayer for guidance on the spiritual path. After all, every request for help is always answered, sometimes by receiving information through books that just "happen" to appear in our life.

If you are like many people during the current "spiritual renaissance," you feel drawn to explore spirituality. Perhaps you've watched a friend become happier and healthier through her spiritual practices. Or you've had a profoundly mystical experience, and you want to learn more about the esoteric nature of life. Maybe a spiritual book or movie has piqued your interest.

Regardless of the reasons you are led to explore spirituality, *The Complete Idiot's Guide to Awakening Your Spirituality* is an excellent guide. The phrase "spiritual path" is a misnomer, implying that there is only one road. Actually, there are countless paths that lead to the discovery of Spirit. In this book, you'll gain understanding about many of those roads that you could travel. Think of this book as a travel guide, giving you an overview of the rainbow of experiences you could explore in greater depth on your own.

Through his travels as both spiritual student and teacher, Jonathan Robinson has learned about the common questions that are asked along the spiritual pathways. He's asked the same questions as you. And although he doesn't claim to know all the answers, he certainly is highly qualified to tell you about the routes that can lead you to discover your own answers.

So, what does spirituality mean to you? By the end of this book, you'll likely have a clearer picture of this complex topic. To me, spirituality means peace of mind and joy. As a psychotherapist, I've found that the only route to inner peace and happiness is through spiritual means. Consequently, all of my personal and professional work involves spiritual practices such as meditation, prayer, yoga, and spending time daily in nature. These actions are the route that I personally have found as keys to my own consistent sense of joy and peace of mind. And my prayer for you is that you find a route for yourself that feels comfortable and natural.

The spiritual pathways aren't a panacea or a feel-good-fast method. There certainly are moments of doubt and sadness as one traverses within. Yet, like any life-altering journey, the best part of the trip is when we return home. Finding our inner joy and peace of mind *is* our return to home. Since our true self—as our Creator made us—is already joyful and peaceful, our spiritual journey doesn't *change* us so much as it awakens us to *knowing who we already are.*

Your homecoming on your journey is a reunion with your true self, and understanding how powerful, creative, intelligent, healthy, and abundant you and your life already are. This realization allows the experience and manifestation of those God-given qualities to come forward. And far from making you arrogant, this insight helps you to appreciate that every living being shares the beauty of the Divine.

So, no matter which of the pathways described in this book you choose to travel, may you enjoy your journey thoroughly!

Doreen Virtue, Ph.D.

Doreen Virtue holds Ph.D., M.A., and B.A. degrees in Counseling Psychology, and she blends spirituality and psychology in her counseling, writing, and speaking work. She is the daughter of a Christian Science practitioner, a fourth-generation metaphysician, and the former director of two inpatient psychiatric hospital units specializing in women's issues and eating disorders.

Dr. Virtue has appeared on *Oprah, CNN, Good Morning America, The View,* and other television and radio programs. Her work has been featured in *Redbook, McCall's, Vegetarian Times, USA Today,* and other publications. Dr. Virtue's best-selling books include *Divine Guidance, Angel Therapy, Healing with the Angels, Divine Prescriptions,* and *Angel Visions.* She gives seminars worldwide on spiritual growth issues. For information on her books, tapes, or workshops, please visit www.AngelTherapy.com.

Introduction

Telling you about spirituality is a bit like talking about water while lying in the middle of the ocean. God, Spirit, whatever you want to call it, is everywhere, but practically no one experiences God's peace and love most of the time. Many people know a lot *about* spirituality (in terms of ideas and beliefs), but have very little experience of what it's like to *feel connected* to their soul or spiritual essence in their daily lives. If that describes you, then this book was written with you in mind. It's a practical guide to knowing various approaches and methods to feeling more connected to "the kingdom of heaven within" while living in a fast-paced world.

Hey, Who Is This Hot Shot?

If I were you, I'd want to know what makes the author of this book think he can "tell me a thing or two" about the ultimate source of life. Good question.

Well, like you, I'm just a regular person trying to find more peace and love in a difficult world. I'm not an enlightened being. Sorry. Yet, for the past 25 years of my life I've been on an intense spiritual search, often spending months or years in spiritual communes or monasteries. In addition, I've been blessed to enjoy time with many of the foremost spiritual leaders of our day. From my interviews with people such as the late Mother Teresa, the Dalai Lama, Deepak Chopra, Marianne Williamson, Wayne Dyer, and dozens of others, I've come to learn what seems to help people know God, and what doesn't. In spiritual growth workshops I lead around the world, I've also noticed what ideas and methods have had the greatest impact in helping people enjoy a deeper connection to their spiritual essence. I'm not a guru, but I hope I can provide you with many practical ideas and methods that will save you a lot of time and energy.

How to Use This Book

Since spirituality *is* such a huge subject, feel free to choose the ideas and methods that feel right to you at this time, and simply skip over what doesn't seem to fit. Although I recommend you read this book from start to finish, you're welcome to do whatever works best for you. If you want to skip to a section or chapter that especially sparks your interest, I promise I won't try to make you feel guilty.

The book is divided into seven parts. Each part includes a combination of helpful ideas and information, as well as specific methods you can do to accelerate your journey toward being a mystic.

Part 1, "What Do You Seek?" describes the importance of first defining what God, mysticism, and spirituality are, so that you'll be able to "hit" your target. You'll learn what to expect on the spiritual journey, and why spiritual growth is important. I'll describe the many benefits you can expect to reap from your spiritual awakening, and the eight essential characteristics of a successful spiritual seeker. You'll discover what keeps you from feeling your soul essence in every moment, and how you can see, understand, and overcome the many inner obstacles that keep you from being fully present in blissful connection to your Creator.

In **Part 2, "Different Shades of Light,"** I'll take you on a whirlwind tour of six different religions and how they view God and mysticism: Christianity, Buddhism, Islam, Judaism, Taoism, and Hinduism. There are many paths up the spiritual mountain. I'll discuss how each path is really a metaphor for different ways to know one's spiritual essence. From this overview, you'll have a better understanding of various ways to view the spiritual journey. I'll discuss the relatively new path of twelve-step programs, and how they can be used on their own or in conjunction with other spiritual systems. Last, I'll explain the path of devotion. In Christian terminology, this means you'll learn how to be more receptive to God's "energy," or "Holy Spirit," and what that feels like.

Part 3, "Spiritual Disciplines," tells you about the importance and techniques for overcoming our ego-based rational minds and sense of isolation. All spiritual traditions agree that service, prayer, and meditation are important components of spiritual growth. I'll discuss why these are so necessary, and how you can incorporate them into your busy lifestyle. We'll look at various ways to meditate and pray, and what to expect when first beginning any spiritual discipline. Finally, you'll learn about six body-centered practices that can help you grow stronger—both physically and spiritually.

Part 4, "Using Negativity to Develop," explains the purpose of negative emotions in one's spiritual growth. I talk about how to interpret negativity in a way that's beneficial, and how to use one's shortcomings and bad feelings as a way to awaken. You'll learn about the power of honesty to accelerate your spiritual progress in your relationships, and about specific parts of yourself that can greatly interfere with your inner journey. I'll discuss how to be aware of your shortcomings in a way that tends to make them shrink in size. Finally, you'll discover the art of inner alchemy—turning your negativity into greater presence and peace through the process of sensing your body.

Part 5, "Experiencing the Sacred in Daily Life," describes the need for quick methods for raising one's "spiritual vibration" and awareness. In the modern world, most of us have little time to spare. Therefore, we need ways to connect with the peace within while sitting in traffic, waiting at the doctor's office, or making dinner. In this section, you'll learn how facing small fears can help create magic moments that aid you to feel more vibrantly alive and closer to God. I'll present how you can make use of gratitude as a practical and effective way to align with the Divine. You'll also learn powerful ways to bring spiritual principles and methods into your pursuit of money, and how your job can be a great training ground for deepening your spiritual connection.

Part 6, "Spiritual Accelerators," offers a brief tour of the pros and cons of spiritual teachers, groups, retreat centers, and workshops. You'll learn how to best make use of such resources, and how to go about finding what's most appropriate for you. You'll learn how to make use of pain, old age, and dying as part of your spiritual journey. I'll discuss the importance of ritual, as well as the benefits of creating sacred space.

Part 7, "Spiritual Inspiration," describes ways to easily stay inspired on your journey so that you'll be motivated to keep moving forward. I'll discuss how to best make use of movies and books, and I'll list some that you are likely to find inspiring. You'll discover how creativity is part of the inner journey, and how you can use your creative talents to bring you closer to the ultimate Creator. The ability to use things such as drumming, dancing, and even sexuality to further inspire you on your spiritual journey is also covered. Finally, the book ends with words of wisdom from more than 20 well-known spiritual experts expressing what they consider to be the most important aspect of the spiritual journey.

Spiritual Wisdom

Throughout this book, you'll find four types of sidebar information to help enhance your spiritual understanding and wisdom.

From Allah to Zen

These boxes provide definitions for spiritually related terms. Contemplating their meaning can be a spiritual exercise in itself.

Cosmic Potholes

These cautionary boxes contain information that can help you avoid making the many mistakes I've made, or the mistakes other spiritual seekers have made.

Heavenly Helpers

These boxes contain simple, practical tips to help keep you on the high road.

Amazing Grace

These boxes contain spiritual anecdotes, miracle stories, or interesting information to inspire, educate, and entertain you.

Acknowledgments

It took a dedicated group of people to put this book together. Although I get credit for being the author, this book and its contents would not be possible without the help, knowledge, and inspiration of many spiritual seekers.

First and foremost, I'd like to thank my teacher, Justin Gold. Your consistent help, caring, and wisdom have changed my life, as well as the lives of many people I love. Thank you. Thank you.

Next, Paula Domalewski's help was indispensable as an overall assistant editor, and as a writer for Chapter 22.

Various people helped me to research, write, or provide comments on various chapters. Along these lines, I wish to thank the following people for the following chapters:

Katy Jacobson for her helpful attitude and immense contribution to Chapters 12, 16, and 24.

Nancy Ingoldsby for her willingness to persevere and contribute via Chapters 5 and 6.

Lisa French for her flawless help with Chapter 10.

Corinne Boyle for her absolute willingness to be of assistance whenever I asked.

Ron Moreland for his dogged determination to get Chapter 7 just right.

Tricia True for her relentless enthusiasm to research and contribute to Chapter 9.

David True for his help and receptivity to learn while researching Chapter 25.

Jim Griffith for committing to Chapter 21 over and over again.

Karen May for being almost invisibly helpful and impeccable with Chapter 23.

And Joe Bernard for growing through the process of getting Chapter 26 completed.

I also wish to thank the people at Macmillan Publishing for their help, especially Susan Zingraf for her support and suggestions, and Mike Thomas for his wonderful editorial assistance.

Technical Editor for Chapters 1 Through 7

Dr. Timothy Conway reviewed Chapters 1 through 7 of the manuscript to ensure the accuracy of information presented.

Dr. Conway received his Bachelor's degree in Religious Studies at U.C. Santa Cruz, and his Master's and Doctorate at the California Institute of Integral Studies. Besides being a noted scholar in the field of Religious Studies and spirituality, Dr. Conway is also the author of the book, *Women of Power and Grace: Nine Astonishing, Inspiring Luminaries of Our Time.*

When he's not writing books, Dr. Conway teaches classes on spirituality at such places as Pacifica Graduate Institute, Antioch University, and Santa Barbara City College. Timothy has been a researcher/participant of spiritual traditions for nearly 30 years, with a special emphasis on Advaita Vedanta, Buddhism, Taoism, Sufism, and Mystical Christianity and Judaism.

Trademarks

All terms mentioned in this book that are known to be or are suspected of being trademarks or service marks have been appropriately capitalized. Alpha Books and Macmillan USA, Inc., cannot attest to the accuracy of this information. Use of a term in this book should not be regarded as affecting the validity of any trademark or service mark.

Part 1

What Do You Seek?

Spirituality can mean different things to different people. In this part, I'll give an overview of what I think people should "aim" for in their spiritual growth. In this fast-paced material world we live in, it's also relevant to explain why someone should invest time and energy in their soul and discuss what some of the benefits will be.

Spiritual seekers are people who are trying to uncover more of their innate goodness. Yet, spirituality is not simply psychological improvement or self help. Instead, it's an invitation to expand awareness, both in the material realm and in other realms. Like a guide providing a map, I will explain what expanded awareness is like, as well as some of the more traditional ways to get there. After reading about states of bliss and ecstasy, you may wonder why more people don't give this "spiritual stuff" a shot. Actually, a lot of it is hard work, and there are many ways to fall off the path. Having fallen off the path a number of times, I feel qualified to tell you about some of the major potholes to avoid!

Chapter 1

Spiny lobster...
spiral...
Ah! Here it is!

Dictionary

Defining the Target

In This Chapter

➤ What spirituality is and is not

➤ Why spirituality is so important in modern times

➤ What to expect from being a spiritual seeker

You've picked up a book on spirituality. Congratulations! It means you have a yearning for something more in life. You may not know exactly what you're looking for, but you're pretty sure there's more to life than just working, watching TV, buying stuff, and going to bed. Perhaps you want more peace, love, or purpose in your life. Perhaps you feel a higher calling, or maybe you've had some "weird" experiences that can't be easily explained in ordinary terms. Whatever your reason for picking up *The Complete Idiot's Guide to Awakening Your Spirituality,* I think you're in for quite an amazing ride.

Let me give you an analogy that describes the spiritual search: Imagine you live in an enormous mansion, with hundreds of wondrous rooms to explore, yet you can't find your way out of the dark, cold basement. Without knowing where the door is, you're stuck in a small space, performing the same routines day in and day out. In the material world, we learn how to better decorate the room we live in. We're taught how to rearrange the furniture and make things more comfortable and secure. But no one ever teaches us how to find the stairs or the door that will take us to higher, more beautiful rooms.

In this book, I'm going to give you a few "flashlights" to help you explore the many rooms of the "mansion" you live in. With these ideas and methods, my hope is that you'll become a daring explorer of your inner world. There is much that is possible once you have a desire to awaken a deeper spiritual experience in yourself.

Show Me the Spirit

One of the things that makes the spiritual journey difficult is that *spirituality* is so hard to define. The things of the material world are easy to measure, define, and control. Yet, spirit is another matter (pun intended).

Knowing Your Target

Historically, people have pursued various religious traditions to explore their spiritual essence. However, nowadays many people find the religious doctrines they grew up with to be of little help or inspiration. Therefore, an early part of your journey should be to decide specifically what you, as a spiritual seeker, are really after.

From Allah to Zen

Spirituality is any practice that helps a person to quiet his mind, open his heart, and connect with a being greater than his normal sense of self.

I first learned of the importance of knowing the target I was after when I was in college. My roommate was a varsity basketball player who was always challenging me to a game of one-on-one. I finally told him, "I'll play you on one condition. I get to place a one-ounce gadget anywhere on the court while we play." My roommate accepted the terms. When we got to the court, I took out a blindfold and placed it in a very strategic location—over his eyes. Then I said, "Let the games begin!"

Admittedly, it still ended up being pretty close. Yet I beat a great basketball player because I knew exactly what I was aiming for, and he didn't. The fact that I kept aiming in the right direction meant that I eventually scored some points.

As it is in basketball, so it is in the world of spirit. If you consistently head in the right direction, you'll be amply rewarded.

Asking Questions, Finding Answers

Many years ago, I wrote a book called *The Little Book of Big Questions*. It became a best-seller when Oprah Winfrey decided to devote an entire show to the questions in the book. When she'd ask members in the audience questions such as, "What is God?" or, "What's the goal of spirituality?" people would give very different answers. Oprah was surprised by the variety of answers, and the discussion was quite enlightening. I think it's important for people to ask themselves such questions, and decide for themselves what it is they seek.

Since I am your tour guide for this journey, I think you have a right to know what *I* feel spirituality is and is not. I think spirituality can be described as …

➤ Any practice that helps a person become more loving and peaceful.

➤ A process by which people connect more deeply with their inner source, whether they call that source their higher self, God, the Creator, or another name.

➤ A system by which people become more aware of themselves, their weaknesses, and the need for guidance from a source beyond their own ego.

➤ The ability to dive more deeply into the present moment, thereby overcoming the ego obstacles that cause us unnecessary suffering.

If any or all of these definitions work for you, you're welcome to borrow them. Because I'm trying to be a good "spiritual" person, I won't even charge you extra for borrowing them! Of course, you're welcome to create whatever definition or goal rings true in your own heart.

Amazing Grace

In India they have a story that says describing spirituality is like three blind men describing an elephant. One blind man, upon touching the trunk, describes the animal to be like a snake. The second man, upon touching the legs, describes it to be similar to a column of a building. The third man, while touching the body, describes it to be like a wall. What spirituality is to you depends upon what part of it you first encounter, and how much of it you explore.

While we're on the subject of definitions, you'll find that there are a lot of terms that refer to something bigger than our normal sense of self. Do words such as *God, Spirit, higher self, Jesus, Buddha-nature, higher power,* and *intuition* all refer to basically the same thing? I don't know for sure. Yet you'll find that I often use them interchangeably, as if they did refer to the same or a similar notion.

Rather than get lost in debating definitions, perhaps we can simply agree that all of these terms refer to some intelligence or power bigger than our ego. I suggest you pick a term that you feel comfortable with, and when I use one of the other terms, just translate it into the term you like.

From Allah to Zen

Religion is a personal or institutionalized system grounded in the belief in a supernatural power or creator of the universe.

Cosmic Potholes

Discussing religion and spirituality with people who feel they know everything can be a frustrating waste of time. Whatever you do, don't become a know-it-all yourself. When talking about God and other such topics, it's always best to have a humble, respectful attitude, and an open mind interested in learning.

Spiritual Without Spirit

In the word "spiritual," there is both the word "spirit" and the word "ritual." Unfortunately, many *religions* have managed to take the spirit out of spiritual—and are left with mere rituals that eventually lose their meaning.

Along with having a sense of what spirituality *is* to you, it's also important to have a sense of what it is *not*. Many people equate spirituality with sitting in a church service, listening to someone tell them how they have sinned. Others believe spirituality has something to do with a bearded old man who watches over them, or who lives in India and talks about transcendence.

People used to kill each other (and in some countries still do) over their differing opinions of the "right" way to follow a spiritual path. Since I'm writing a book on the topic, I admit I also have opinions on the right way to follow a spiritual path. You're welcome to believe whatever you feel works for you. However, I do feel there are some ideas, behaviors, and practices that may slow you down rather than help you along on your journey.

In my opinion, the *core* of spirituality is *not* related to any of the following:

➤ UFOs, aliens, or beings from the planet Vulcan

➤ Astrology, the zodiac, or what sign you were born under

➤ Following a dogmatic moral code (although spiritual people tend to have high moral standards)

➤ Psychic powers, occultism, or supernatural powers

Twenty-Five Guidelines for Spiritual Growth

1. **Find help.** Find a person or, better yet, a group of people who inspire you, challenge you, and can help you to become the person you want to be.

2. **Practice humility.** Try to avoid feeling better than people who are not consciously on a spiritual path. If your path leads you to feel more separate from others, you're probably moving in the wrong direction.

3. **Take risks.** Having an attitude in which you're willing to experiment, try new things, and face small fears is helpful in accelerating your growth.

4. **Practice honesty.** The more honest you are with yourself, the more likely you can avoid the problems of arrogance and separation that can hinder your spiritual progress.

5. **Develop humor.** An ability to laugh at yourself and at the many absurdities in the world is a great ally on the spiritual path.

6. **Nurture positive qualities.** Kindness, courage, compassion, sincerity, and curiosity are great allies on the spiritual journey. Nurture these qualities in yourself.

7. **Listen to intuition.** Your intuitive wisdom, or "still, small voice" within will feel "right" to you and is a way of keeping you honest and headed in the right direction.

8. **Watch your mind.** As you grow in awareness, your prison of thoughts becomes more obvious. Seeing your prison is a first step to becoming free of it.

9. **Observe devotion.** Opening your heart to God through the use of various devotional methods can be useful to many seekers.

10. **Experiment with prayer.** There are many ways to pray or converse with Spirit. As you try different approaches, note the way(s) that feel right or deepest to you.

11. **Practice service.** All spiritual traditions emphasize the importance of service. It helps to lessen one's sense of importance and connect more deeply with one's heart.

12. **Meditate consistently.** If prayer is talking to God, meditation is listening to God. Try different meditation methods, but choose one that helps you to consistently connect with the silence within.

alpha
books

13. **Develop body awareness.** By increasing your connection to your body through body-centered spiritual practices, you can increase your health, energy, and receptivity to Spirit.

14. **Use negative feelings.** Your negative feelings can be a signpost alerting you to shortcomings in yourself and can be a helpful "wake-up call" to become more present.

15. **Learn from relationships.** Relationships can be wonderful mirrors that help you to see yourself, and through the power of total honesty, can be a helpful path toward opening up to deeper levels of intimacy and vulnerability.

16. **Discover inner obstacles.** The "kingdom of heaven" is already within you. Your job is to identify the obstacles you have inside yourself that prevent you from feeling more connected to Spirit.

17. **Explore religions.** Each religious tradition is like a unique path up the spiritual mountain. By learning from them, you can find new ways to explore your spiritual self.

18. **Live simply.** Money can help or hinder your spiritual growth, depending on how you use it. Fortunately, by living a simple life, you can have less stress and more time for spiritual practices.

19. **Seek experts.** Constantly look for people who can teach you to be more kind, help you to increase your knowledge of a specific spiritual discipline, or enhance your wisdom.

20. **Find your calling.** By listening to your intuition and the messages the universe sends your way, you can better know what type of work you are best suited for and what work will lead to the greatest contribution.

21. **Practice appreciation.** You can feel more aligned with the Divine by focusing on gratitude and the beauty in people, nature, art, and music.

22. **Seek frequent inspiration.** If taken in with a reverent attitude, spiritually focused books and movies can be a helpful tool along the spiritual path. Nowadays, there is an immense amount of information and inspiration readily available.

23. **Explore creativity.** When you create, you come closer to the Creator. Let your ability to sing, write, dance, paint, or even cook a meal be an act of opening to Spirit.

24. **Create sacred space.** In this fast-paced world, you need to make sure you create both the internal and external space you need to commune with your soul.

25. **Prepare for the end of life.** Learn to use sickness, aging, pain, and the knowledge of death as a motivator and method for going deeper within the part of you that doesn't die.

➤ Positive thinking or attaining outward success

➤ Converting people to your way of thinking

➤ Creating nice surroundings or dressing in flowing robes

➤ Pretending to be nice when you feel a different way inside

➤ Going to a religious service because you're "supposed" to go

➤ Performing rituals that don't mean anything to you, such as mechanically reciting a prayer from a book

You could probably come up with a dozen other things that people often mistake for spirituality. The less time you spend on fringe "spiritual" pursuits, the more time you'll have to explore the real McCoy.

Wayward Hope

In this day and age, we place a lot of our hope for the good life on the pursuit of money. Most people feel that the more money they have, the more in control they are, and the better their life will be. Money and the world of control may take you to a comfortable life. But they can't take you to bliss, God, or a life of depth.

Besides being an author, I'm a psychotherapist and hypnotist. It never ceases to amaze me that hypnosis works so well. Unfortunately, hypnosis doesn't just work for people going to a therapist. You and I have also been hypnotized, since we were little kids, to believe certain things about ourselves. For example, in this culture we've been "hypnotized" to believe that happiness is best achieved by making more money or finding a perfect relationship. Then, when we wake up one day surrounded by our TVs, electric gadgets, and mate of 20 years, it's hard to understand why we're not truly happy and fulfilled.

I believe we're given life in order to grow spiritually. That is our inherent purpose. Yet, we're hypnotized to think that our purpose is to look beautiful, or make a living, or impress others, or all the other things we spend our time doing.

It's true that we do need a basic grounding in order to feel ready for spiritual exploration. We need a stable "launching pad" such as food, shelter, and a few friends. But once we have our launching pad,

Amazing Grace

One spiritual teacher I know said that people in the industrialized Western world are "money-realized beings" instead of "God-realized beings." He went on to explain that money is what's most real to many Westerners, whereas God is what is most real to many Easterners. He suggested that the West has to focus more on God, and the East more on finances in order to find the balance they each need.

Cosmic Potholes

There is always the temptation that, if we could simply change one thing in our life, such as our job, our mate, our health, and so on, we could find the peace we yearn for. Yet such thoughts are not true. There's always going to be unpleasantness in life, but peace is possible if you look for it where it truly exists—inside yourself!

it doesn't do much good to keep redecorating it—especially when there is so much to explore! We need to use our launching pad to launch a rocket ship to explore the cosmos. Once we place our hope in the world of Spirit rather than the world of control, life takes on a whole new possibility; we can explore the cosmos.

We live in the busiest culture in the history of humanity. Whereas we used to have a lot of time just to relax, enjoy our family and nature, and commune with Spirit, nowadays it seems that everybody is rushed. We're constantly distracted by the TV, the ringing phone, our to-do list, and a host of minor emergencies. In such a chaotic and busy era, it's necessary for us to come up with practical ways to reconnect with a deeper meaning, love, and peace that cannot be found in the material world.

The many methods and ideas in this book are aimed to help you awaken and explore your innate spiritual essence—even during a busy life.

The Cosmic Carrot and Stick

In my psychotherapy practice, I see a lot of people who are just beginning their spiritual search. They are often in the throes of a midlife crisis and don't know exactly what's wrong. My clients frequently feel a vague sense of failure and dissatisfaction. Often an event such as the loss of a job, a divorce, or the death of a loved one triggers their search for a deeper meaning to it all.

While they may feel like failures, to me, such people always look like successes. After all, they have reached a point where they have seen through the illusion of finding happiness in the material world alone. In a sense, they have reached a higher level of awareness.

Perhaps you are like many of my clients who feel unsatisfied with the daily grind. If so, your disappointment in the material world can be a great help in your spiritual search.

I have found that two things help to motivate people to really explore their spirituality. The first is a sense of dissatisfaction with how things are. The second is a longing for a deeper connection to God, love, and peace. The experience of suffering is like a prodding stick that can help you search for deeper truths. On the other hand, the heartfelt longing for Spirit and an eternal love can be like a cosmic carrot enticing you to stay on the path.

It can be helpful to write down specific reasons why you want to awaken your spirituality. What are the "sticks" in your life that motivate you to pursue something more? Likewise, it's also useful to write down what your hopes or wishes are in the world of Spirit. Do you want more peace, a deeper connection with people, a sense of wonder and magic? What exactly do you long for?

Making a list of the pain that provokes you and the hopes that you have can help you stay motivated and on course for your journey. Since we all have so many competing priorities, a written list can be a helpful reminder. If you don't want to make a written list, then consider discussing with your mate or a friend the sticks and carrots in your life. Some helpful questions to ask a friend or yourself in this regard are …

➤ What do I find disheartening about modern life?

➤ What do I dislike or find unsatisfactory about myself?

➤ When was a time my life had more depth and meaning, and what was I doing differently then?

➤ What is my hope or dream of what awakening spirituality could do in my life?

➤ What type of person would I really like to become?

As you ask yourself, or have someone else ask you these questions, feel free to talk about related questions or concerns. Part of a spiritual search is to *search,* and seek out hidden answers inside yourself. To use a cliché phrase from the old *Star Trek* television series, as a seeker your job is "To boldly go where no one has gone before."

What to Expect When You're Expecting

Being on a spiritual path can be a lot like being eternally pregnant. In some mysterious way, you may feel different than the people around you. You may find yourself going through rapid changes in your life, and the people close to you won't always be able to relate to what you're going through. It's tempting to begin to feel separate from people, and even self-righteous because you're growing and they're not. Sometimes, especially at the beginning of the spiritual journey, an increased sense of separation is inevitable. Yet the goal of spirituality is a lessening of separation—from other people as well as from God.

How to Be a Spiritual Jerk

When I began on my path at the age of 16, I quickly became a real jerk. While in the woods, I had a spontaneous mystical experience that proved to me that God existed. I was filled with bliss and ecstasy for a full day. It was like Paul on the road to Damascus.

Of course, the first thing I did was become an arrogant brat, making fun of all my friends and family for how meaningless their lives were without a spiritual foundation.

Heavenly Helpers

To know if you're getting off course on the spiritual journey, it can help to ask yourself, "Do I feel more separate from people?" If you do, you're probably faced in the wrong direction.

Needless to say, they did not enjoy my taunts. I took their lack of receptivity to mean I was clearly superior to them, which just made me feel even more isolated from everyone. My humble advice is to avoid doing what I did.

When pursuing your spiritual path, it's important to avoid feeling "better than" all the people who are not similarly inclined. Going to high school is not better than elementary school, it's just different. In a way, everyone is on a spiritual path, whether he knows it or not. It may be that your friend or mate, as part of his path, really needs to become a stockbroker before he can see through the illusions of the material world. It's hard enough to know your own path, much less the journey of another soul. Self-righteous indignation is never the sign of an enlightened soul, but merely the sign of a lack of compassion.

Out of Control

Another thing you can expect from being a true spiritual seeker will be extreme highs and lows in how you feel. Part of being a seeker is exposing yourself to a process outside of your control. That's how spiritual growth differs from self-help or psychological growth. In self-help, you're always in charge. Yet awakening your spirit means that you are forming a partnership with God (or whatever term you want to use). The Lord can work in mysterious ways, and sometimes the process can feel a bit out of control. You don't always get your own way.

Amazing Grace

According to polls, 95 percent of Americans believe in God, and about 50 percent have had a "transcendent mystical experience" at some time in their life. Since 1969, a movement called "transpersonal psychology" has attempted to validate and study higher states of consciousness and union with God.

I learned this lesson when a girlfriend unexpectedly left me. Using my psychology training, I had tried everything to keep the relationship together. I wanted it to go the way I wanted; I wanted to be in control. Yet, the Creator had different plans. After becoming exhausted by trying to keep the relationship together, I prayed to God to "do whatever was best." Lo and behold, the relationship soon totally fell apart.

Secretly, I was mad at God for not doing what I felt was best. But after about two months of intense grief, I noticed that I felt more compassionate toward people. I was kinder, and felt softer inside. Soon I was led to another partner who was much more appropriate for me, and who encouraged my spiritual pursuits (unlike my former partner). Had I gotten my way, I would have missed out on one of the most heart-opening experiences in my life.

Of course, being on the path is not always difficult. As you use the ideas and tools in this book, I hope you will experience more spontaneous moments of joy, intimacy, and union with a higher power. The good news is that you were born a spiritual being. You don't have to become something you're not. You need only take off the layers of falseness and protection that at one time served you, but which now keep you from a deeper connection to your source. At its core, spirituality is the art of becoming who you really are, more open to the childlike innocence that exists underneath your fears.

Being a Spiritual Scientist

In the last 100 years, science has made amazing progress toward discovering the secrets of the universe. Its main tool for doing so has been the use of experiments to prove or disprove various hypotheses. On the other hand, in the last 100 years, humanity has not progressed very much in terms of spiritual growth. I believe that part of the reason for this is that most seekers do not have an *experimental attitude* toward awakening their spirituality.

Having an experimental attitude means seeking answers the way a scientist would. You try various things to see what effect they have, even if you're pretty sure they won't have the effect you want.

Unfortunately, many seekers stop being seekers once they find a single thing that works for them. Then they fall into the routine of what they already know and find comfortable, and fail to keep moving forward. However, a true seeker is someone who is always trying to expand and deepen his knowledge of himself, his higher power, and the mysteries of the universe. To do that requires a humble heart and the willingness to try things out as an experiment, even if it is difficult, uncomfortable, or seems weird.

From Allah to Zen

Having an **experimental attitude** means trying something for a short period of time in order to learn new things, or have new experiences.

Many years ago, a well-respected spiritual teacher strongly suggested I try singing devotional songs to God. Being a rather intellectual person, I hated the idea. I always cringed when I saw other people sing those "mushy" songs. On my list of spiritual methods to try, singing devotional songs was just one notch above committing suicide. Yet, armed with an experimental attitude, I was willing to try it a couple of times.

Heavenly Helpers

To help you have more of an experimental attitude, you can ask yourself, "What might be a beneficial experience for me to have that would help me to grow?" Listen to your intuition, and be willing to explore new ideas, groups, and experiences that you used to avoid.

The second time I sang devotional songs with a group of people, I had the experience of being struck by an unexpected jolt of grace. I felt an energy surge through every cell in my body, then I began crying for more than 20 minutes. As my tears subsided, I looked at the teacher who suggested I try singing and said, "I think this method might be workable."

You just never know what method or idea will work for you until you give it a try. My hope is that you'll use the methods and ideas in this book with the same attitude. Give them your best shot. If they move you forward, great. If they don't, at least you'll have learned what doesn't work for you.

To awaken your spirituality, you have to keep moving forward. If you rest on your laurels too long, you start to lose your connection to "the kingdom of heaven within." Unfortunately, higher states of consciousness have very little shelf life. Therefore, it's important to always be looking for new, challenging, and growth-filled opportunities to become a wiser, stronger, more peaceful and loving person.

The Least You Need to Know

➤ Spirituality is the art of quieting your mind, opening your heart, and connecting to a deeper love and peace.

➤ It's important to know what you want in your search.

➤ People often place all their hope in the material world, and have little or no energy left for spirituality.

➤ Nowadays, because our culture is so busy and rushed, methods for quickly reaching a deeper love and peace are more necessary than ever.

➤ Try to avoid feeling better than other people who are not on a deliberate spiritual search.

➤ Having an experimental attitude and a willingness to try new things is helpful to accelerate your growth.

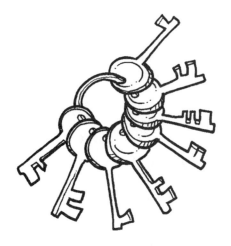

Chapter 2

Keys to the Kingdom

> ### In This Chapter
>
> ➤ What the spiritual experts agree on
>
> ➤ How and why to use honesty, humor, and humility as part of your guideposts along the spiritual path
>
> ➤ The importance of kindness, curiosity, courage, and a sense of urgency while pursuing your inner journey

For my book *The Experience of God*, I asked 40 spiritual experts 10 questions about their relationship with the Divine. I wanted to see if people from different religions or backgrounds really did things differently. For example, does a Christian pray in the same way as a Buddhist or a Muslim? Do they meditate in the same way? To my surprise, I found a surprising range of answers to the 10 questions I asked these spiritual leaders.

Although I found a wide variety of answers to my questions, I did find *some* areas of agreement. When people as different as the *Dalai Lama*, Pat Boone, Marianne Williamson, Deepak Chopra, and Wayne Dyer agree on something, you probably have an eternal truth! I believe that listening to such people is a great way to learn about spirituality, and when the experts agree on something, so much the better.

In my interviews with these 40 spiritual notables, one theme seemed to underline many of the answers I received. In almost every interview, they stressed how important it was to move toward certain character traits when pursuing the spiritual journey. By discussing in detail the seven core traits that almost all religious and spiritual notables agree on, I think you'll discover some valuable keys to the kingdom within.

From Allah to Zen

A **Lama** is a Buddhist monk of Tibet or Mongolia. The **Dalai Lama** is the exiled spiritual and political leader of Tibet. He is thought of as the 14th incarnation of the Buddha of compassion. In 1989, he won the Nobel Peace Prize for his efforts to peacefully resolve differences between Tibet and China.

Amazing Grace

Imagine a bicycle wheel with a lot of spokes all attached to a central hub. All the spokes enter the hub from different directions, yet they still unite at the hub of the wheel. In a similar way, each spiritual path has ideas, or "spokes," that start from a different place, but ultimately lead to the same central spiritual core.

Honesty Will Set You Free

In the Bible, Jesus says "the truth will set you free." Of course, he was right, but he left out an important point. The truth *will* set you free, but at first it will be as scary as hell, and will likely make you miserable. I assume Jesus knew that truth was scary, but thought it best for people to discover that part of the equation on their own!

Self-honesty is indeed difficult. Most people rationalize their behavior to avoid seeing their own faults. Yet, honesty is critical to spiritual growth. Unfortunately, it's easier to imagine you're a good person than to actually *be* a good person. Self-honesty can keep you from getting lost in your imagination and thinking you're making progress—when in fact you're not.

Many years ago, I lived in a spiritual growth commune that had a very wise, compassionate leader. Every once in a while, he would give someone in the group very honest feedback about his faults. Although his feedback was, in my opinion, always right on, the person in the "hot seat" would inevitably argue with him. He would rationalize his behavior, make excuses, and generally not see what was so clear for everyone else to see. After listening to all his excuses, this teacher would say, "If you think my description of this person is accurate, raise your hands." Everyone's hands would rise.

Of course, every now and then, *I* would end up in the hot seat. The leader of our spiritual group would tell me my faults—but he was always incredibly wrong about *me!* I would try to explain myself, but he'd simply ask others in the room to raise their hands if they thought I was the way he described me. Inevitably, every hand would rise. At first I thought it was a conspiracy, but I finally realized that I had hidden my faults from only one person—myself.

Since self-honesty is so hard to attain, you might try to get some help. Ask trusted friends or family members for their honest feedback on what your faults or shortcomings are. Tell them you're interested in being a better person, and that you'd appreciate their feedback on what you need to improve. They might give you great insight into yourself.

14

The Power of Humility

A friend of mine once said that the spiritual path is just one big humiliation after another. In a way, he was right. Our egos are the main thing that keep us feeling separate from each other and from God. Part of the goal of spirituality is to dismantle—or at least to not identify so strongly with—our ego. Unfortunately, that requires a lot of honesty, which inevitably leads to humility.

Humility is not self-hatred. It is simply a recognition of how vast our shortcomings are, how limited our abilities are, and how boundless and pure Spirit is.

In interviewing many spiritual leaders, I was often most struck by their *humility*. You might think that the Dalai Lama or the late Mother Teresa would give the impression that they know something you don't. However, that was not the case. Rather, what impressed me about such people was their childlike innocence and humility. It was their vulnerability and humanity that seemed to, ironically, imbue them with an aura of divinity.

Allah to Zen

Humility is the experience of being unpretentious, and being able to honestly see your own shortcomings. In addition, humility is the ability to put others "above" you by learning from them and serving them.

Amazing Grace

In an effort to remain humble before God, Saint Francis of Assisi would often give himself spiritual challenges. Since he was initially repulsed by lepers, he spent time caring for them. Once Francis started to become known as a great saint, he would sometimes put the newest member of his order in charge of his every action. Avoiding the leadership position helped Saint Francis to remain a humble servant of God.

In order to be humble, you not only have to be incredibly honest with yourself, but you also must be able to face personal challenges on a consistent basis. All great spiritual adepts, from Saint Francis to the Dalai Lama, have had to face great difficulty. From such challenges, a recognition of one's limitations and small place in the universe naturally results, and one becomes truly humble.

Troubles, tragedies, and challenges are akin to going to a spiritual gymnasium. When at the gym, it would be ridiculous to curse at the weights. After all, by lifting the weights, you grow stronger. The same is true in the gym of your life. As you rise above the weighty challenges that come your way, you become stronger and more humble. Many of the spiritual leaders I've met over the years attributed their connection to Spirit to the immense challenges they had faced in their lives.

In the material world, we're encouraged to be totally in charge. It feels good to be a big dog among smaller dogs. Yet, in the world of Spirit, being a small dog among bigger dogs is a more humble and better position for growth. After all, we *are* just little dogs in a big universe. A person who has faced difficulties and has been humbled by life exudes a power that touches the hearts of all he encounters.

Use Humor to Become More Fully *You*

If you're honest with yourself, and if you consistently face personal challenges, you'd better have a sense of humor. Otherwise, you could fall into cynicism, hopelessness, or a bunch of other attitudes that just aren't very funny. A sense of humor about yourself helps honesty and humility to develop. It makes life a little easier to handle. It can provide you with an instant hit of perspective, which is often needed as you grow spiritually.

Amazing Grace

The great Indian leader Mahatma Gandhi once said of himself, "I have only three enemies. My favorite enemy, the one most easily influenced for the better, is the British Empire. My second enemy, the Indian people, are far more difficult. But my most formidable opponent is a man named Mohandas K. Gandhi. With him I seem to have very, very little influence."

Imagine a black dot the size of a quarter on the page in front of you. If you brought the page up to your face until your eyeball touched that black dot, it would look as if your entire world were black—despite the fact that most of the page is white. In modern life it's easy to lose perspective. We tend to focus our eyes on the black dots in front of us, and miss the bigger picture. A sense of humor about life can be a great way to step back from the black dots that come our way. From a foot away, a quarter-sized dot isn't so dark and scary; from across a room, it's hardly noticeable. Spiritual adepts often use humor to gain this larger perspective.

When you can laugh at yourself and the many absurdities of life, you become more fully *you*. Almost all children laugh a lot, and their laughter makes it easier for them to recover from life's challenges. If you don't have a sense of humor, steal one from someone else. Like the measles, good humor is contagious and learnable. Listen to modern-day gurus of humor such as Bill Cosby, Jay Leno, Jerry Seinfeld, or whoever tickles your funny bone. Learn to look at the world in the slightly warped way that they do.

Recently I was speaking to a group of people on the importance of kindness and compassion. I gave the workshop participants an exercise to do while I made a telephone call in the next room. Unknown to me, my clip-on microphone was still on while I made the call, and the people in the lecture hall could hear every word I said to the travel agent who had managed to completely foul up my airline reservations. I was, shall we say, not exactly modeling kindness and compassion as I slammed down the phone. When my girlfriend (who was in the lecture hall) ran in with a horrified look on her face, I instantly knew what had happened.

As I walked back into the lecture hall, everyone's eyes glued to me, I knew that making excuses was not going to help. Only the ability to laugh at myself was going to restore my serenity or credibility. With a smile on my face I told the participants, "I have recently prayed to be more humble, and isn't it glorious how rapidly God responds!" We all laughed, and I apologized for failing to walk my talk.

A spoonful of laughter makes the medicines of life go down a lot easier.

Cosmic Potholes

Laughing at *yourself* lessens separation between you and others, but laughing *at* others increases it, and can be very hurtful. Be careful about using humor to make yourself feel superior at others' expense.

Ya Gotta Have Courage

In the movie *Damn Yankees,* there is a song that starts, "Ya gotta have heart." It's true, a good heart is a must on the spiritual path. Yet, you also "Gotta have courage." Your ability to face fears is a big aspect of the spiritual path.

You may have thought that spirituality was all about retreating from the world and creating a safe little haven. If so, you were mistaken. To unlock the basement of your mind and move to more beautiful rooms higher up, ya gotta face your fears. (Sorry. If I were God, I'd have created the world differently, but I wasn't consulted when the whole thing was set up.)

Since I'll be talking about how to grow spiritually by facing your fears in Chapter 20, "From Fear to Magic," for now I'll just say that courage can be an acquired trait. I used to be one of the most shy, fearful kids in the world. At age 12, I was so afraid, I couldn't even order my own ice cream cone at Baskin-Robbins. I would whisper my order to my dad, who would relay it for me. Yet once I understood that facing small fears was the accelerated path to growth, I began to take more risks.

I've also learned that courage is contagious. You can catch it by hanging around brave people. Despite my best efforts to stay stuck in my fears, as I began to hang out with spiritually advanced souls, a bit of their courage rubbed off on me.

Catch 'Em with Kindness

We all know that spirituality has a lot to do with love, kindness, and compassion. The Dalai Lama once said, "Kindness is my only religion."

An open and giving heart is often the most obvious characteristic of a spiritually advanced soul. Being kind and caring is in direct opposition to the selfishness we witness all around us. Fortunately, being kind to others almost always feels good, has no calories, is enjoyed by everyone, and has no negative side effects. Not many things in life can fit all those criteria!

Amazing Grace

Marianne Williamson, a popular New Age author, once said, "We were born to make manifest the Glory of God within us. As we are liberated from our own fears, our presence automatically liberates others." Nelson Mandela liked these words so much that he used them as part of his inaugural speech when he became the leader of South Africa.

In Chapters 8, "The Way of Devotion," and 10, "The Significance of Service," I'll go into more depth about the value and methods of growing a kind and generous heart. For now, just know that it can be a good measure of your spiritual progress. If over time you feel kinder and more compassionate toward people, you're probably on the train bound for glory. On the other hand, if you find that your heart beats only for yourself, then you're missing an essential ingredient of the "God formula."

Several years ago, the van several passengers and I were riding in hit a patch of ice and overturned. While glass was breaking and people were screaming, I was temporarily knocked unconscious and had what is often referred to as a near-death experience. During this experience, in which my life was being reviewed in front of my eyes, I was asked two questions by my higher self or God. Later, I found out that most people who have a near-death experience are asked the *same* two questions. Fortunately, none of us were permanently hurt, yet the two questions I heard still affect me today.

I want to tell you what those questions are so you can better study for the "final exam" of life. The first question was, "How well did you learn about being a kind and loving person?" The second question was, "How well did you use your gifts to contribute to other people and the world?" In a way, both questions are about love, compassion, and acting on our kind impulses. I think it's no coincidence that almost all spiritual paths have love and compassion as a central part of their teaching. You should, too.

Amazing Grace

According to many studies, people who are clinically dead for a short period of time seem to have remarkably similar experiences. Even people from different religions and atheists report similar experiences. For example, most people hear similar sounds, feel like they're going through a tunnel, see their life in review, are asked the same two questions, and observe a bright light that feels totally loving. Studies also show that people who have such experiences are greatly affected by them for the rest of their lives.

The Fervent and the Urgent

Many of the people I interviewed noted that a sense of urgency is a great assistance on the spiritual journey. One of the best spiritual growth tools available is to have a doctor tell you that you have three months to live. It's amazing how spiritually moti-vated a person can get under such circumstances! Unfortunately, such a motivational method has the unpleasant end result of having to die. The question is, "How can we have a sense of urgency without being so close to death?"

One way to obtain a sense of urgency is to simply *pretend* that you're close to death. Since none of us know when our time is up, it can be a helpful exercise to ask yourself, "What would I be doing if I had only six months to live?" When we have limited time, we tend to focus on what really matters to us, rather than on the trivialities of everyday life.

So, I'm asking you: What would *you* do with your last six months? As you do more of those activities, you will likely find a greater depth and spiritual connection in your life.

A famous story tells of a student who asks a spiritual teacher for the way to know God. The teacher says, "Meet me at the lake and I'll show you the

Heavenly Helpers

In his workshops, author Steven Levine asks people whom they would call if they had an hour left to live, and what they would say to them. Then he tells them to make the call right now. Whom would you call with an hour left to live, and what would you say? Try it. It will likely deepen your relationship to both God and the person you talk to.

19

Cosmic Potholes

While it's fine to feed a sense of urgency in yourself, trying to do so in others usually just leads to more separation. The best way to convince others of the urgency and value of spiritual growth is to become a loving, inspiring person yourself.

way to God." The student meets the teacher at the lake, and together they walk into the water until they are neck deep. Then, the teacher suddenly grabs the student's head and thrusts it underwater. After 30 seconds, the student struggles for air; after 60 seconds, he fights for air with absolutely all his effort. Finally, after 90 seconds he gets out from under the teacher's hold and gasps desperately for air. As he is gasping for air, the teacher calmly says, "When your desire for God is as urgent as your desire for that first breath, you will know God."

In my own spiritual search, I have seen that nothing is more important than a sincere and urgent desire for true connection to one's source. Whatever you can do to feed a sense of urgency in yourself is going to help quicken your growth.

The One in Wonder

Long-time adherents of a spiritual path tend to be constantly curious and full of wonder. The world is their sandbox, and like an innocent child, they enjoy exploring every nook and cranny. The advanced spiritual beings I've met have often seemed very childlike. They ask questions about things that most of us never think about. With the tool of curiosity as their guide, they are constantly learning about themselves, others, and the mysteries of creation.

Heavenly Helpers

To reawaken your sense of wonder, spend time with little kids, especially three- to six-year-olds. Try to see the world through their eyes. When they ask questions, attempt to feel the wonder they feel when discovering the answer to one of life's mysteries.

Curiosity is something we are all born with, but after many years of schooling, most people stop looking at the world through the eyes of wonder. I think curiosity allows us to grow at an accelerated rate during our first few years. Think about it. The difference in wisdom and maturity between a three-year-old and a five-year-old is vast. That's because, when we're young, we're constantly curious and desirous of new learning. However, the difference in wisdom between a 30-year-old and a 32-year-old is usually nothing. Somewhere along the line, we stop being inquisitive. We stop learning.

There are a host of things you can do to reawaken your innate sense of wonder. Many of the methods in this book will help you release the protective layers of mind that keep you from your natural curiosity. I have found that simply going through life with a desire to better understand what's going on has helped me live in wonder. Some of the questions I currently find interesting to explore, and which help me live in wonder, are …

➤ Why are people so afraid to speak more honestly and say what's going on with them (like kids do)? What exactly are we afraid of?

➤ Why does the average American spend the majority of his waking life watching TV, when it brings him so little satisfaction?

➤ Why do people worry about money, even if they have never gone without food or shelter in their entire life?

➤ How do radio waves travel through buildings and walls and somehow find their way to my radio—and get converted into music?

➤ What are my nighttime dreams trying to say to me, and why do I get fooled into thinking such bizarre situations are actually real?

The list could go on and on. Once you enter the realm of curiosity, the world becomes a more magical place. You start to see the deeper truths behind the world of appearances. It will help you to keep learning.

The famous scientist Sir Isaac Newton once said, "I know not what I may appear to the world, but to myself I seem to have been only like a boy playing on the sea-shore … whilst the great ocean of truth lay all undiscovered before me." Besides being one of the greatest scientists who has ever lived, it would seem that Mr. Newton was also a closet mystic.

The Least You Need to Know

➤ Self-honesty and humility are difficult to maintain, but can keep one from a host of spiritual potholes.

➤ A sense of humor can help you keep a larger perspective on life when the going gets tough.

➤ Courage or fearlessness is necessary to keep facing your limitations and moving consistently forward.

➤ Kindness is something that every spiritual path agrees is central, and is a good measure of progress in the right direction.

➤ Sincerity and a sense of urgency can keep you motivated to cut through the muck of ordinary life.

➤ Curiosity and wonder are hallmarks of a seeker who is still learning and discovering the magic of existence.

Chapter 3

Diving into Now

In This Chapter

➤ Embracing the present moment

➤ How to know true intuitive guidance

➤ How to become fully immersed in an activity

➤ Self-remembering: a higher level of consciousness

When a person goes to jail, he's required to stay for a specified amount of time. However, when a person begins to realize he is in the jail of his own mind, it's possible for him to leave at any time.

That's the good news. The bad news is that, without the right training, few people leave the jail of their mind for more than brief moments. This need not be the case. Years of planning your escape are not necessary. You could be free in an instant. The key to leaving your ego-based world is to dive into the present moment.

The Present of the Present

The present moment is like a magical portal to another world. Although the present is the only moment we ever actually live in, it's unexplored territory for most people.

There are two distinct ways to more fully enter the present moment—through the inner doorway and through the outer doorway. I refer to these two approaches as "inner presence" and "outer presence." As you concentrate on one of these two doorways, you begin to transcend the ego-based way you normally perceive your life. As your thoughts quiet and the prison "bars" disappear, you step into an inner world of love and peace.

From Allah to Zen

Inner presence or **mindful-ness** is the ability to watch your thoughts, feelings, and behaviors in a way that helps you to feel separate from them. In this state, your own thoughts and feelings are objectified, and you start to identify yourself with the part of you that *is* watching.

Heavenly Helpers

To use your body to dive into the present moment, simply re-port your bodily sensations out loud for a few minutes. For ex-ample, you might say, "Now I feel a tightness in my chest, now a coolness in my throat, now an ache in my knee ..." and so on. As you keep reporting your moment-to-moment sensations, you'll become more present and internally quiet.

Into Inner Presence

The goal of *inner presence* is to watch your thoughts, feelings, or behaviors rather than simply experience them. You focus so thoroughly on watching them that you enter a state called present-time awareness. You become the watcher, rather than the actor or doer. In spiritual traditions this state is referred to variously as "the witness," or "pure awareness," or even "the soul." Instead of identifying with every thought and feeling you have, you watch it almost as if it were happening to someone else.

One technique Buddhists use to elicit this state of con-sciousness (which they refer to as *mindfulness*) is to simply label your moment-to-moment thoughts and feelings. Therefore, while cleaning your house, you might think, "I am feeling in a hurry. I am worrying about what to cook for dinner. I am feeling a tightness in my shoulders. I am feeling angry that I have to do the dishes." Eventually, this practice of labeling what is going on for you helps to bring you more deeply into the present moment. In addition, the simple act of being aware of what you're doing tends to dispel inharmonious thoughts and feelings.

As you enter into inner presence by being mindful of what you experience, you begin to taste the world of Spirit. The part of ourselves that can watch our thoughts and feelings acts as a doorway to Spirit. By watching our manifestations, it's possible to be "in the world, but not of it." In Chapters 4, "The World According to Awareness," 15, "Selves of Lead," and 16, "Turning Lead into Gold," I'll discuss several more methods to help trigger this state of consciousness.

"Be still and know that I am God," says a famous pas-sage in the Bible. It sounds easy enough, but thoughts are clever and tricky things. Fortunately, underneath all the mental garbage that keeps us in a thought prison is an ocean of pure peace. As you experience moments of dipping into the ocean of silence within, you become a different person. You start to spontaneously manifest the seven traits outlined in Chapter 2, "Keys to the Kingdom." Instead of trying to *be* a spiritual person, you simply *are* one. Beneath the thoughts and superficial roles each person plays is a being of innate goodness.

Normally we bounce around between many thoughts each minute. Yet when your mind is quiet, it's easier to feel a deeper connection or "knowing" that people refer to as God, the higher self, or intuition.

Into Intuition

Intuition is a term used by many people to indicate a way of knowing things that is not based on thinking. Normally we spend all of our time in analytical thinking that clouds our direct way of knowing information. By becoming quieter and more present, we can begin to access this deeper (and wiser) way of being.

A first step in recognizing your intuition involves simply listening to your thoughts and feelings. Many people are so busy and distracted that they don't really *know* how they feel about things. Instead of listening to the discomfort they feel in a relationship, for example, they watch TV, or use

some other form of distraction. As you learn to trust your intuition or "inner guidance," you become motivated to make the time to listen to your thoughts and feelings. They can tell you a lot.

While your thoughts and feelings are in the right general direction of your intuitive wisdom, they are not synonymous with true intuition. As your thoughts and feelings settle down (using any of the quieting methods described in this book), it's possible to discover an even deeper way of knowing.

Some people actually hear a "voice" of intuition that seems to speak to them differently than their normal thoughts. Other people, upon trying to listen to their intuition, see images or symbols that seem to come from a deeper part of themselves. However, most people receive intuitive guidance in the form of a "feeling of rightness." They just feel that they know something, although they may not know how they know.

You've probably had an intuitive experience before. Perhaps you just knew someone you cared about was hurt, or perhaps, when faced with an important decision, you somehow knew what choice to make. We've all heard stories of people who had intuitions about car accidents and so forth. More commonly, people have intuitions about smaller matters, like what to say to a friend in need. When you've had such experiences, how did you know what to say? Was it a voice, an image, or simply a feeling of sureness? By remembering how you've received intuitive guidance in the past, you can better recognize it in the future.

From Allah to Zen

Intuition is the capacity of knowing without the use of rational thought processes. It is a direct knowing usually attained by quieting one's mind and connecting with an intelligence greater than one's own.

Amazing Grace

When I was in college, whenever a certain friend of mine would call on the phone, I somehow knew it was him. After a while, I would just answer the phone, "Hi Jeff." That would generally freak him out because he didn't believe in "intuitive mumbo jumbo," as he put it. Eventually he started to have the same intuitive sense when I would call him, which finally got him to explore spirituality for the first time.

Is It Intuition?

In seminars I lead on listening to intuition, the most common question participants ask me is: How can you know the difference between true intuition and normal thoughts? I can't give you a surefire way to always tell them apart, but I can give you some helpful guidelines.

Cosmic Potholes

Since you can never know for sure if you're receiving true guidance or just mental garbage, don't ever assume intuition is definitely correct. Once you receive an intuition, use your rational mind and the guidance of those you trust to help you determine if the guidance you've received is useful or correct. In general, the more information you have, the better.

First of all, the quieter your mind is, the more likely you will be able to reach the bedrock of intuition hidden underneath your thoughts. By watching your thoughts and feelings as described in the previous "Heavenly Helpers" or by using other methods to quiet your thoughts, such as the ones presented in Chapters 11, "The Art of Meditation," 16, "Turning Lead into Gold," and 19, "Aligning with the Divine," you are much more likely to receive true guidance.

Second, intuition is clearly different than our normal rational thought process. If you feel like you're consciously trying to figure something out, or if your thoughts are attempting to convince you that you "should" do something, that's probably not the voice of true intuition speaking. Intuition feels right, even if you don't like what you "hear." It feels like the obvious and deepest truth behind all your conflicting thoughts. It's similar to a sudden "aha!" experience. You just know that you know.

Listening for Intuition

To hear your intuition, you need to let go of thinking about the past and future, and just be fully present with your deeper self. You must also let go of any preferences or agendas you may have. If you have a clear-cut agenda or preference about a subject, it's almost impossible to hear what your intuitive guidance says.

Let me give an example of how I might go about gaining an intuitive answer to a problem I have. Let's say I want intuitive guidance on what to do in a problematic relationship. First, I would find a quiet room and simply pose a question to myself, such as, "What do I need to know in my relationship with Martha?" Then I would focus on becoming more present by listening to my thoughts and feelings. I could ask myself, "What is going on with me?" I might note some resentment, fear of losing Martha's friendship, and feelings of hurt for how she's been treating me. (To become even more present, I could try quieting my mind by meditating, listening to some music, or any other method that helps me feel more relaxed.)

Once my mind is somewhat quiet, I would try to listen to my intuitive guidance. I'd ask myself the question again, but this time I would attempt to let go of my thoughts and just receive any sudden insight or information my deeper being presented. If I noticed myself trying to figure things out, I'd take a deep breath and try once again to let go of my rational thought process, and simply wait with a sense of quiet expectation. Usually, within a few minutes, some deeper knowing arises.

Sometimes answers do not come right away. When this happens to me, I ask that an answer be forthcoming in the near future. An answer to a specific question might come in the form of a dream, something a friend says to you, or very unlikely places.

Amazing Grace

It's been said that prayer is a form of talking to God, while hearing your intuition is like listening to God. Spiritually advanced people are always listening to what their deeper being or God is suggesting they do. Instead of trying to think through and plan everything out, they dive into the present moment and tap into a wellspring of nonstop intuitive guidance.

One time I asked my intuition if I should go to India. For a week, I received no clear feeling of what I should do. Then, as I was flipping through channels one night while watching TV, I heard a preacher clearly say, "Jonathan, you need to go to India!" I practically fell out of my chair. Even if I had hallucinated this statement, I figured it was a clear message to go. You just never know how a question posed to your deeper self will become clear to you. (I made the trip, and it was phenomenal.)

When your mind becomes quiet and focused on the present moment, it's as if you suddenly tap into a very wise being that lives within you. That being has always lived within you—it is your soul, and it is usually drowned out by all the stimulation you are constantly bombarded with. It takes practice to quiet your mind, open your heart, and let go of the rational mind long enough to let a deeper intelligence—God, or whatever you want to call it—"speak" to you. But it is a very rewarding experience.

Going out of Your Mind

The second way a person can become more focused on the present moment is through what I call "outer presence." In this approach to being more aware, rather than diving into your thoughts and feelings, you pay full attention to whatever activity you're doing.

Outer presence is a far more common experience than inner presence. When people become fully absorbed in a movie or piece of music, they experience this form of presence. Since it feels good to lose *self-consciousness* and become fully immersed in an activity, people seek out such experiences. Making love, watching a movie or TV, or enjoying a beautiful sunset are all activities that can transport us out of our thinking mind.

While it's fun to watch a good movie or see a sunset, you can't create such powerful events every moment of your life (although many have tried). With practice, you can get better at experiencing outer presence even while doing mundane activities like vacuuming the carpet or washing the dishes.

From Allah to Zen

Self-consciousness is a term that refers to the tendency to feel concerned with how one appears to others, or even oneself. Losing self-consciousness feels good because you can become so absorbed in an activity that you no longer are concerned with how you look.

Staying Awake

Normally, for most of the activities of our life, we're not fully present with them. As we eat a meal, go for a walk, or open our mail, we're busy thinking about the past or future. We mechanically run through the motions, never suspecting that we are living in the midst of wonder. Occasionally, something temporarily "wakes us up" from our thought-imposed slumber, but we soon fall back to our habitual routines. How can we stay awake?

The first step out of undesirable behavior is to become more aware of exactly what it is you're doing, such as being lost in thoughts or negative feelings. The second step is to switch your focus to what is currently happening around you. As you see the possibility that you could be more fully absorbed in any activity, you'll have moments where you experience it. The technique for accomplishing this is so obvious that it's usually overlooked: Just pay close attention to whatever you're doing. It's not as easy as it sounds. Paying attention implies that there is a payment, and indeed there is. It takes effort to get out of your thoughts and into the subtleties of whatever activity is at hand.

When doing any activity, there is always an infinite amount of subtle sense impressions you receive. For example, when going for a walk, you can hear birds sing, nearby traffic, and the sound of your feet against the path. As you tune into all the sounds you hear and all the sights you see, you'll begin to feel more present—and more alive.

Try it right now. How many sounds can you hear as you stop reading for a moment? Focus on them. Now, how many colors can you see around you? Try to take them in all at once. As you do, you'll start to get out of the prison of your mind and into the world of outer presence. It'll likely feel good.

Heavenly Helpers

To more closely focus on any activity you're doing, choose one sense (such as hearing, seeing, or tasting) and see how much more you can take in than you usually do. The more you focus on subtle sense impressions, the more likely you'll experience outer presence.

Getting Lost

Whenever you notice you're lost in thoughts (which is most of the time), make an effort to pay attention to whatever activity you're engaged in. At first you might seesaw back and forth between your thoughts and what you're doing. But don't give up. If you keep making an effort, you'll eventually find yourself noticing subtle elements of the activity you're engaged in. Eventually, you may find you get lost in what you're doing. Success!

Know About Flow

Research psychologist Mihaly Csikszentmihalyi (I have no idea how to pronounce his name) has studied the factors that help people achieve a state of outer presence. In his best-selling book *Flow,* he outlines various ingredients that help people experience total immersion in an activity.

For example, Dr. Csikszentmihalyi states that competitive games, sports, or activities such as creating music make it more likely a person will slip into the flow experience. Indeed, many practices associated with spirituality are simply activities where "flow" is more likely to occur. Singing, drumming, dancing, and various rituals are all conducive to creating an experience of outer presence, or flow.

Going with the Flow

While it can be fun and mind expanding to engage in activities where outer presence is likely to occur, it's a good idea to understand how to turn *any* situation into a flow activity. As I've mentioned, focusing on subtle elements of the present moment can be very helpful. Dr. Csikszentmihalyi describes other methods and aspects conducive to experiencing flow.

Amazing Grace

A spiritual teacher once told me how, at a talk on cosmic consciousness, one elderly woman stood out from the crowd of mostly hippies. No matter how metaphysical his talk became, this old woman nodded her head in agreement. After the talk this teacher went up to the elderly lady to find out her spiritual background. He said, "How did you get interested in cosmic consciousness?" She politely replied, "I could relate to everything you said because I have explored in depth the art of crochet."

For instance, by turning something into a challenge or a game, you are more likely to become concentrated and present. If you find brushing your teeth to be boring, you can turn it into a challenge by brushing with the opposite hand. The more focused you are, the greater the chances you'll fall into flow.

Besides having a challenge, some of the other elements conducive to creating a flow experience, elements potentially within your control, include ...

➤ Having a task that you have a chance of completing.

➤ The ability to fully concentrate on what you're doing (not doing two things at once).

➤ Having a clear goal with immediate feedback.

➤ Having a task (or challenge) that is well matched to your level of skill.

➤ The ability to go beyond self-consciousness and forget about how well you're doing.

➤ The ability to enjoy an activity for its own sake, and not just for the results (such as winning a game or completing a project).

The combination of the right situation, attitudes, and effort makes the experience of outer presence much more likely to occur. Like a muscle that grows stronger over time, it's possible to "train" yourself to go into flow. Fully immersing yourself in a conversation, a game of tennis, or crocheting a sweater will help you develop the skills that are a prerequisite for the flow experience.

Feeling the Flow

What does the experience of outer presence or flow feel like? People describe it differently, but many report that their sense of time is dramatically altered. Most people report that hours seem to pass in minutes (hence the adage "Time flies when you're having fun"). Other common descriptions of the experience are feelings of total ease, unself-consciousness, and euphoria, and a tendency to perform at the peak of one's ability.

To train yourself to experience more "flow moments," simply set a clear intention to pay full attention to whatever you're doing. Start with tasks that have, in the past, helped you experience such moments before. For example, you probably have an easier time being present during a tennis game than when cleaning your house. Over time, you can learn to turn almost any activity into an opportunity to become attuned to the present moment. Relax, and be present with what you're doing.

Cosmic Potholes

Since outer presence experiences can alter your perceptions in unusual ways, do not attempt to create them while driving your car or doing any other potentially dangerous activity.

Creating a More Perfect Union

Inner and outer presence are both wonderful experiences. They are each difficult to maintain, yet with a little effort, you can get glimpses of them throughout your everyday life. After practicing each of these spiritual "skills," it's possible to advance to an even higher level of consciousness: experiencing both inner and outer presence at the same time. Although I am not *enlightened* (and am in no immediate threat of becoming so), I hear that enlightened beings consistently experience inner and outer presence simultaneously.

What is it like to experience both presences at once? In the moments I've experienced it, it has felt very peaceful, relaxed, and even blissful. Although it is a rare thing for me to experience, for people who are enlightened, it is a very natural, relaxed state. It is what we'd experience all the time if we weren't so caught up in our thoughts.

G. I. Gurdjieff, a twentieth-century Russian mystic, referred to this state as "self-remembering" or being "awake." While different teachers and traditions have different names for it, it is often thought of as one aspect of the goal of the spiritual path. Experiencing inner and outer presence at the same time makes you feel vitally alive.

From Allah to Zen

Enlightenment is a state of blissful awareness characterized by the self being fully absorbed into a sense of oneness with the universe. In Hinduism it is called samadhi, and in Buddhism it is referred to as nirvana or satori.

Heavenly Helpers

When practicing outer presence or flow, try stating a specific goal out loud, such as, "While washing the dishes, I'm going to focus on the sound of the water and the dishes being scrubbed." That will help you to know what to go back to when you get lost in your thoughts.

From Allah to Zen

Self-remembering is the ability to be aware of one's own body, thoughts, and emotions while simultaneously being fully aware of one's environment.

There is no simple method for experiencing moments of simultaneous inner and outer presence. Sometimes they just happen, such as when walking in the woods, making love, or facing an emergency. Often quite suddenly, you feel as if you have just arrived on the scene—as if waking up from a dream. What makes the experience unique is the simultaneous awareness of your being both an actor and an observer in a particular scene in your life. In such a state of being, there is little room for thoughts, or anything else that takes us away from a direct experience of the present moment.

Such moments of *self-remembering* or wakefulness are rare, but by practicing the skills of inner and outer presence (one at a time), you'll be building up your concentration abilities and paving the way toward more such moments.

In order to experience deliberate moments of wakefulness, you might try focusing intently on one form of presence (inner or outer), then expanding to include the other form. For example, let's say you're cleaning your house. You might focus on the subtle shadows and shades of light of the objects you're cleaning. After a while, you'd likely be very present with your environment. That's outer presence. Once there, you could then try to be aware of the sensations of your body moving through space, while also being present in your surroundings. It's hard to do, but quite an experience when it happens.

My personal preference is to first attempt to experience inner presence, and once I have that, expand outward to include outer presence. Using any of various methods outlined in this book to become aware of my thoughts, feelings, or body, I become internally oriented for a period of time. This slows down my thoughts. Then, once I have some inner presence, I tune into the sights and sounds around me, while attempting to not totally lose my sense of self in the process.

A favorite way I have of self-remembering is to look closely at a person's face and eyes when talking with him. That helps me to become outwardly present. Then I become aware of what his eyes are looking at—namely, me. That helps me to become aware that I "exist." I become vitally aware of both me and him at the same time—which is the essence of self-remembering. Experiment for yourself to see if you can create this experience.

Throughout history, spiritual masters have said that we spend most of our lives in a state of "waking sleep." Lost in a world of thoughts, we lose touch with our body, our feelings, our surroundings, and most important, our connection to Divine Spirit. By practicing inner and outer presence, and finally both together, you can go from being "nowhere" to being "now here." Although there is just a little space between "no-where" and "now here," that small space (between your thoughts) can make a world of difference.

Amazing Grace

When in India I met an enlightened guru named Papaji. He told me to sit in front of him, and he looked me in the eyes and asked me a simple question: "Who are you?" Every intellectual answer I came up with seemed stupid, so my thoughts just shut down. With my mind quiet, I stared into his glowing eyes. The room seemed to fall away. I became simultaneously aware of my own body and the presence of this master's eyes—connected by what felt like a loving energy. It was very blissful. I began to cry. As my tears flowed into his lap, he patted me on the head and said, "Now you know who you are."

The Least You Need to Know

➤ There are three ways to dive into the present moment: inner presence, outer presence, and both together, called self-remembering.

➤ By becoming internally present, you can better contact your deeper wisdom, known as your intuition or higher self.

➤ Your intuitive wisdom will feel right to you, and is a way of knowing things beyond the rational thought process.

➤ By becoming externally present, you can enter into a "flow" experience in which you feel fully alive and immersed in whatever you're doing.

➤ As you get better at enjoying inner and outer presence, you might find you can experience both forms of awareness simultaneously.

Chapter 4

The World According to Awareness

In This Chapter

➤ The battle of the selves

➤ Growing your present-time awareness

➤ Going from being a somebody to a nobody

➤ Escaping from the prison of the mind

In Woody Allen's movie *Annie Hall,* there is a great scene where Woody is talking to Annie for the first time. In the conversation, they're exchanging pleasantries and trying to find out about each other, but in subtitles the "real" story is unveiled. As Woody Allen's character chitchats about photography, the subtitle states, "I wonder what she looks like naked?" Meanwhile, as Annie speaks about her approach to photography, the subtitle reads, "I hope he doesn't turn out to be a schmuck like the others."

The two conversations ensue simultaneously: the one you hear and the one taking place inside their heads. It's a funny scene because we all recognize it as a truer version of what's really going on.

What if you lived in a world in which you were aware of both conversations—the one you could hear and the "real" one? Well, that's pretty much a typical experience for me. There's the outer world of "show" in which everyone (including me) constantly jockeys for position, tries to look good, and subtly manipulates things to get maximum attention. Then there's the "inner" world in which we're usually just vulnerable, out-of-control kids, often feeling insecure, afraid, and alone, wanting our mommy.

The Parade of Selves

Before the invention of the microscope, there were many theories of what made people sick. Once we could see germs and viruses, we could pinpoint what *actually* led to disease.

In a similar way, in order to truly know oneself, it's helpful to have an "internal microscope" to pinpoint who we actually are. An internal microscope isn't a machine you stick down your throat, but rather a description of ourselves that helps us to see things more accurately and discover what inside us could lead to spiritual *dis*-ease.

From Allah to Zen

A **tool** is any technique or idea that has a practical application in learning about oneself, or practical use in bringing a person closer to a higher state of consciousness.

Heavenly Helpers

By occasionally saying out loud the thoughts you are thinking, it can help to make a relationship more intimate. Such "being yourself" is rare in today's world because it's often a little scary, but it can be a valuable way to deepen a relationship with your friends and family.

A description of reality that is helpful for consciousness growth is called a *tool*. Like tools we use to build a house, an "internal tool" is useful in building greater awareness of who we are, as well as helpful in climbing to higher levels of consciousness. The "Selves Diagram" I am about to describe is a tool that can powerfully help you to understand yourself better. In addition, in Chapters 15, "Selves of Lead," and 16, "Turning Lead into Gold," I show how the concept of selves can be used to help you awaken to your spiritual essence.

In Western society, we are led to believe (through our schooling and religious training) that we're basically in control of our own behavior and thoughts. Of course, if you've ever tried to quiet your mind for even 10 seconds, you've seen that your mind is completely out of control and it never shuts up. If I *were* in control of my mind, I'd choose to love everyone, not have any bad habits, and be in perfect peace all the time.

Once I saw how inaccurate a notion society had given me about my own psychology, I was primed to make use of a better, more precise description of myself. I have found a concept known as "The Selves Diagram" to be an amazingly useful tool in describing precisely who I am, and in helping myself and others transcend normally neurotic states of mind.

The Selves Diagram is like an internal microscope that describes the specifics of what is motivating you at any moment. Its origin is unknown, but it is currently used in many spiritual systems, as well as in certain psychological therapies.

Normally we think of people as more or less consistent over time. We might say that Bob's a "good person," or that Mary's a "sweet person." The Selves Diagram helps us to see that everyone is different from moment to moment.

The basis of the Selves Diagram is that each person is made up of dozens of different selves or "subpersonalities." Each of these selves is almost like a distinct person, with unique motivations, desires, and perceptions. The only commonality the selves have is they all reside in the same body. This can cause much confusion and trouble.

Since people normally don't consider that they are made up of a lot of selves that barely know of each other, they sometimes have a hard time explaining their own behavior. For example, one self will sign a contract while another self hates the idea. One self will tell his mate how much he cherishes their relationship (and really mean it), while another self leads him to have an affair. One self values honesty and integrity, while another self will lie instinctively to avoid a small embarrassment. As you learn to watch these selves in action, you will see more clearly the obstacles to a deeper connection with Spirit.

Cosmic Potholes

Do not use the concept of having different selves as an excuse to avoid responsibility for your own behavior. Although you have a lot of different selves that affect what you do, you are morally and legally responsible for all of them!

The Selves Diagram.

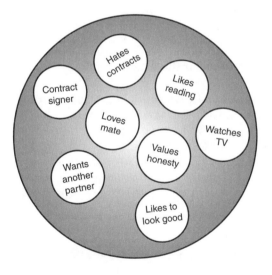

Taking Off the Tinted Glasses

Although the selves can act to filter a person's view of the world, people also have the capacity to see things without any filtering or judgment. When a person experiences inner presence, as discussed in the last chapter, he can "watch" his own thoughts and feelings from a detached state of awareness. This experience is often called pure or present-time awareness.

Amazing Grace

Many sages of the East routinely speak of being liberated from the play of opposites—pleasure and pain, loss and gain, fame and shame. These externals arise and pass away, but the sage is unbound by them, ever-free of their pull and push because he lives in the realm of present time, or pure awareness.

As my spiritual teachers taught me ways to experience present-time awareness, I began to see things from a new perspective. Previously I had taken everything very personally. From the point of view of pure awareness, however, our behaviors, thoughts, and emotions are not things we control, but rather things that *happen to* us.

With practice I was able to watch my selves in a very impersonal manner, as if watching people go by on a movie screen. Instead of thinking, "I'm bored," I would think "a self is up that is proclaiming things are boring" when I was in "pure awareness." Soon I noticed that whenever I connected with present-time awareness, I began to feel very connected to Spirit. I felt compassionate, blissful, at peace.

One of the many advantages of seeing things through the eyes of pure awareness is that one's shortcomings become more obvious. As the obstacles to compassion and peace are more clearly seen by pure awareness or the "witness," they become smaller. Before developing my ability to be a witness, when someone pointed out a fault of mine, I'd get defensive. When I was in the state of pure awareness, I saw that various selves in me were harmful to my peace.

From Allah to Zen

The **ego** is our normal sense of who we are. It creates a feeling of separateness from other people that is slowly dissolved on the spiritual path. As infants, we need to develop a strong separate sense of self or ego in order to survive. Yet, when an ego becomes *too* strong, it interferes with the connection between people and God.

As Paul says in the New Testament, "For what I do is not the good I want to do; no, the evil I do not want to do—this I keep on doing." Paul definitely knew what it was like to be made up of a lot of selves in constant battle with each other. If you grow your ability for present-time awareness, you will see how specific selves control you in much the same way a ventriloquist controls a dummy. Do not be alarmed by this. It means you are becoming more aware of how things actually are.

How to Be Nobody

In Western culture, we're taught to become an important "somebody." We're encouraged to develop a strong ego and are lauded for its accomplishments. The whole point of spiritual traditions is to transcend the *ego*.

Fortunately, when in pure, present-time awareness, you go beyond identification with your ego. You become what some teachers refer to as "a nobody."

Instead of being somebody important, you start to feel like you're a mere servant of a higher force. Although your sense of importance is much smaller than usual, you feel more connected to your source—and therefore quite blissful.

Our ego, or normal sense of self, is analogous to the wave of an ocean. Like a wave that momentarily separates from the ocean it's part of, our ego separates from the ocean of Spirit to be born into a body.

Consider how ludicrous it would be if a wave, upon briefly rising above the ocean, proclaimed, "I'm a special wave, separate and unlike the rest of the water around me," before it dissolved back into the ocean a second later. That's pretty much what you and I do by stressing our individual (ego) importance.

Becoming a somebody isn't bad or wrong. In fact, part of our job as spiritual beings is to fully develop our separate sense of self. In order to survive and mature, we first need to develop a strong, capable ego. But that's not the end-all of life. Once we've done that (usually accomplished by the age of 20 or 30), our next task is to feel our connection to the ocean of spirit *while still being* an individual "wave."

One way to accomplish this is through growing our ability to experience pure, present-time awareness. Such an ability is like possessing an electrical cord that allows a person to "plug into" the ocean of energy that's always been inside him.

The spiritual path is not a matter of attaining something you don't have, but of discovering something you already possess. It is a process of letting go the defenses that keep you from being fully present and relaxed. As you progress along the spiritual path, you do not lose your individuality. Instead, you learn to play the role of being an individual wave while maintaining a connection to the ocean of love of which you were born.

Waking Up in Jail

G. I. Gurdjieff, the famous mystic, was known for saying, "You can't escape from jail until you know you are in it." As you *wake up* and learn to see the selves that run you, the first thing you'll notice is how imprisoned you are. The constant demands and complaints of the selves become very evident. It's as if a bunch of people are fighting to tell you what to do. Of course, if dozens of people were yelling demands at you, you'd probably tell them to get lost. Because these "people" are inside your head, telling them to get lost isn't so easy.

From Allah to Zen

Waking up refers to the process of being able to see, from a transcendent perspective, the emotions, motivations, thoughts, and selves that literally run our lives. As a person wakes up, he realizes his ego, or multitude of selves, filters his worldview and determines his experience of life.

Amazing Grace

When I first began the spiritual path, I was afraid of losing my individuality and becoming a boring person. As I met spiritually advanced teachers, I noticed that they all seemed so completely different, unique, and alive. I finally realized that not being attached to your ego is different than becoming a boring, uninteresting person.

Cosmic Potholes

It's easier to see how neurotic and controlled by internal selves other people are than it is to see it in yourself. Telling people that their suffering stems from their own neurotic selves can be hazardous to your friendship. As Jesus once said, "Why do you look at the speck of sawdust in your brother's eye and pay no attention to the plank in your own eye?"

Let me give you a personal example: Right now a self is insisting I get some ice cream, despite the fact that "it" just got me to eat a whole cup of ice cream a few minutes ago. Another self is telling me that I'm an indulgent slob for eating so much ice cream, and insists I go for a bike ride to burn off some calories. Another self rationalizes that I don't need to exercise because I exercised yesterday. The next self triggered in this ongoing game of internal dominoes is the thought that I'd better get back to writing. The battle between the selves rages on.

Instead of seeing that our internal selves create our experience, and keep us in a state of turmoil, we project the reason for our suffering onto the world. We say it's a certain person's fault, or the fact that our job is dull, or it's the weather, or whatever. While it is true that certain events and people are difficult to appreciate, in the end it is our internal thoughts and selves that filter and create our experience.

It can be depressing to see how our different thoughts and selves keep us in prison. That's why it's so important to be able to watch your selves in an impartial, detached manner through various methods described in Chapters 11, "The Art of Meditation," 15, and 16. If you can watch or laugh at how screwed up you are, you're halfway to being free of the endless muck that keeps you in a small room.

Breaking Out of Jail

Once you realize you live in a thought-based prison of battling selves, the obvious question is, "How do I get outta here?" To a large extent, the rest of this book is an answer to that question. Fortunately, there are many ways out of prison, yet all of them require a certain sincerity. If you want to escape from prison, it does little good to shake the bars and yell "Let me outta here!" Getting out of the thought/selves prison we live in requires a lot of help, persistence, and clever techniques.

Adding to the difficulty of escaping from our ego prison is an unfortunate cosmic law: Anything you do to try to escape from prison can easily make matters worse. (Once again, don't blame me for these cosmic laws; I didn't create them!)

The reason it's hard to escape from our self-imposed prison is something I call "self-importance." When we decide to be a better or more spiritual person, it can actually reinforce our ego or sense of separateness, instead of diminish it. Have you ever known someone who becomes a religious convert and immediately turns into an even bigger pain in the butt than they were before they "became spiritual"? I sure have. Speaking from personal experience, it's not a pretty sight.

Amazing Grace

Thinking that you're important can be quite a problem—even when you see it in yourself. I once heard a humorous story of a priest who, upon seeing his own self-importance, prays out loud to God, "Show me I'm just a 'nobody.'" The assistant priest, upon hearing this sincere prayer, falls to his knees and asks God for the same thing. Finally, the custodian, upon hearing these two men, falls to his knees to ask God to show *him* that he's also a "nobody." Upon seeing this, one priest elbows the other and says, "Look who is trying to be a nobody."

A long time ago I saw one of the original *Star Trek* episodes in which Spock and Captain Kirk are in a prison. The bars of this particular prison are made of energy drawn from their bodies. The more Kirk and Spock struggle to get out, the thicker the bars become. Spock finally escapes the prison by letting go of his effort to escape. He quietly watches his mind and becomes fully present to the moment he is in. He enters into the realm of pure awareness, and as he does, the bars simply disappear.

It's a good analogy for the situation you and I are in. If we create a bigger, more important ego by trying to be a spiritual person, our bars just get thicker. We feel even more separate from everyone around us. But if we stop struggling to be spiritual and simply relax and focus on being fully present, the bars that hinder us vanish, and we draw closer to God and each other.

To avoid building up massive amounts of self-righteousness, you must work slowly but surely to free yourself from "prison." As in the story of the tortoise and the hare, the people who patiently but quietly move in the right direction are usually the ones who make the most spiritual progress.

Over the years, as I've learned to enter the state of present-time awareness, I've felt the euphoric feeling of being free of my own internal obstacles for brief periods of time. Entering pure awareness is like taking your finger off the panic button of life.

Heavenly Helpers

One simple way to detach from the thoughts in your mind is to say, "The mind is now thinking (fill in the blank)" each time you notice a new thought pattern. When you keep repeating this formula out loud, it will help you to stop identifying so strongly with your thoughts, and may help you to start to feel what "witness consciousness" is like.

You can relax. You can open up to the beauty all around you. You can enjoy yourself without falling into a thought pattern (a self) that carries you away into an ongoing negative fantasy. It's a wonderful feeling.

Witnessing or watching your life creates a sense of perspective or spaciousness around each self that arises. As I've become more aware, I've often felt that watching myself through the eyes of present-time awareness is like watching the conductor of an internal orchestra. Normally, each self makes its demands, regardless of the effect it has on my other selves. The self that wants to stay up late and drink alcohol has little awareness of the self that will resent getting up early the next morning. A hundred selves all acting without thought of each other, like 100 musicians each playing his own tune in the same room, is bedlam.

Pure awareness, like a conductor of an orchestra, helps to establish order and harmony. A conductor creates beautiful music by watching over the orchestra and signaling to each player when he should play. In a similar fashion, by occasionally watching over the group of selves manifesting through me, I maintain order and foster harmony within my being as well as in my actions.

The Least You Need to Know

➤ We are made up of many parts or "selves" that filter and determine our experience moment to moment.

➤ We also have the capacity to see things through the eyes of pure awareness, without any filtering.

➤ When seeing through the eyes of pure awareness, we see more clearly that we live in our own thought "prison."

➤ By growing the ability to see things with present-time awareness, it's possible to create harmony and escape from our self-imposed prison.

Part 2
Different Shades of Light

Each religion or spiritual tradition is like a path up a "spiritual mountain." While they all converge at the top, at the bottom it can seem like they approach things from completely different directions! Yet, by explaining the unique wisdom of various traditions, you'll get a better map or picture of the spiritual mountain you are trying to climb. In this part, we'll look at six of the most known Eastern and Western religions, with special attention to what is unique about each one.

In the last 60 years, there has been an explosive growth of twelve-step programs and renewed interest in the power of devotion in various religious traditions. I'll do a whirlwind tour of these approaches up the mountain and offer insights from them that are applicable to seekers pursuing any path.

Chapter 5

The Way of the West

In This Chapter

➤ Why understanding other religions is important

➤ How the three main Western religions are connected

➤ The joy of Judaism

➤ The cry of Christianity

➤ The *is* of Islam

To grow spiritually, it's important to learn about the various religious and spiritual practices of the world. There are a couple of reasons for this.

First, the world needs it. It is growing smaller every day. In the United States, which admittedly has a head start in the mixing of cultures, interracial and interreligious marriages are common. Knowledge enables such qualities as tolerance, acceptance, and brotherly love to grow. Considering that more people have been killed in religious wars than in all other wars put together, the world certainly needs the tolerance and acceptance such knowledge can bring.

The second reason it's important to learn about various traditions is its potential spiritual benefit. Learning about the many great religions of the world gives our own spiritual understanding an added dimension. If you were brought up in one tradition, it may have given you blinders to the value of other paths. Each of the major religions has immense wisdom to offer, and it can be helpful to extract their unique perspectives. Learning about many different religions has helped me to see what I lack or have somehow missed in the path I have chosen to follow.

I believe there are many paths up the "spiritual mountain." The major religions of the world are all paths one can take to reach the summit of the kingdom of God. Knowing about the various sights and vistas different paths offer along the way can help you to better appreciate the mountain being climbed.

As a seeker, your job is to appreciate wisdom and truth wherever you find it. In this chapter and the next, we'll examine some of the main principles and wisdom of six major religions in the world today—Judaism, Christianity, Islam, Hinduism, Buddhism, and Taoism. This chapter will focus on the Western religions: Judaism, Christianity, and Islam.

Amazing Grace

One of the most universal religious tenets is the Golden Rule. Here is how it is phrased in Judaism, Christianity, and Islam.

Judaism: "That which is hateful to you, do not do to your neighbor. That is the whole Torah; the rest is commentary." (Rabbi Hillel)

Christianity: "Thou shalt love thy neighbor as thyself." (Jesus)

Islam: "None of you truly believes until he wishes for his brother what he wishes for himself." (Muhammad)

One Family

It's interesting to note that most people are not aware of the common origins of Judaism, Christianity, and Islam. Followed by more than half of the world's population, they all began with a tiny migrating Hebrew nation around 3000 B.C.E. "In the beginning, God …" is the root of Western civilization. *Monotheism,* largely unknown to the ancient cultures of both East and West, became the force that changed the course of human history.

Judaism, Christianity, and Islam all believe that there is only one God. Each of these religions, although similar in origin, ethics, and beliefs, views the spiritual world and man's relationship to it from slightly different angles. In addition, although many of their teachings are the same, the importance they place on various teachings differ.

The Jew sees the importance of obedience to God's law as vital. The Christian emphasizes that loving God and his children is the key to heaven. The Muslim focuses largely on how humility is the ultimate spiritual attribute.

These points of view are not at odds with one another, but are, when considering the whole, inseparable. Law, love, humility—mind, heart, and soul. How can one exist without the others?

Judaism: The Ultimate Legal Contract

One of the greatest puzzles of history is how that little nomadic tribe of ancient Hebrews had, and continues to have, such a great impact on the development of the world. The odds against the survival of the Jews has been great, yet they have flourished. You may be surprised to know that the percentage of Jews in the world is a meager 0.2 percent! Yet the Jews have played a dramatic role in the history of the Western world, and continue to do so. Why? It started in the ancient world, with the beginnings of the worship of one God rather than multiple gods.

God Makes a Deal

Abraham was born in Babylonia around 1800 B.C.E. He came to believe that there was only one God, and began to teach his beliefs around town. A few years later, while Abraham was praying to the one God, God spoke to him. He wanted to make a deal. If Abraham would leave his home and family, God would make him the founder of a great nation and bless him. Abraham accepted the offer, and the covenant between the Jewish people and God was established.

From Allah to Zen

Monotheism is a doctrine or belief that there is only one God. In the time of the ancient Hebrews, almost all other people in the world believed in and prayed to many gods. The Babylonians, Syrians, Greeks, Indians, Chinese, Africans, Native Americans, Anglo-Saxons, Indonesians, all believed in and prayed to many gods and idols.

Amazing Grace

The Torah consists of the first five books of the Old Testament. To the Jew, there is no "Old Testament" because the books that Christians call the New Testament are not part of Jewish scripture. The Torah contains the whole body of Jewish law and teachings.

The next major deal God made with the Jewish people involved Moses. Enslaved by the pharaohs in Egypt, the Jews were poor and for the most part badly treated. God told Moses to set them free and lead them to the Promised Land. This Moses did, through a series of miracles and prophecies, locusts, droughts, and plagues.

Led by a flame of light, eating food called manna that dropped out of the sky, the Hebrews finally came to Mount Sinai where God revealed the entire Torah to Moses. Most Westerners are familiar with the *Ten Commandments*. Yet Moses was also given and recorded the first five books of the Torah and the Old Testament, which include 613 other laws called mitzvoth.

From Allah to Zen

The **Ten Commandments** contain the ethical prescriptions for most of the world today, certainly the Western world. Jews, Christians, and Muslims all abide by them, and ascribe them to Moses.

From Allah to Zen

Kosher means ritually fit for use according to Jewish law. You will usually see it in reference to Jewish food. Kosher slaughtering is designed to be as fast and painless as possible. If there is anything that happens during the process that indicates the animal has suffered, the flesh may not be eaten.

After Moses came back down from the mountain, he began to hear cases and judge them according to the laws. This soon became too much for one person, so Moses instituted a judicial system. Moses was literally the first lawyer!

Law Leads to Love

Although laws are at the heart of Judaism, a large part of Jewish law is about love and brotherhood. The law, which was revealed by God to Moses, is not only the Ten Commandments, but 613 specific instructions for creating a just and ethical society. They are called mitzvoth, and are so much geared toward charity that the word *mitzvah* is commonly used to mean any good deed.

The law commands the Jew to help those in need, and charity is an essential part of life. Called tzedeakah, charity is considered by some rabbis the highest of all the commandments. Jews are required to give one tenth of their income to the poor. (This is where the Christian idea of tithing comes from.) The obligation includes giving to both Jews and gentiles. It can include charitable institutions such as health care or education. Jewish law even goes so far as to break down tzedeakah into levels of merit.

Some of the most stringent laws have to do with the proper treatment of animals. Judaism has always recognized the link between the way a person treats animals and the way a person treats human beings. The scriptures say clearly that God chose Moses because of his skill in caring for animals! Although man has the right to use animals for legitimate needs (Jews are allowed to eat meat), it must be done in the *kosher* way, the way that causes the animal the least suffering. Even the taking of eggs from a hen must be done when the hen is not around, so that she does not suffer the psychological pain of loss.

What happens if you break the law? Depending on the specific branch of Judaism one follows, sometimes there can be some forms of social censure. Unlike many other religions, there is no mention of hell, or "divine" punishment. Nor would you ever hear a Jew say, "The devil made me do it." The concept of right and wrong in Judaism is an internal one, and man always has the freedom to choose.

The nature of man is dual, meaning he has both a good impulse and an evil impulse. At the age of 13, a Jew becomes responsible for making the right choices. He has studied the law and goes through a rite of passage called a bar mitzvah, or in the case of Jewish girls, a bat mitzvah. If, after knowing the law, you choose to do wrong, there is no one to blame but yourself, and you are fully responsible for the consequences.

Heavenly Helpers

By reading any holy book, and discussing favorite passages with like-minded seekers, it's possible to learn many valuable things. In addition, a "back and forth" discussion with others can help each of you discover important new insights that you may have missed on your own.

When I was in Israel, I met with Jews who spent virtually every moment they could studying and debating each line of the Talmud—sacred books that have commentaries on the books of the Torah. The reverence they had for every word was awe inspiring. Just as physicists study physical laws to understand the nature of reality, Jews study the spiritual laws said to bring about a harmonious and righteous existence. It is thought that by following the laws and fulfilling your obligation to God, God will keep and fulfill his obligation to you.

So is Judaism a dry, intellectual religion? No. What the Jews have is a practice, which, if followed, brings about the good life. When life is lived righteously, there can be a relaxed attitude of joy and harmony. Judaism is unique in its inclusion of this material life as a part of God's creation. It is unique in its celebrations of life and family. The rewards of obeying the laws are many, but the obvious one is harmony!

Christianity: Love Fulfills the Law

It was around 4 B.C.E. that the Jews were in a desperate situation. Although Judaism was a religion based upon human contact with God, it had been many centuries since the prophets spoke with the angels of the Lord. Judaism had become a body of knowledge devoid, for the most part, of Spirit.

It was during this time that a wild man named John the Baptist roamed the desert preaching repentance to the Jews, and baptizing them to prepare them for the coming of the Messiah. According to some scholars, when John baptized Jesus, he proclaimed him to be the coming Messiah. Most Westerners, be they Christian, Jewish, or Muslim, know the general outline of the rest of the story.

Cosmic Potholes

The fact that Jesus was scorned by some of the religious Jews of his day shows how easy it is to fall off the "narrow path." Although following spiritual laws can be helpful, more than that is necessary to stay connected to Spirit. Whether Christian, Jew, or Muslim, spiritual knowledge isn't as important as true humility, love, and sincerity.

Think what it would be like today if a person came along and shook up our world by saying, "I have been sent by God to tell you …." There would be some definite skepticism. That was how it was for some of Jewish leaders at the time. Jesus came and shook things up.

What Jesus preached was not new to the Jews. He was a Jew himself. But though his message was familiar, his emphasis was different. What was so special about Jesus was that he didn't only preach a message of love and humility, he lived it. He himself was the message! The Christians saw him as a part of God because of his holy example.

This was one of the aspects that revolutionized Christianity away from mainstream Judaism—the worship of the man Jesus. Many Christians believe that Jesus is not only a doorway to God, but an incarnation of God in human form. They call the experience of letting Jesus into their heart being "born again." With rebirth comes the bliss of the presence of the Holy Spirit, or the state of grace.

Love Fulfills the Law

Jesus, in his Sermon on the Mount, revised the laws of the Hebrew commandments from "thou shalt" and "thou shalt not" to "blessed art thou." The language itself moves the listener from the law to love. The people who are blessed are the poor in spirit (the humble), pure of heart, people who mourn, those who are merciful, those who are hungry for righteousness, those who are peacemakers, and those who get persecuted in the name of God. These are the chosen people; being chosen has nothing to do with whether people are Jews or gentiles, men or women, sinners or saints.

The Jewish law at the time of Jesus drew distinctions between the Jew and the Gentile, calling the latter unclean because they didn't observe the Jewish prescriptions for righteous living. Jesus went against such social prejudices, reinterpreting "clean" and "unclean" in terms of the soul. Once Jesus ate with some Jewish rabbis without first washing his hands. The rabbis were appalled, as this was one of their laws. Jesus replied, "Now do ye Pharisees make clean the outside of the cup and the platter; but your inward part is full of ravening and wickedness" (Luke 11:39).

Jesus moved the kingdom of God from without to within. He ate with the poor, the sick, the sinner. He healed the Greeks and Romans and Arabs, and often on the Sabbath day of rest. He protected a prostitute from the law of being stoned, asking the people, "Who among you is without sin?" No one was able to meet this challenge, and they all walked away. Jesus was a true practitioner of nonviolence.

Jesus resisted evil, but did not judge anyone who was evil. He separated the person from the act. That is why he could practice forgiveness. He said that we must love our enemies and forgive those who hurt us. The Jewish law said that after 7 times of offense you didn't have to forgive, but Jesus said to forgive 70 times 7, probably meaning forever. That sounds like a big call, but Jesus expected a lot of himself and his followers.

The Cry of Christianity

The path of love is also the path of pain. Love and pain are inseparable. Many Christians consider finding love through suffering a great gift of God. Painful struggles are considered blessings. What greater proof is there of love than a willingness to sacrifice? Even performing a small kindness for another, instead of for yourself, is considered an act of sacrifice. According to Christians, Jesus was even willing to sacrifice his life for the benefit of others. Through the process of sacrifice, one becomes more humble, and thereby closer to God.

Amazing Grace

There are people who identify with Jesus' pain so completely that they bleed mysteriously. This is called the stigmata. Stigmatics have included Saint Francis of Assisi, the first known stigmatic, as well as more than 100 others, mostly Catholic and mostly women. Therese Neumann, a German peasant who lived in the twentieth century, was one such stigmatic. She experienced the suffering of Christ almost every Friday. She would go into a trance, have visions of the crucifixion, and bleed from her head, breast, hands, and feet. She neither ate nor drank anything but one consecrated wafer a day.

Opening to Spirit

According to the Bible, there were 12 main disciples of Jesus, but the person we know the most about is Paul. Paul became a Christian months after Jesus' crucifixion. He wrote most of the last chapters of what later became known as the New Testament. These chapters mainly consisted of letters he wrote to other apostles teaching in the Mediterranean area.

Much of the church is built upon Paul's teachings. Paul was convinced, through the miracle of losing and then regaining his sight, that Jesus was the Messiah. Paul had been a Jewish Pharisee actively engaged in persecuting and arresting people who believed that Jesus was the Messiah. Yet he became a healer and a great teacher in the name of Christ.

There is a powerful message in the fact that Paul was chosen to spread Jesus' message. The fact that he could be redeemed and picked to spread the gospel of love would seem to indicate that no one, no matter what they've done in the past, is beyond redemption. A person can, through the power of God, always have a change of heart.

Heavenly Helpers

If there is something you've done that you feel is hard to forgive yourself for, just remember that Paul persecuted Christians—and God forgave him. Perhaps you can, in prayer, ask God to forgive you and for you to forgive yourself. It does little good to be carrying unneeded baggage around when you seek heaven within.

One of Paul's most famous writings is Corinthians 1:13. He says that even if you speak in the tongues of the angels, and you don't have love, you have nothing but the sound of brass or a tinkling cymbal. He said that you can teach knowledge beyond anything anyone has ever heard, but without love it is meaningless. He is speaking from his own experience of Jesus' love, and the experience he had of being filled with the Holy Spirit.

One of the things that Christianity is known for is its emphasis on the Holy Trinity. According to Christianity, Jesus, God, and the Holy Spirit are one. Through being receptive to the Holy Spirit, Christians can learn to feel the love of God within themselves, and pass on this love of God to others. Therefore, their faith in Jesus is based on a direct experience, not simply an ideology. That is part of the power of Jesus' message—seek and you will find the "kingdom of heaven within."

Islam: The Way of Surrender

Islam is a religion greatly misunderstood by the Western world, even though it is quite similar to Judaism and Christianity. When many Westerners think of Islam, they think of warring terrorists and underprivileged women. These images are far from the truth of this great religion, which was transmitted to the prophet Muhammad in the seventh century C.E.

Islam is the religion of more than 20 percent of the world's population. Its roots lie with the ancient Hebrews and Abraham. Muhammad was born in 570 C.E. He became disillusioned with the corrupt and degenerate society of the Arabs, and turned inward to find truth. At that time, there were a few contemplative people who worshipped only one God, whose name was Allah, the creator and supreme provider of the people. Muhammad was one of them. He would go off to a cave on the outskirts of Mecca and meditate and pray.

Over time, Muhammad's communion with Allah became more and more intense. Then, in 610 C.E., Muhammad heard a voice from an angel telling him to "Proclaim!" Muhammad protested three times, saying he could not do this, but the angel insisted. From that point on, Muhammad's life was not his own. This was the beginning of the Koran, the sacred book of Islam, which the Muslims believe to be the last word of God.

The People of the Book

The Muslims consider the Koran to have been transmitted to Muhammad by the angel Gabriel, and the words are no less than God's words. It is, in essence, very similar to the Old and New Testaments, including the stories and laws of the Jewish prophets, as well as the story of Jesus as the Messiah. Muslims believe in the prophecies of the Judgment Day and in heaven and hell. In the Koran, God speaks in the first person. Allah describes himself and makes known his laws. So Muslims obey the Koran, and consider it to be God speaking directly to them.

Translations of the Koran are not considered to be the real Koran, and this could be one of the reasons we know so little about the religion of Islam. There seems to be some mystical presence in the original language of Arabic, which, when recited or heard, transports the worshipper into a state of grace. Its essence being untranslatable, what I present of Islam here are merely a couple of the main concepts and ideas.

Cosmic Potholes

The media often characterize "foreign" religions in stereotypical and unfriendly ways. The only way to really know what a religion is like is to meet with practitioners of that religion, study it for yourself, and be open to its teachings. The ideas and images you can pick up from the TV about any religion are usually totally inadequate.

Amazing Grace

Most Bibles, and many English versions of the Koran, have been translated from Arabic to Greek to Latin to English. A lot is lost in the translation process. For example, the Lord's Prayer, which begins with, "Our father," translates directly from Aramaic as, "O cosmic Birther of all radiance and vibration! Soften the ground of our being and carve out a space within us where your presence can abide." As you can see, even the words of God can easily be interpreted in different ways.

The Is of Islam

In *Islam,* God is referred to as Allah. Much of the Koran describes Allah and man's relationship to him. Allah is omnipotent and at the same time merciful. Allah is feared by the Muslim, not because he is tyrannical, but because fear is the only human emotion that could be evoked in the presence of something so grand and so intimately aware of man's thoughts and actions.

From Allah to Zen

Islam means "the peace that comes when one is surrendered to God."

The other emotion that is evoked when worshipping Allah is gratitude. Gratitude comes with the peace of the state of dependence and surrender to this mighty power. The Muslim thinks that most people are unable to truly believe, and that all we can do is surrender and commit to obey the laws as laid down in the Koran.

Part of the beauty of Islam is that it is completely interwoven into the Muslim's daily life. It is not enough to worship on the Sabbath. To Muslims, Allah is the most important aspect of life, and is remembered before and during every significant act, including eating, sleeping, washing, working, and even sex!

The Five Pillars

The Five Pillars of Islam are the strength of the Muslim people, a proof of their commitment to Allah and belief in the holy word of the Koran.

- ➤ **Faith.** There is no god but Allah, and Muhammad is his messenger. This is called the Shahada, and it is the basic declaration of faith in Islam.

- ➤ **Prayer.** Salat is the name for the obligatory prayers, which are performed five times a day: dawn, noon, mid-afternoon, sunset, and night. The Muslim will stop whatever he is doing and pray facing Mecca.

- ➤ **Charity.** Zakat is the name for charity. The Muslim believes that all things belong to God and so it is man's duty to share his wealth. Most Muslims give away 2.5 percent (or more) of their wealth annually.

- ➤ **The Fast.** Every year in the month of Ramadan, all Muslims fast from first light until sundown, abstaining from food, drink, and sex. It is regarded as a way of self-purification.

- ➤ **Pilgrimage.** Every year about two million Muslims make a pilgrimage to Mecca. This is obligatory only to those who are physically fit and can afford it. However, to most Muslims, this is the highest point in their lives.

In addition to these five pillars, Muslims should not gamble, steal, lie, eat pork, drink intoxicants, or be sexually promiscuous.

Sufism, the Mystical Branch

There is a more inner, contemplative, and devotional aspect of Islam, called Sufism. The Sufis are less concerned with the formalities of worldly laws and duties, and more concerned with the inner surrender and love of God. The Sufis are not satisfied with being good in the world so that they can reach heaven in the afterlife. They want to know heaven on earth, to see God directly, now.

One of the big differences between Sufism and Islam proper is the centrality of the Shaykh. This is a spiritual master, under whose guidance the disciple follows his path to God. It is vitally important to have a teacher, as the path to the summit of the spiritual mountain can be treacherous. The disciple must completely surrender to the master. Therefore, humility is considered to be the first requirement to come near to God.

From the foundation of humility, the disciple can begin his journey of love. The Sufis dwell on their feelings of longing for God. The Sufis feel those pangs of separation, and believe that such feelings can draw God closer. They become ecstatic with love, sometimes completely losing consciousness of the world around them. These states are ways to open what is called "the eye of the heart."

By understanding each of the three major Western religions, a seeker can begin to feel an affinity with people who practice faiths other than their own. In my own case, I used to feel disdainful of people from other religions when they did things I thought were "weird." Yet, as I began to see their practices as sincere attempts to know their beloved Lord, I began to feel closer to them.

As Muhammad once said, "None of you truly believes until he wishes for his brother what he wishes for himself." Whenever possible, learn from, pray for, and understand the wisdom in faiths other than the one you know best. It will do your heart good.

The Least You Need to Know

➤ Every religion is a doorway to the heaven within. By understanding them better, you can open yourself to new ways of knowing God.

➤ A major focus for the Jewish faith is the understanding and application of spiritual laws that lead to a harmonious and righteous life.

➤ Jesus diverged from his Jewish background to emphasize the importance of love, sacrifice, forgiveness, and humility in knowing God's "kingdom."

➤ Islam emphasizes the significance of surrender, humility, and the interweaving of spiritual practices, such as prayer, in daily life.

Chapter 6

The Way of the East

In This Chapter

➤ The value of the Eastern perspective

➤ The uniqueness of Hinduism

➤ The spiritual science of Buddhism

➤ The flowing nature of Taoism

I grew up in an American middle-class household. The purpose of my life was to *become*—become successful, become educated, become a good person, become strong and independent. This was justified and encouraged by my religion and the culture I grew up in. If I became successful, I would be loved by God and go to a good place after this life. My spiritual and material life were focused on future reward.

When I was 16, a friend loaned me a copy of *Siddhartha,* by Herman Hesse. It was my introduction to Eastern philosophy and religion. Soon afterward, I read the Eastern classic *Autobiography of a Yogi,* by Paramahansa Yogananda. I was hooked! For the first time, the idea of *being*—rather than becoming—entered my world of possibility. What would life be like if I could relax into the present moment? According to the sages of the East, it would be *nirvana,* pure bliss.

The Eastern approach to God is an inner journey toward the center of one's being, not an outer journey toward the goal of heaven. The Eastern seeker is not satisfied with knowing God sometime after being good for 80 or 90 years. He wants to know God now. The Eastern religions teach many ways to know God, and have many role models of saints and sages who have traveled the path. Although there are many different Eastern religions, they all agree that the path to peace requires diving deeper within your being while here on Earth.

The Here of Hinduism

Hinduism is a very old religion, going back at least 5,000 years to the Indus Valley (part of present-day Pakistan). The ancient Vedas, Hindu scriptures memorized and chanted in a language called Sanskrit, are at least 3,500 years old. Hinduism is the main religion of India. It has managed to gain the respect and recognition of philosophers and scientists, as well as the attention of spiritual seekers here in the West.

From Allah to Zen

Nirvana is a Buddhist term for the state of pure bliss attained upon recognition that the self is an illusion and nonexistent.

How could something so old still have relevance for us today? The answer lies in Hinduism's all-inclusiveness. Hinduism is a religion of many paths. It recognizes that different people have different needs. Some people are intellectually inclined, for example, while others are more emotionally or mystically inclined. Hinduism offers distinct methods of seeking for different types of people traveling different paths.

The path laid out for those who are of an intellectual bent is called Jnana *yoga*. The path of Bhakti-yoga is for people who are more emotional, who seek feelings of bliss and devotion. For seekers interested in taking action in the world, and serving mankind, there is the path known as Karma yoga. And last, for people who are primarily attracted to the intuitive and mystical realm, there is the path known as Raja yoga.

Amazing Grace

When I first traveled to India, I quickly saw the positive and negative aspects of a less goal-oriented, more accepting way of life. At the airport, the baggage conveyer got stuck, so no luggage came out. No one seemed to be uptight or concerned about it. Finally, after an hour, I reported it to the airport authorities, and they quickly fixed it. Had I not mentioned it, who knows how long people would have sat there! Whereas I had been quite upset about the situation, the Indian people seemed accepting of what came their way, and weren't inclined to do anything about it.

The Many Faces of God

Along with a choice of paths according to temperament, there is a choice of personal god. Hinduism is a polytheistic religion, a religion of many gods. The sophisticated multiplicity of the gods can be likened to the refraction of light in a prism. There is the One, known as Brahman. This one undivided, unbounded unity can take on infinite forms. From the one unity comes three forces, known as Brahma, Vishnu, and Shiva. These three make up the forces that create, maintain, and destroy the universe.

The refraction of the one Brahman continues into every color, form, sound, smell, and taste. God pervades everything in the Hindu world. A houseguest is considered a visit from God. Mother and Father are to be treated as God by the children. And the teacher, or guru, is none other than God. Around every corner in India you will find a sacred place. Often you will see a small temple built over the home of a cobra, as the snake is also considered sacred. Cows are revered, and their horns are brightly painted and decorated with ribbons and bells. They are never eaten. There is a lot of room to see God wherever one wants to, and to worship God in whatever manner best fits a person's preferences.

From Allah to Zen

Yoga means "union." The end of all the paths of Hinduism is union. Union with what? Hindus believe that man is capable of a state of consciousness wherein the individual self is merged with infinite Being. This state, called self-realization, is the ultimate knowing of God, by awakening one's identity as God (or Brahman).

Amazing Grace

Once, in India, I visited a small village in Gujarat State. It was a time of drought, and the farmers of the village had barely enough water to tend their gardens and animals. As a guest in their home, they insisted on giving me a bath. They heated precious water on an open fire and filled an entire bathtub! I was moved to tears by their generosity, but to them my visit was a great honor. They saw me as God coming to visit them and treated me accordingly.

The Final Goal of Liberation

The ultimate truth to the Hindu is that God (or Brahman) and man's soul (known as the "atman") are really the same, the Supreme Self. Until a person realizes this ultimate truth, he will continue to repeat the cycle of birth and death, called reincarnation. He will act and react, doing good and doing evil, a cycle called karma. Making mistake after mistake, he eventually tires of the cycles. Becoming tired, he renounces his attachment to the world, follows a path, and finds moksha, or liberation.

When a person reaches this stage of evolutionary advancement, after many cycles of being born and dying, he will choose one of the paths of yoga. He will need a personal teacher or guide, called a *guru*. A guru is one who has been to the top of the mountain of spirituality and has come back down to lead others to the summit. This is one of the unique aspects of Hinduism. Talking with God is done face to face. You don't talk with an invisible savior, nor do you have to interpret old texts. The enlightened living teacher provides immediate feedback when you have strayed off course. There is little or no room for self-deception.

From Allah to Zen

A **guru** is a spiritual teacher who assists a student toward enlightenment. The Sanskrit word literally means "dispeller of darkness."

Since Hinduism offers different approaches to God for different types of people, there are also a variety of spiritual practices to pursue. A follower of Bhakti-yoga, for example, might use devotional singing and chanting as part of his daily spiritual practice. A Jnana yogi might use the tools of philosophical logic and self-observation. A Karma yogi would likely be involved in some form of selfless service, and a follower of Raja yoga would probably choose to perform daily breathing and meditation exercises. Of course, no regimen is fixed in stone. Seekers typically do whatever their guru and their inner guidance feel is most appropriate at the time.

Cosmic Potholes

If you go to India, be careful of false gurus. There are many imposters who prey on tourists. They usually try to sell you beads or read your palm or follow you until you give them money. A true guru would never do this. You are pretty safe if you go to established ashrams (spiritual centers run by specific gurus) to meet a teacher. It is highly unlikely to meet a true master on the street.

Whatever method or approach the Hindu seeker uses, the goal is the same—union with the Supreme Self. It is said that when one realizes his Supreme Self, the material world and all its suffering falls away as if a dream. What is left is infinite Being, infinite consciousness, infinite bliss.

The Science of Buddhism

The foundation of Buddhism, which began almost 2,500 years ago, is the teachings of an Indian prince named Siddhartha Gotama.

When Siddhartha was born, in a small Hindu kingdom in what is now Nepal, he had many visitors. One of these was a sage, Asita. Asita told Siddhartha's father, the king, that the boy would grow up to be either a great king or a great sage. The king, of course, wanted the prince to carry on his royal legacy, so he gave the boy everything he could possibly want—every delicious food, toy, material thing, and, when his son was a little older, any woman he wanted. But one thing was denied Siddhartha. He was not allowed to go outside the palace. The king thought that if Siddhartha saw poverty or pain, he would question the meaning of life, and therefore take the path of the sage.

The prince grew up, intelligent, kind, happy, and strong. But he wondered what the world was like outside the palace walls. His father finally consented to allow him to go on a journey, but endeavored to make sure that on the road Siddhartha traveled, he would not encounter sickness, poverty, or anything that might make him question the meaning of life.

The king thought he had removed all the old and sick people from Siddhartha's path. He had not. On his first journey outside of the palace, Siddhartha saw an old man, then a sick man, then a group of mourners carrying a coffin. Siddhartha had never known that people grew old and died. He quickly fell into a deep gloom, and spent day and night contemplating the meaning of what he had seen.

From Allah to Zen

Buddha means "the awakened" or "the enlightened" one. It commonly refers to Siddhartha Gotama, who became enlightened around 500 B.C.E., but it can also refer to anyone who becomes enlightened.

From Allah to Zen

Enlightenment, also known as **samadhi** in Hinduism and **nirvana** in Buddhism, is that perfect state of supreme bliss in which the self is completely absorbed into a sense of oneness with the universe.

From Allah to Zen

Many religions teach that self-denial is holy. Extreme self-denial is called asceticism. In India, some **ascetics** sleep on nails, stare at the sun, or stand on one leg for weeks. The Christian church had monks who wore burlap and flagellated themselves to endure pain.

Siddhartha took one more journey outside the walls of the palace. This time he saw a saint meditating under a tree. He learned that this man had also seen the suffering in the world, and sought to put an end to it by attaining *enlightenment.* Siddhartha came home, sure of his calling. He sneaked away from his family late at night, rode his horse into the forest, cut his hair, and donned the robe of the *ascetic.* At the age of 29, his journey had begun.

After six years of severe fasting and meditation practices, Siddhartha still had not found the cause of suffering. Going against the protests of the other ascetics with him, he gave up his fast and ate a good meal. Making one last attempt to understand, he sat down under a tree, vowing not to get up until he died or found the end of suffering. Under this tree, called the Bodhi tree, Siddhartha became the *Buddha,* the Enlightened One. He went on to become a great world teacher, as Asita had prophesied, and from his teachings, Buddhism was born.

Buddha's Teachings

Buddha's first teaching was in a deer park, a little north of the city of Sarnath. He taught that all humans are caught in the wheel of reincarnation. They go through lifetimes in a cycle of birth and death, creating situations that carry consequences, known as *karma.* Until an individual can free himself from this wheel of birth and death, he will be subject to the ups and downs of suffering.

From Allah to Zen

Karma is a Sanskrit word referring to the law of cause and effect, or universal balance. It is normally thought of as a law that makes it so everything you do, say, or think has an effect on the universe that, in some way, eventually reverberates back to you.

The Buddha taught his first disciples The Four Noble Truths. These truths form the bedrock of Buddhist belief:

➤ **Dukka: The Noble Truth of Suffering or dissatisfaction.** Life is full of suffering, and full of sickness and unhappiness. Although there are passing pleasures, they vanish in time, hence, they too are dissatisfactory.

➤ **Samudaya: The Noble Truth of the Cause of Suffering.** People suffer for one simple reason: They desire things. It is self-centeredness and greed which bring about suffering. Desire is never satisfied.

➤ **Nirodha: The Noble Truth of the End of Suffering.** It is possible to end suffering if one is aware of one's own desires and puts an end to them. This awareness will open the door to lasting peace.

➤ **Magga: The Noble Truth of the Path.** By changing one's thinking and behavior, an authentic awakening from self and its problematic desires can be reached. This is called the Middle Way and can be followed in the Eightfold Path.

Cosmic Potholes

Buddha found that the methods of ascetics only increased self-importance and pride. The Middle Path, he said, is the way to freedom.

The Eightfold Path was the Buddha's "map" for how a seeker can best progress spiritually. In this same sermon in Deer Park, Buddha laid out the requirements of the Eightfold Path:

1. **Right Understanding.** Strive to understand clearly the Four Noble Truths. Strive to understand the workings of your own mind.

2. **Right Thought.** Think kindly of others and avoid dwelling on the past or future.

3. **Right Speech.** Speak kindly and truthfully.

4. **Right Action.** Act kindly toward all living things. Do not be attached to the results of your actions. The five precepts could be included here: Do not kill, do not steal, do not lie, do not be unchaste, and do not take intoxicating drugs or drink alcohol.

5. **Right Work.** Have a vocation that does not harm others.

6. **Right Effort.** Be determined to cleanse your mind.

7. **Right Mindfulness.** Buddha said, "All we are is the result of what we have thought." He sees sin as the result of ignorance. To gradually overcome this ignorance, Buddha calls his disciples to take up a very difficult step, one of continuous self-examination. Mindfully watching mental states and bodily sensations, the aspirant becomes aware of the patterns of the mind and body, its constant state of change, and finally sees that there is nobody behind these thoughts and sensations. With this discrimination, the belief in a separate self begins to dissolve.

8. **Right Concentration.** Clear, one-pointed concentration on an object of meditation, such as the breath. This step is very similar to the Hindu path of Raja yoga.

Is Buddhism a True Religion?

Some people say Buddhism is a philosophy and not a religion. This is because Buddha did not talk about a personal God, and maintained that there is no such thing as a soul or the atman. He remained silent when asked about God, because God is beyond description.

The closest he came to describing God is his depiction of nirvana, or liberation. He said that nirvana is "permanent, stable, imperishable, immovable, ageless, deathless, unborn, power, bliss, and happiness." He said that it is "the Good, the supreme goal and the one and only eternal and incomprehensible peace." If the meaning of God is a being that creates, Buddhism is atheistic, in that the Buddha does not believe such a being is the most ultimate state possible. But if God is considered as the One, indivisible, then Buddhism can be called a true religion. But if God is considered as the One who simply *is*, indivisible, then Buddhism can be called a true religion.

Heavenly Helpers

The Buddha's Eightfold Path contains many similarities to Jewish, Christian, Islamic, and Hindu ideas. Whenever there is widespread agreement on a spiritual principle, it's likely to be especially important. Notice the similarities between these religions and try to put special emphasis on such teachings.

Buddha argued that the world, because it is ever-changing, is virtually unreal. In fact, Buddha's ideas about the natural order of the material world in many ways resemble the ideas of modern science and physics. Nothing in nature is unchanging from moment to moment. Everything is a chain reaction of events. Broken down into its smallest known particles, it is nothing but space and energy.

The Buddha included thoughts, emotions, and the sense of self in this ever-changing parade of action and reaction. What we think of ourselves is also an illusion, for it has no permanence. The grasping for permanence in a world of impermanence is the cause of pain. Freedom from pain can be achieved only through freedom from these illusions. Stripped of these beliefs, we experience the eternal bliss of Being.

Buddhism Today

Buddhism soon spread to South Asia, Central Asia, China, Tibet, Korea, and Japan. It has also become widespread in the West, primarily because of the exile of the Tibetans and the Dalai Lama in 1959, and Western exposure to Zen Buddhism. With the expansion of Buddhism came some differences in how it was practiced. It eventually split into two primary sects, one self-described by its practitioners as the Mahayana, or "Big Raft," and the other self-described by its adherents as the *Hinayana,* "Little Raft," or "Way of the Elders."

In the countries I've traveled in which Buddhism is the main religion, I've noticed a great respect for the Buddha's teachings, and reverence for those engaged in spiritual work. For instance, before becoming the president of Thailand, the presidential candidate has to kiss the feet of a random Buddhist monk begging on the streets. This ritual is meant to symbolize that even the president is "below" a begging monk in terms of status.

Having spent time in several Buddhist monasteries, I have always been impressed with the scientific precision of Buddhist teachings, as well as the earnestness in which meditation and mindfulness are practiced by its followers. Buddhism is a very logical, practical, and methodical approach to becoming free of suffering.

From Allah to Zen

Hinayana, or Little Raft, does not mean it is a lesser path. It is a narrower path, open only to those who want to be monks or nuns, and it sticks conservatively to Buddha's original teachings. It is also known as Theravada, or the Way of the Elders.

The Now of Taoism

Taoism (pronounced *dowism*) is an ancient philosophy and religion of China. It is said to have originated with a man named Lao Tzu around 500 B.C.E. Lao Tzu means Grand Old Master, and was a name of endearment and respect. Much of Lao Tzu's life is a mystery—his birth name remains unknown—and some people say he did not even exist. Most probably he was a solitary recluse who was absorbed in meditation, but some stories portray him as a sage consulting at the imperial court. His story ends as mysteriously as it begins, with Lao Tzu riding his water buffalo westward into central China.

Amazing Grace

The Tao Te Ching, as well as other Taoist writings, is very poetic to read. Simply reading the Tao Te Ching can transport you into a higher state of being. In fact, it is said that the Tao Te Ching is the most widely read and translated book in the world next to the Bible. It is quite short, but each line is pregnant with meaning. Even read slowly, it can be completed in a couple of hours.

From Allah to Zen

The **Tao Te Ching** is a book supposedly written by Lao Tzu. Roughly translated, the book title can be interpreted as "The Way and Its Power." The word "Tao" (pronounced *dow*) can be roughly translated as "the way," or, in other contexts, as "the supreme formless or God."

Lao Tzu was saddened by the conditions of humanity and the reluctance of people to follow the way of goodness that he taught. So he went far away to seek solitude. At the farthest gate of China, he was stopped by the gatekeeper, who tried to persuade him to turn back. Lao Tzu refused, but consented to leave behind a book representing his knowledge of Truth. This book is all we know of him today. It is called the *Tao Te Ching,* The Book of the Way and Its Power, and is the basic text of Taoism.

Contemplative Taoism became an influential philosophy for both laypeople and kings. Over time, it also became a religion. Yet, as a religion, it veered from its basic philosophical ideas, and began emphasizing the possibility of immortality, the worship of deities, the building of temples, and so on.

The Contribution of Chuang Tzu

The philosophy of Taoism laid out in the Tao Te Ching was further developed by the mystic writer Chuang Tzu, who was born around 370 B.C.E. Like Lao Tzu, Chuang Tzu felt it was important for people to transcend all dualities, or ideas that we are separate from everything around us. They both felt that it was mankind's desires that were the problem, and advised people to turn from their strivings and return to their natural state.

Both Lao Tzu and Chuang Tzu believed in the philosophy of wu-wei, which literally means "doing nothing," as a way to find peace. It's not that they advocated never acting on anything, but rather that people should discern and follow the natural forces and order of things. In this sense, wu-wei means not interfering with the spontaneous, intelligent, powerful action of the Tao. By following the Tao, or the natural way, all could be accomplished without striving.

The Tao Te Ching consists of 81 short chapters, each advising people in the way of the Tao, often using metaphorical language. For example, here is Stan Rosenthal's translation of chapter eight:

The Way of Water

Great good is said to be like water,
sustaining life with no conscious striving,
flowing naturally, providing nourishment,
found even in places
which desiring man rejects.

In this way
it is like the Tao itself.

Like water, the sage abides in a humble place;
in meditation, without desire;
in thoughtfulness, he is profound,
and in his dealings, kind.
In speech, sincerity guides the man of Tao,
and as a leader, he is just.
In management, competence is his aim,
and he ensures the pacing is correct.

Because he does not act for his own ends,
nor cause unnecessary conflict,
he is held to be correct
in his actions toward his fellow man.

Much of Taoism and Tao Te Ching can be summarized in a single passage from Chuang Tzu:

> "To regard the fundamental as the essence, to regard things as coarse, to regard accumulation as deficiency, and to dwell quietly alone with the spiritual and the intelligent—herein lies the techniques of Tao of the ancients."

The Importance of Yin-Yang

The philosophy of Taoism is often represented by the yin-yang symbol. This symbol, which represents the interconnectedness of dualities, looks like this:

The yin-yang symbol.

This ancient symbol contains many secrets. It shows the relationship of opposites and how they make up all that we experience. There would be no goodness if there were no evil. There would be no light if there were no darkness. It is something's opposite that makes it a distinguishable, knowable thing. The opposites intermingle somewhat, flowing into each other gracefully with no rigid delineation. Each even contains a suggestion of its opposite, the dot at its center.

This circle represents the Tao in its eternal wholeness. Inside this circle, the pairs of opposites turn endlessly in cycles, night and day, summer and winter, each exchanging its place for the other. This cycle is never resolved, only transcended through the realization that all is one, the meaning of the circle that surrounds them. That is why a distinguishing characteristic of Taoism is its stance on good and evil. Taoists do not see a contradiction in these two, or one as being "better." They are only relative to the mind that entertains them. Ultimately, all opposites are seen as balancing each other. The Tao Te Ching and the Chuang Tzu invite people to transcend all sense of egotism, both the egotism that indulges in evil and the egotism that inflates itself with being a do-gooder.

The Eastern religions are practical paths to finding what lies beyond the world of opposites. They, each in their own way, can lead you to "the kingdom of heaven within." They hold human beings in an ultimately positive light, and give hope for the realization of our true nature. They maintain an optimism of human potential, which is as limitless as the eternal space within. The soul or self is unfathomable, and yet it can be experienced. God is within our reach here on Earth.

The Least You Need to Know

➤ Eastern religions emphasize selfless *being*, rather than selfish striving, or goal-oriented behavior.

➤ Hinduism has many different approaches to help liberate seekers, depending upon the disposition of the person who wants to know God.

➤ Buddhism is a practical, logical teaching and series of methods to help eliminate the cause and experience of suffering so that one can awaken to the spiritual state beyond all greed, hatred, and delusion.

➤ Taoism is a philosophy that also gave rise to a religious development, that emphasizes the importance of returning to our natural spiritual state, and the ultimate uselessness of our ambition, control, and strivings.

Chapter 7

Twelve Steps to Transformation

In This Chapter

➤ The history of Alcoholics Anonymous

➤ How to use the Twelve Steps in daily life

➤ Why the Twelve Steps are effective

➤ The nature of addiction and recovery

In 1935, Bill Wilson was on a business trip to Akron, Ohio. Bill was an alcoholic who had been seeking to overcome his alcoholism with the help of a spiritual group called the Oxford Group. The business part of the trip was going badly and Bill was considering having a drink. Instead, he picked up the phone and called a local group minister. That phone call brought together Bill and Dr. Bob Smith, who became the founders of Alcoholics Anonymous. With the help of the Oxford Group, A.A. grew rapidly.

Today, there are more than two million people around the world participating in twelve-step programs or related support groups. Though the aim of these programs is addiction recovery, thousands of members would claim that the program is also their spiritual path. The twelve-step program is probably one of the most effective methods known for creating change based on spiritual growth principles. The combination of straightforward, commonsense goals, a flexible view of God, and a network of peers for both support and accountability is a path that has worked for millions.

Although A.A.'s spiritual roots are Christian, founded in the teachings of the Oxford Group, its flexible definition of God allows people who would otherwise be turned off by traditional religion to benefit from the program. All twelve-step organizations disavow their own affiliation with any religion or particular view of God or spirituality.

Amazing Grace

The Oxford Group was founded in 1908 by a Lutheran minister, Frank Buchman. Buchman's vision was to revive the methods and beliefs of the apostles. He worked to create small, dedicated groups that held very high spiritual standards and worked with each other to maintain those standards. The Oxford Group was particularly successful among affluent Americans. The group's popularity was at its peak in the 1930s and 1940s, and it was during this time that A.A. founders Ebby T., Bill Wilson, and Dr. Bob Smith found sobriety using methods and teachings rooted in the Oxford Group. Among these methods were group support, meditation, personal inventory, and deep honesty. The Oxford Group continues today; its name changed in the 1940s to Moral Re-Armament (MRA).

A Framework for Recovery

One of its practitioners describes A.A. as "a ridiculously simple, jerry-built, noisy, fiercely loved, and joyous kind of vehicle." Of evangelical Christian roots, it passed through the Oxford Group into the hands of pragmatic alcoholics who knew that to save themselves, they had to throw out what didn't work—trying to convert people to evangelical Christianity—and retain what did. They combined psychology with the medical view of alcoholism, and, most important, persuaded people who were in trouble to work with and care for one another.

The result is an inclusive, flexible, and focused approach not only to achieving sobriety, but to staying sober. Staying sober is the most important goal for an addict, and the Twelve Steps are flexible enough to accommodate whatever it takes for a person to achieve that goal.

The Twelve Steps Approach

The Twelve Steps approach gently opens a door to the desire for connection and peace that is inside everyone. A twelve-step recovery program consists not only of following the Twelve Steps but of going to meetings, reading the A.A. Big Book, sometimes reading the Bible, and sometimes talking with a sponsor. Daily prayer and meditation are encouraged. This practice often takes the form of a morning prayer for guidance and silent self-assessment.

One of the reasons twelve-step programs have such broad appeal is that they allow people to come to personal understandings at their own pace. Newcomers are encouraged to read, listen, and share their thoughts about how the program is going for them. If something works, use it; if it doesn't, leave it for now. People are not generally put on the spot and confronted for their drinking. Instead, by listening to the stories of others, each person comes to see, in his own time, the value of A.A. and the Twelve Steps.

Cosmic Potholes

The Twelve Steps is a lifelong process. Every person who chooses to try them isn't expected to accept or embrace them all. Don't look at them and say, "I can't do all that!" Do what you can.

Step by Step

The Twelve Steps were assembled and distilled during the first years of A.A., originating from principles taught by the Oxford Group. The Oxford Group focused on changing people's lives by creating a powerful, personal relationship with God. Some of the group's principles adopted by A.A.'s founders are ...

➤ Recognizing a power greater than ourselves.

➤ Surrendering one's will to that power.

➤ Rigorous self-assessment.

➤ Restitution of wrongs.

➤ Confession to God and to each other.

➤ The method of relating personal stories as a way to spread the word.

➤ Passing on what God has done for us.

Almost all the steps echo a point of view found in Oxford Group teaching.

From Allah to Zen

We live in a culture that promotes the idea of "personal power." The illusion that we have the power to control our lives is an impediment to spiritual growth. **Powerlessness** is not being a victim of situations, but a recognition of our place in relationship to God.

The Twelve Steps of Alcoholics Anonymous

1. We admitted we were powerless over alcohol—that our lives had become unmanageable.

2. Came to believe that a Power greater than ourselves could restore us to sanity.

3. Made a decision to turn our will and our lives over to the care of God as we understood Him.

4. Made a searching and fearless moral inventory of ourselves.

5. Admitted to God, to ourselves and to another human being the exact nature of our wrongs.

6. Were entirely ready to have God remove all these defects of character.

7. Humbly asked Him to remove our shortcomings.

8. Made a list of all persons we had harmed, and became willing to make amends to them all.

9. Made direct amends to such people whenever possible, except when to do so would injure them or others.

10. Continued to take personal inventory and when we were wrong promptly admitted it.

11. Sought through prayer and meditation to improve our conscious contact with God as we understood Him, praying only for knowledge of His will for us and the power to carry that out.

12. Having had a spiritual awakening as the result of those steps, we tried to carry this message to alcoholics and to practice these principles in all our affairs.

As you can see, the steps are not simply intended to keep a person sober. They are a process for living a set of spiritual principles. Therefore, while many people get into twelve-step programs because of addiction, they often stay in the program for the spiritual support it offers. In addition, while you may not have a clear-cut addiction, I believe that any sincere seeker would find the Twelve Steps to be a helpful framework for spiritual growth.

Using the Steps

God is mentioned in seven of the Twelve Steps. Language such as "powerless," "turning over our lives," and "making amends to them all" can seem pretty heavy and intimidating. Fortunately, you are free to interpret each step in accordance with your view of God. It is your relationship to God that you are trying to build and are accountable for. You can use the steps as a guide to assess the condition of your spiritual life, whether you have an addiction or not.

For example, take Step One, "We admitted we were powerless over alcohol—that our lives had become unmanageable." I'm not an alcoholic—my worst addiction is to television, and I don't think my life is unmanageable because of it. However, I can still look at my life in relationship to the First Step. Since I can't even control my own thoughts, any belief I have that I'm in control of anything is an illusion. The time and energy I put into worrying about how a stock investment will go, or how my next book will do, is wasted—gone forever.

I've seen that by admitting I'm powerless over various elements of my life, it has opened up more "room" for God to enter.

Here's another example of applying the steps to your life. Step Eight says: "Made a list of all persons we had harmed, and became willing to make amends to them all." When reading such a statement, it's easy to become overwhelmed. You might think, "How can I possibly make such a list, and then *make amends* to everyone on it!" Perhaps you can't make *that* list, but you can make *some* list on which there would be people to whom you could make amends.

Recently, I tried making such a list. On the list of people I have hurt, there were many small instances that I was able to easily amend. For example, I neglected to return a phone call. So I picked up the phone and apologized to the person I didn't call back. In making amends with only a few people, I learned something about forgiveness and the sweetness of humility. It helped me to see how much my fear and pride has cost me. It helped me to look at other names on the list and feel remorse about the hurt I've done to some relationships. Just a little bit of effort with this step showed me how powerful it can be.

Heavenly Helpers

Some A.A. groups, more than others, stress a relationship with God. In some groups, God is hardly mentioned, while in others, you might think you're in a Bible study. If you're looking for spiritual transformation, find a group that matches your level of aspiration. This may mean checking out a few different twelve-step groups.

From Allah to Zen

To **make amends** in A.A. means to fix or improve something. Amending a wrong usually means saying, "I'm sorry." Yet apologies, while nice, are sometimes meaningless. Another way to make amends is to change or amend *yourself.* Resolve that you will never bring harm that way again.

Caring for Others

One of the most important parts of a twelve-step program is bringing together people with a common problem. They learn that by caring for and thinking about someone else, they help themselves.

From the start of A.A., service to others has been a key to the twelve-step path. Bill Wilson, A.A.'s founder, believed that only by helping another alcoholic get sober could he himself stay sober. Service to others balances the amount of self-examination that takes place, keeping the process from becoming dry and self-absorbing.

It might seem odd or ironic that in order to help ourselves, we have to help others. It is not that helping others becomes self-serving, but that service to others helps connect us to something bigger than ourselves—and in the process, we benefit. We become less "me" oriented, and thereby link ourselves to grace. It seems to be one of the cosmic laws of Spirit that, to ease your own suffering, you need to help someone else ease his suffering.

I am not a participant in a twelve-step program, but I am part of a spiritual group. I know the value and importance of having good companions on the path with me. I want to be a better person, yet my desire for this is not always enough to keep me headed in the right direction. I need help.

I know that my personal addiction, television, is devastating to my spirit. Yet if I plant myself in front of the TV, I will sit there for hours. My housemates know me and they know how to help me with this addiction. We have an agreement that I can't watch TV unless they're watching (which is almost never!). Having the support of others is key in almost all spiritual endeavors.

Amazing Grace

The average American watches 4 hours and 20 minutes of TV each day! Yet most people don't even view it as an addiction. In my own case, since I know I'm addicted to TV and need help to avoid overdoing it, I make sure my housemates help me avoid getting stuck in front of the tube. Struggling with this addiction, and using the Twelve Steps to confront it, has made me better appreciate the value of the twelve-step process.

There is a tangible atmosphere of equality and acceptance in an A.A. meeting. This is part of the magic of the process. In twelve-step programs, addicts help each other, primarily by sharing their life experiences. The belief is that an addict can only be helped by another addict, because help from anyone else is a well-intentioned put-down. While this point is debatable, it is true that you're likely going to give more credibility to someone who has been through the experience you're struggling with.

Seeing It as It Is

It is an act of courage to take the first steps—admitting your condition and honestly assessing yourself. Whether it's seeing the ruin an addiction has brought, or seeing the emptiness of a life pursuing material happiness, honest evaluation of ourselves inevitably leads to seeing our need for spiritual growth.

Upon being honest with themselves, what many people see are abandoned families, failed love, lost jobs, damaged health, amassing debt, and gathering depression. Many people who begin the twelve-step process find an honest assessment of their moral behavior to bring shame and embarrassment. People are ashamed to admit their pettiness, selfishness, and level of daily indulgence. The desire to deny, blame, or wallow in self-pity can creep in. It takes consistent courage to not turn back from self-honesty.

In the Twelve Steps, this honest look requires admitting that we are entangled in something that is beyond our control. Rather than depend on one's own willpower, the first steps state that we need God's help to get us out of the mess we're in. The commitment to "turn our will and our lives over to the care of God" may seem extreme to some, particularly Westerners, who can be more controlled by needs and cravings than they realize. Yet in an addict's case, his life is already surrendered to the object of his addiction. It is only through the surrender to a positive "addiction," namely God, that hope can be restored.

Cosmic Potholes

When honestly evaluating your life, it's easy to become overwhelmed, which can lead to self-pity or giving up. Remember that you're on a path of recovery. The worst is over! Hang in there. Self-evaluation is hard work, and sometimes you may need to take it slowly, rather than all at once.

Heavenly Helpers

To make amends in the moment that something happens, all you need to do is say what you're thinking and feeling. For example, you might say, "I'm sorry I was impatient with you. I guess I must be pretty stressed. I feel bad that I took my frustration out on you." People almost always react positively to this type of sincerity.

The Flip Side

A.A. and the Twelve Steps have their detractors. It's a big organization that sees its job as changing people's lives. That's a tall order, and some people don't like the way A.A. carries it out.

Some criticize A.A.'s flexibility in its view of God. Since God is defined by each individual, some Christians oppose the program because accepting Christ is not central. Fundamentalists of any religion would probably oppose the program since it invokes God, but doesn't recognize their God as *the* God. A.A., however, does not preclude anyone in the program from participating in another religious organization. In fact, participation is encouraged if it helps the person keep with the program. "Whatever works" seems to be their motto.

Cosmic Potholes

Anyone can use spirituality to hide from the world. It can happen in a twelve-step program, or in any spiritual organization. The nurturing and understanding environment of an A.A. meeting is needed for a person in recovery, but it is not intended to protect someone from the real world or from learning his spiritual lessons.

Some *addiction* professionals, Dr. Stanton Peele for example, feel that A.A. substitutes one addiction for another. The premise that addicts are "powerless" places the person in a victim position, and according to some people, this is psychologically unhealthy. People could become dependent on the A.A. program.

That's certainly a possibility, but it's a possibility in any method of recovery or spiritual growth. No matter what twelve-step program a person chooses, each person must eventually assess and take responsibility for his or her life. God will give strength, and programs like A.A. will provide help, but the work of cleaning up their life is theirs.

What Is Addiction?

Addiction has become one of the buzzwords of this age. A simple definition of addiction doesn't exist. Byron Lewis, author of *Sobriety Demystified,* defines it this way:

> Any compulsively repeated behavior, whether drinking, using, gambling, eat-purging, certain sexual activities, etc., which negatively impact an individual biologically, psychologically, socially, or spiritually is an addiction.

Everyone likes to feel good. Feeling good is not a problem. It only becomes a problem when the experiences we choose become limited and compulsive. The world we've created is often stressful and painful. It's necessary to find relief. Common ways we find relief are television, Web surfing, shopping, and working. Although these may not seem harmful, they can take a toll on our soul. They keep us busy, distracted, and away from a deeper connection with our spirit.

So why do we become addicted? Why do so many people spend their lives fulfilling a craving? Well-known medical doctor Andrew Weil suggests that craving is a fundamental part of human life. It's easy to believe. We are separate from God, and re-union with the creator is something we all want. Some people try to fill this need with drugs, ciga-rettes, or alcohol, to the point of physical and psychic destruction, while others fill it with sex, money, or life-risking activities. What we each are trying to get is that fix that will make us feel all right—some high that will carry us through this moment of barely tolerable separation. Yet all these efforts to achieve the peace we crave will fail. The peace that we want can only be filled by reunion with God.

Fixing What Is Broken

What any spiritual path teaches us is to become ad-dicted to simple methods to get the "fix" we need.
The twelve-step programs teach people to become addicted to truth, service, connec-tion with God, and surrender. Other paths teach people to become addicted to quiet meditation, breathing exercises, or feeling the unity of themselves with all creation.

The ultimate "fix" is the peace within our own soul that connects to the heaven within. No drug, no thought, no thing outside ourselves can match the intoxication of connecting with the source of our existence.

Heavenly Helpers

Nowadays there are literally dozens of twelve-step programs offered in most cities. You can find programs for any addiction, even programs for being related to someone who has an addic-tion problem (such as Al-Anon). To find an appropriate twelve-step program in your area, look in your phone book under "Alcoholics Anonymous."

The Least You Need to Know

➤ Almost everyone is addicted to something, such as work, television, Web surf-ing, or shopping.

➤ The Twelve Steps, and twelve-step programs such as Alcoholics Anonymous, provide not only a process for breaking out of addictive behavior, but a help-ful framework for spiritual growth.

➤ If your life is in crisis because of an addiction, get help; don't try to fight it alone.

➤ We are all addicted to feeling good. Try to find many different ways of feeling good. Learn to appreciate subtler joys that can be found all around us all the time.

Chapter 8

The Way of Devotion

In This Chapter

➤ How Hindus create and express devotion toward many deities

➤ The way Buddhists venerate their best teachers

➤ How a guru can be a useful focus of devotion

➤ How to open up to Christian devotion and the Holy Spirit

➤ Methods and expressions of devotion, such as rituals and chanting

All major religions and spiritual paths emphasize the importance of *devotion*. While they may use different methods, or call their God by different names, the common theme among all the paths is the need to focus on love. Not love in the normal human sense, but rather an intense longing, a total burning to know the Creator more intimately. To help build a powerful emotional connection to God, various paths have created ingenious rituals, beliefs, and methods for expressing and expanding devotion to something bigger than ourselves.

Devotion is not something that usually comes naturally to Westerners. In a society based on science and materialism, the faith necessary to maintain intense devotional energy can be hard to come by. By learning how several religious paths create and express an inner longing for God, you can begin to incorporate many of their ideas and methods into your own journey. Whether you're a Christian, a Jew, or simply a brand-new spiritual seeker, an understanding of the many ways of devotion can help enliven your longing for Spirit.

The Hindu Science of Devotion

Perhaps more than any other religion, Hinduism has developed a sophisticated science of devotion, referred to as *Bhakti-yoga*. This path of devotion offers a variety of concepts and methods to help the spiritual aspirant more fully love and surrender to his beloved God.

From Allah to Zen

Devotion is an ardent loyalty, love, respect, and/or allegiance to a person or deity. When people experience devotion, it opens up their hearts and can help them have a deeper experience of their spiritual essence.

From Allah to Zen

Bhakti-yoga is the science of devotion to God, emphasizing the importance of surrender, love, service, and an intense personal relationship with whatever form of God one is worshipping. Bhakti adherents often use chanting, prayer, various rituals, and pilgrimages as part of their spiritual practice.

The Devoted

The seeds of devotional sentiment sprouted in India sometime around 200 B.C.E., when the Bhagavad-Gita, one of the most important texts in the Hindu tradition, was likely composed. The Bhagavad-Gita built on the two paths to liberation popular at that time—the path of action (Karma yoga) and the path of wisdom (Jnana yoga). It offered a new approach to liberation as well—that of devotion. In the text, the God Krishna tells Arjuna, a warrior, to fight the battle he must fight, but to devote the fruits of his action to Krishna. By following the path of devotion, Krishna teaches, one achieves liberation from the endless cycle of rebirth. Besides the Bhagavad-Gita, Hindus have a rich oral tradition and countless other texts containing stories, mythology, and poetry that point to the joy, intensity, and fruits of devotion. Poets and saints throughout India, male as well as female, have composed devotional verses to their beloved Lord. These verses are well known and well loved by devout Hindus.

In the following centuries and up to the present day, Hindus have approached their deities from a variety of devotional standpoints. In order to foster feelings of love and devotion, Hindus say that one may approach God in the manner most suited to one's personal inclination. For example, a Hindu may relate to God as a servant to a master, as a son to a father, as a parent to a child, as a friend to a friend, or as a lover toward his or her beloved.

The One in the Many

Because Hinduism has so many forms of God, a superficial look at the religion can make one think it is polytheistic. Yet each deity, such as Krishna, Ram, or the goddess Devi, is seen merely as an aspect of the one singular, absolute God. By appealing to deities who "specialize" in various aspects of life, devotees are better able to form closer devotional relationships with them.

For instance, if a person is starting a business, she might pray to Lakshmi, the goddess of wealth. Or a student preparing for exams might pray to Saraswati, the goddess of learning. As a devotee focuses his energy on a chosen deity, he develops a deeper "relationship" with the deity—and he hopes that the deity will thereby smile upon him.

Hindu devotees have many other ways of deepening their intimacy with God. They might go to a temple to pray before an image of the deity and make an offering of food or money. They may make a pilgrimage to a site that is sacred to their chosen deity. They may construct a special altar in their home, say heartfelt prayers, read devotional literature, or simply consider that in all their actions they are serving their beloved form of God.

In these and other ways, the feelings of connection and devotion are intensified. Eventually, a devotee can begin to see all people and life situations as gifts emanating from his chosen deity. Through this process, he can see and appreciate God in each situation in his life.

While the idea of a deity in charge of different areas of life may seem childish to a Western mind, one must remember that it was a common concept even in ancient Greece. Human beings have often segmented a formless, all-powerful God into various parts, from Apollo to Zeus. By putting a "face" on God, many seekers throughout history have found it easier to develop a more intimate relationship with the source of life.

Emotional Buddhism

Buddhism is known for being a very rational and logical approach to spirituality. Therefore, it may surprise you to know that it has a major devotional element in its modern-day practice. Although the

Cosmic Potholes

Although relating to God in the way that comes most naturally can be a great help, it can also be a profound limitation. For example, in Western culture, many people only relate to God as a father. Yet, relating to God through the filter of other types of relationships can help to expand one's sense of God, and thereby deepen one's relationship to him.

Heavenly Helpers

In opening your heart to God, you might try pretending or imagining that God is your friend or lover. Try talking to God as if God were your imaginary friend or invisible lover. It can be easier to pray to and relate to a God who loves you unconditionally rather than a God who is remote or distant.

Buddha himself seemed to shun devotion and worship, various sects of Buddhism have made use of devotional elements as part of the journey toward enlightenment.

While Buddhism is a nontheistic religion, that fact has never stopped adherents from performing acts of reverence. For instance, it is common for some Buddhists to pilgrimage to the tree beneath which Buddha supposedly became enlightened, to make devout offerings at Buddhist temples, or to pray to Buddhist images. Certain sects of Buddhism, such as Tibetan Buddhism, focus on particular aspects of the Divine that they personify as various deities—as in Hinduism. In their meditations, Tibetan Buddhists attempt to become one with a particular deity and its corresponding qualities.

In the fifth and sixth centuries, partly due to the Bhakti movement spreading across India, personal devotion to the Buddha and *bodhisattvas* became more common. With increased devotion came the inevitable focus on faith and the healing powers of the Buddha and bodhisattvas. Although Buddhism in its most pure form emphasizes the importance of diligent effort, the masses soon popularized the notion that simple devotion to a favorite Buddhist saint could lead to salvation. For example, in a religious sect of Buddhism known as "Pure Land Buddhism," the recitation of the names of certain Buddhist saints or short sacred texts (or sutras) became a popular method of devotional Buddhism.

From Allah to Zen

A **bodhisattva** is like a saint in the Buddhist tradition. They seek enlightenment purely for the benefit of mankind. Bodhisattvas devote their lives to the service of others, and even vow to forego their own personal enlightenment in order to make sure they can continue to help all beings.

Although traditional Buddhism does not worship various deities as in Hinduism, it does have a strong history of venerating Buddhist teachers and bodhisattvas. For example, there are many legends about the intensity of Bodhidharma, the man credited with bringing Zen Buddhism into China.

One such legend has it that Bodhidharma cut off his eyelids to prevent himself from falling asleep while meditating. Other Buddhist teachers, such as the Dalai Lama and many other lamas, are often objects of devotion for devout seekers. When I interviewed the Dalai Lama, he humbly referred to himself as "a simple monk." Yet for millions of Buddhists around the world, he is more aptly to be worshipped as the fourteenth reincarnation of the Buddha of compassion.

Devoted to the Guru in You

Starting in the 1960s, a lot of Westerners went to India in search of an enlightened guru. Nowadays, the word *guru* is a common, though largely misunderstood, term in the West. For one thing, there is a difference between a teacher and a guru. A teacher points you toward the path of enlightenment, whereas a guru *is* the path to enlightenment. A person can potentially be a teacher to some people, and a guru to others.

For instance, some people relate to Jesus as a very wise teacher, whereas others see him as God in human form—able to "save" devotees through his divine intervention.

In the Hindu tradition, there is a concept known as "gurukripa." In essence, guru-kripa is the path of seeing the guru's hand in all things. The events, people, and circumstances of one's life are seen as gifts given by the guru to help the seeker find God. In India, where certain gurus are known to have miraculous powers, it is easy for many people to believe that their guru is "behind the scenes," dealing each devotee certain life lessons for their benefit.

This point of view is very different from Western thinking. In Western thinking, if you lose your job, it's because of bad luck, a bad economy, or the fact that your boss is a jerk. For devotees practicing gurukripa, it's because of the guru's grace and will. A devotee, rather than be upset by the loss of a job, would see it as his teacher's will and grace. Since it's his beloved teacher's will, he would try to understand the meaning behind it, and make use of it spiritually as best he could.

Amazing Grace

When I was at a big ashram in India, I stayed at a small local hotel. While paying my bill, I noticed that the desk clerk got very nervous. He began praying to his guru. Finally, the manager stepped in and took care of my bill. I asked the manager why the clerk was praying. He said, "He didn't understand how much change to give you, so he prayed for his guru's help." I was amazed that this man surrendered to his guru in even such a minor, worldly matter. I realized that, because of cultural differences, I could never practice devotion and surrender as fully as this innocent man.

Besides gurukripa, there is also a concept in Eastern religions known as "shaktipat," which refers to the flow of grace from a teacher to a student. Some people believe that the simple touch or look of a guru is enough to trigger someone to become enlightened.

I used to think that was hogwash until I met a person named Joyce who had spent many years in a state of bliss due to a single look from her guru. Joyce told me how she was just a normal housewife until her guru, Sai Baba, sent some kind of energy to her upon their first meeting. Once she received his magical look, she was catapulted into a state of unconditional love that lasted about five years. When I met her, three years after she first saw Sai Baba, she radiated unconditional love like no one I had

Cosmic Potholes

Some people, upon hearing of the powers of certain gurus, end up visiting many of them in hopes that they'll be "blasted" with spiritual energy. Such blasts of energy are usually short lived. To truly progress spiritually, it's best to dive into the guru's teachings, rather than just "feed" off his energy.

ever met! Inspired by the stories I had heard of Sai Baba, I decided to travel to India myself. Sai Baba is well known for being able to produce things out of thin air, such as rings or ashes. As an amateur magician, I vowed to see if he could do real magic, or if he was just using sleight of hand. Although there were tens of thousands of people at his ashram, Sai Baba stopped in front of me and held out his hand five inches from my face. Ashes started to manifest from his hand. Fortunately, I had the presence of mind to see if he was manifesting the ashes the way a magician normally would. I carefully concluded he was not using any sleight of hand to produce the ashes.

After about five seconds of manifesting a lot of ashes before my eyes, Sai Baba looked at me mischievously and said, "Satisfied, magic man?" Then, before I could regain my composure, he bent down and seemingly "sneezed" on me. When he did this, it was as if a hurricane of energy blasted through me. I felt like I was going to die. I surrendered to the energy, lost all sense of my body, and entered into a realm of pure bliss. To my amazement, I "came to" about three hours later. Although I felt elated for a couple of days, I then came "down." It hadn't been as long-lasting as what Joyce had experienced, but it was a powerful occurrence. From this experience, I could better understand how and why so many people have become so fervently devoted to this guru.

Now that I've had several experiences with teachers who can clearly send energy, I no longer doubt the potential power of shaktipat. It's easy to fall into the trap of just hoping that some guru will save you—with little or no effort on your part. While I think a guru and shaktipat can be incredibly helpful on the spiritual path, spiritual growth still depends on our level of discipline, consistency, and sincerity. However, in an age of selfishness and closed hearts, opening up to a guru, or receiving his "energy," can be a good beginning to spiritual faith and development.

The Devotional Christian

Islam and Judaism, like every other major religion, have their devotional elements. Sufism, the mystical sect of Islam, is especially ripe with devotional poetry, dance, and worship. Yet neither Islam nor Judaism is, at its core, as devotional as Christianity. After all, the basis of Christianity is that God's only son came to earth in the form of a man—to save us from our sins. Since Jesus is seen as God in human form, the possibility of developing a devotional relationship with Jesus is expanded. While it is rarely the case today, the early Christians practiced many methods of devotion and worship as part of their daily routine.

The Bible is made up of the Old and New Testaments, both of which are really quite different. Except for the biblical books of Psalms and The Song of Songs, there is very little in the Old Testament that speaks of love, devotion, or worship of God. The New Testament is quite different. It is filled with such passages, such as when Paul writes in 1 Corinthians 13 how "If I give all I possess to the poor and surrender my body to the flames, but have not love, I gain nothing." It would seem that one of the aims of Jesus was to remind the religious of his day of the importance of love and worship in traveling the spiritual path.

Cosmic Potholes

If you feel drawn to express more devotion in whatever religion you adhere to, go for it. See if you can use the ideas from this chapter to further open your heart to God. Don't insist that others worship in the same manner as you. Devotion is a very personal thing. It has to come from within—not from proselytizing.

Western culture is primarily Christian, and almost anywhere you go there are Christian symbols and reminders of the love Jesus has for humanity. Since I grew up in a Jewish home, I long avoided anything having to do with Christianity or Jesus. I particularly didn't like the way some evangelical Christians implied that Jesus was the *only* way to true salvation, that all other people "burn in hell." Yet, a non-Christian spiritual teacher I respected suggested that I open my heart to Jesus. I did my best to see what that might be like.

My experiment with Christianity was difficult at first. It took a lot of pain—and letting go of my pride—to become humble enough to receive the grace of Jesus and the Holy Spirit. Although I didn't like the "our way is the only way" attitude of some Christians, I figured there *must* be some experience they were having that I was not. Therefore, I attempted to learn from the "born again" Christians I met, hoping that the experience would open me up to new levels of spiritual understanding.

After just a week of fully immersing myself in the concepts, songs, and prayers of the born-again Christians I met, I started to share their experience of devotion. With all the strength I could muster, I attempted to become vulnerable to God—in the form of Jesus. In my vulnerability I was often filled with the Holy Spirit—which felt incredibly blissful and joyous. Based on such occurrences, I could finally understand why people would want to convert others: to share such a powerful experience.

Nowadays, I still don't believe that Jesus is the *only* way to spiritual salvation. Yet, because I've spent a few years exploring Christian devotion, I can usually open up to Holy Spirit "energy." I greatly enjoy Christian stories, the New Testament, and hanging out with Christians. While I don't agree with some of the beliefs of many Christians, I don't let that get in the way of understanding the spiritual experience that unites us as part of one human family.

I don't know how you feel about Jesus, Christianity, or the Holy Spirit. In this culture, most of us have a lot of baggage from the past that can interfere with our relationship to God. The fact that many churches are spiritually "dead" can be especially detrimental to forming an alive, vibrant relationship to Jesus.

While I don't consider myself an expert on the subject of Jesus and the Holy Spirit, I've seen that seekers who sincerely want to deepen their relationship with Jesus can get the divine help they need. In your relationship with Spirit, as with all relationships, sincerity, vulnerability, consistency, and persistence ultimately are rewarded.

The Technology of Devotion

While religions have different objects of worship, their methods for increasing and maintaining devotion are basically the same. Throughout history, humans longing to open their heart to Spirit have used many of the following methods:

➤ Cleansing rituals

➤ Singing and chanting

➤ Creating and sitting before an altar

➤ Pilgrimages to holy sites

➤ Imagining a relationship with a form of the divine

➤ Having a relationship with a living guru

➤ Sacrificial rituals such as fasting

➤ Certain types of prayer

➤ Certain types of meditation

Cleansing rituals and chanting are two of my personal favorites.

Heavenly Helpers

To become more receptive to the Holy Spirit, and to develop a deeper devotion to Jesus, try to find a church or a person who inspires you. You may have to search out many churches to find the one that seems to fit. Devotion to God is contagious. To a large extent you catch it from spending time with those who already have it.

Cleansing Rituals

There are endless variations of what I would call cleansing rituals. In general, a cleansing ritual is anything you do that helps you let go of the past and become more receptive to divine guidance or energy.

Since we tend to live in a rather distracted and intellectual state of mind, many cleansing rituals have been created to help people focus on the power and love inherent in God's grace. For instance, Catholics go to confession and take communion as a way to let go of past wrongs and reconnect with the teachings of

Christ. Hindus often perform *pujas,* which are ritual offerings to their favorite deity, in order to purify themselves and receive divine blessing.

Although cleansing rituals have been around for thousands of years, it's possible to create your own. The first goal of a cleansing ritual is to help you let go of thinking about the past. Once you're more present, the second goal of a cleansing ritual is to open you up to a deepening intimacy and union with God.

By experimenting with activities such as reading holy texts, taking a cleansing bath, listening to music, or burning incense, you can discover what works best for you. Notice which rituals help you to let go of the past and become more relaxed, spiritually attuned, and focused on the here and now. When it comes to cleansing rituals, imitating what works for others is second best. Experiment and find what works for you.

From Allah to Zen

A **puja** is a ritual offering, usually made to a specific deity, to purify oneself and receive the deity's blessing. In puja one offers sweets, waves incense, bows before a picture of the chosen deity, or performs other rituals.

Chanting

Another great way to increase a sense of devotion toward God is to sing to him. Playing music and singing are two of the strongest ways to stir up the emotions. By writing love songs to Spirit, or singing chants that others have written, you are likely to experience an outpouring of powerful feelings.

I mentioned previously that I had always disdained people who sing chants. Once I tried it, however, the experience was incredible. There is a certain magical energy, especially in a group, that can be created when singing worshipful songs to God. It's as if God wants people to come together to sing to him, and all those who do so are rewarded by divine grace.

Singing and chanting are very similar, with the main difference being that chants tend to be much shorter and repetitive. In Hindu and Buddhist devotional songs, usually there are one or two lines that are repeated. This repetition can be boring or intoxicating, depending upon how much you allow yourself to surrender to the chant.

There are also Christian, Jewish, and New Age chants, or you can make up your own. To get the most out of any type of devotional singing, it often helps to close your eyes and imagine singing directly to Spirit.

In my exploration of singing spiritual songs and chants, I've found that little things can make a big difference. For example, some people totally open their heart and soul to gospel music, while others find it too emotional. If you like to sing, it's worth checking out various churches or spiritual groups that play different types of music. When you find the one that's right for you, you'll know it. It's worth more than diamonds to find fellow seekers who can sing in a way that opens your heart to God.

The Least You Need to Know

➤ Bhakti-yoga is the Hindu science of increasing devotion to God through various practices.

➤ In Buddhism, worshipping respected teachers and bodhisattvas is a common practice.

➤ Through a guru's sending of energy and life lessons, devotees often experience profound devotion.

➤ By letting go of past baggage, Westerners can open themselves up to a deeper connection with Jesus and the Holy Spirit.

➤ There are many methods for deepening devotion, such as various rituals, singing, and chanting.

Part 3
Spiritual Disciplines

While there are seemingly an infinite number of spiritual paths, there are, fortunately, not that many respected disciplines to help seekers deepen their growth. Among the most common practices used in virtually every tradition are those of prayer, service, and meditation. In this part, you'll learn ways to practice and benefit from these disciplines as well as ways to overcome common obstacles people face when attempting them.

Some spiritual traditions use the body as a vehicle for transcending the mind. Among them are yoga, T'ai Chi, and various martial arts. Even if you're too lazy to practice these on a consistent basis (as I am), you may find they can add helpful spiritual nourishment to your regular spiritual practice. In addition, as you try out these "body-centered" practices, you may find you have more energy and discipline for your other spiritual exercises.

Chapter 9

The Wonderful World of Prayer

In This Chapter

➤ Questions and answers

➤ How people from various faiths pray

➤ How to make space for quiet prayer time

➤ Learning to pray more effectively

In this chapter, we'll embark on a journey to another world. As your guide on this journey, I will provide you with some pathways to consider, pitfalls to avoid, hints to follow, and a map to your destination. Remember that on your journey toward *God*, with each step you take, you should listen to your heart.

People have many questions about *prayer*. Am I ready to pray to Spirit? Will I be heard and answered? How does one pray? Before we can answer such questions, we need to discern what prayer is and what it is not. We'll look at what prayer means to people of different religions. And finally, we'll look at how to turn various ideas about prayer into a practical, vibrant, and alive connection to the source of all being.

Questions Are the Answer

Asking questions can be considered a form of prayer, although in this culture it is rarely thought of as such. Questions are a quest for something unknown, an opening to exploration. Whether you are a scientist researching the effects of prayer (refer to

From Allah to Zen

God is defined as the absolute, omnipresent, living Being in all things, the source of all existence.

From Allah to Zen

Prayer is devout petition, addressed to God or another deity. It can also be a sincere attempt to remove the obstacles that keep us from recognizing our dependence on each other and on God.

Dr. Larry Dossey's book *Healing Words*), or a poet who enjoys the subjective aspects of prayer, a questioning attitude can spark opportunities for discovery. Questioning, like prayer, can be a lifelong process that opens the door for grace to enter.

Questions may not always provide the answers you expect or hope for, but they can foster an expansive and cosmic view of things. They can help you connect with something bigger than your ordinary sense of self.

I used to hold on to many unexamined concepts about God, prayer, and grace. Questioning my unexamined concepts helped me to loosen up and free myself from rigidity and narrow-mindedness. Coming up with the questions for my book *The Little Book of Big Questions,* and trying to answer them, helped me to realize how little I actually knew. The feeling of humbleness that resulted from pondering many "big" questions helped me feel closer to God. Therefore, for me, asking questions about the nature of life, God, and death, has been a type of prayer.

Besides asking questions of yourself, you can ask questions of those you care about as a form of both service and prayer. Since it's difficult for us to see our own shortcomings, which are obstacles to greater union with God, asking questions can be a great way to open the eyes of those you care about. Rather than merely pray that someone you love become more open to Spirit, you can pray for him by asking him helpful questions. Of course, this kind of "service" requires that others have a willingness to receive or ponder the questions you ask.

Let me give you an example of using questions as a form of prayer for those you care about. Over the years, I've noticed that I sometimes keep my feelings from my partner—in order to gain a sense of power. Inevitably, this creates a barrier between our being more intimate. My friends know I have this shortcoming, and when they see it, they "pray" for me by asking me certain questions. Questions help me to see that I am being manipulative, and that I'm isolating myself and blocking intimacy. By asking me questions, they open me up to going beyond my hurtful ways.

For instance, recently my girlfriend and I were talking about a doctor's appointment she said she'd make, but failed to do so. Although I was upset by her actions, I didn't say anything. Fortunately, my housemate asked me, "If you're not telling her how you feel when she does that, how do you think that'll impact the relationship?"

From her question, I could see that I was trying to look "cool," but my behavior was ultimately counterproductive.

If you're in the presence of someone who is open to helpful questioning, to moving beyond his limiting concepts or behaviors, you might try asking him questions such as the following:

➤ What do you think will be the result of (the behavior you're questioning him about)?

➤ How do you think that person reacted or felt when you did (the behavior you're questioning him about)?

➤ What price do you think you pay for behaving like that?

➤ What price do you think others pay when you behave like that?

➤ What other ways might you have handled this situation that may have been more harmonious?

Cosmic Potholes

Don't attempt to force questions down someone's throat. If he is not receptive to your questions, try to help him in some other way. If people don't want to answer your questions, it means they don't feel safe enough being vulnerable around you. Instead of putting them on the defensive, try to help them feel safer while around you.

Questioning a negative behavior is prayer in action. We are not here to puff ourselves up about what is good in us, but to learn about what is "off course" from our innate goodness. When I feel remorse over the price I pay for my manipulations, I receive a great gift, a true desire to change. Then I can experience humility and vulnerability. When I get in touch with such feelings, a desire to move closer to God and his grace naturally wells up within me. Questions can lead to remorse for our actions, and true feelings of remorse are like a silent cry to God for help.

Prayer as a Cosmic Proposal

When I turned 19, I came down with a bad case of mononucleosis; I was so weak I thought I was going to die. I prayed to God that if he would return my health, I would devote the rest of my life to service, either by joining a monastery or by working in a field that helped people. Fortunately, I did regain my health. I was blissfully grateful! I set out to play my part of the deal that I had made with Spirit.

I believe grace operated in my life on this occasion because I was willing to offer service as my part of the deal with Spirit. I recognized that in order to live, I was dependent on God. This helplessness made me become a beggar of divine intervention.

How do we get grace to enter our lives? Can we simply ask for it? I don't think that enticing, seducing, flattering, persuading, or trying to manipulate God will bring grace to us. Instead, I believe that grace comes when we recognize that we need the help of God (or people). Through that realization, we become willing to surrender some of our independence and control. Having a good intention is a jump-start to prayer, yet it is only part of the formula. By making a clear promise to God, you may find that it helps to complete a cosmic circuit that allows magic to happen. I know that in the times I offered something for the changes I requested, my prayers were answered. Perhaps my "offering" merely helped provide evidence to *myself* that I meant business—and really wanted to change. However it worked, I have noticed that making a clear promise as to what I'll do or give up for the changes I want has been a useful practice for me.

Rather than look at prayer as a way of getting something for nothing, I think it's more accurate to look at it as an exchange. What you offer may be a simple letting go of worry or negativity, but it's still an exchange. The old spiritual adage "Let go and let God" implies that God can only "take over" if at first we let go.

Amazing Grace

I once prayed that God would tell me if I should get married to a certain woman. The answer to my prayer was that I should be more honest with this woman about the problems I saw in the relationship. I promised God that I would speak to her in this way. When I did, this woman made it clear to me that she no longer wanted to get married to me. To my surprise, we soon broke up. Although this process was painful, I felt that my prayer was answered because I kept to my part of the agreement. God had showed me that I really shouldn't get married to this particular woman.

The Many Faces of Prayer

At its most basic level, prayer is a way to become closer to God. Each culture and each religion has emphasized certain modes of prayer that are considered to be the "proper" way to pray. Yet ultimately we each must come up with a form of prayer that feels right to us.

In order to discover the form of prayer that works best for you, it's helpful to be exposed to the many types of prayer that have existed throughout history. What follows is a brief tour of how people from different religious backgrounds look at prayer.

How Hindus Pray

The Hindu tradition consists of a variety of gods and goddesses who represent different aspects of the Divine and who are worshipped for various purposes, each with his or her own elaborate mythology. Some popular Hindu deities are Krishna, a world savior who is often portrayed as a beautiful flute-playing cow-herder; Ram, the king of righteousness; Ganesha, the elephant-headed god who clears a path by removing obstacles; Saraswati, the goddess of learning; and Kali, the fierce demon-slaying goddess.

Hindus often have a deity they worship. A *devotee* will position himself before a picture, or upon entering a temple, will stand reverently before a statue and gaze into its eyes. Hindus believe that some portion of the deity actually inhabits the image they pray to, and indeed looks out through its eyes to see who has come before it to make offerings, requests, or give thanks. Therefore, this viewing of the deity, called *darshan,* is in fact considered to be seeing—as well as being seen by—God. Darshan is believed to give one spiritual strength and awareness, and to help one achieve the qualities of the deity.

For puja, Hindu prayer and worship, the devotee may use a variety of gestures: decorating the deity with garlands of fresh flowers, burning incense, building sacred fires, waving lights, meditating, or painting designs on the walls of the home. Sweets are sometimes set on the altar of a statue or near the picture of a deity as an offering while fasting, as if to say, "I will fast and give you sweets; please grant me my request." If a woman has been unable to bear children, she may perform a fast as a sign of her sincerity and of the importance of her request. She may also make a vow that if her wishes are granted, she will make some specific offering in the temple of the deity to whom she addressed her prayers.

Offering sweets while fasting is an example of making a covenant with a deity. Gazing into the eyes of an admired deity to achieve its qualities is a more subtle proposal. Although this form of prayer is generally not practiced in the West, you can get a taste of it by trying to focus on absorbing the magnificent qualities of someone you admire. You can do this with someone living, such as a friend or role model, or someone who is no longer living, such as Jesus or Gandhi. Ask yourself, "What characteristic does this person have that I would like more of?" As you focus on the person, you are literally praying to be receptive to the traits he or she has to offer you.

From Allah to Zen

A **devotee** is a student or disciple of a philosophy or guru. **Darshan** is translated from Sanskrit as "seeing and being seen by God," or an act of respectful worship.

Heavenly Helpers

Consider yourself an alien who has just landed on Earth. You need help to find your way back to your true home—your soul. As an explorer, you are looking for the maps previous navigators of the inner realms have used to find their way back. Try their maps. See if they help you find the home within.

How Jews Pray

Prayer is central to the Jewish tradition. Prayers are largely congregational, and spoken in the first person plural, "we," as opposed to "I." In the synagogue, it is said there is no room for selfish prayers. These congregational prayers should not be a passive experience, however, as each individual is encouraged to express his own devotional fervor. Daily prayers may also be offered in Jewish households, such as before and after meals.

While the English word *pray* comes from a root meaning "to beg" or "to entreat," the Hebrew verb for praying means "to judge oneself." As one famous Rabbi taught, your prayer will not be heard if you are not at peace with the world. And as the Jewish philosopher Maimonides stated, "Prayer without devotion is not prayer .... He whose thoughts are wandering or occupied with other things ought not to pray." Ideally, all deeds should be filled with thoughts of God, and each action should be performed for the sake of God, with pure intentions.

The Jewish faith teaches that God watches our every action. This awareness of being observed causes the person to ask, "How does my action serve God?" Imagine becoming aware that God is watching your every move! You may ask yourself, are the conversations I have an indulgence in entertainment for myself? Am I writing to benefit the reader with new perspectives? How would God see this done? The ability to observe oneself through the eye of God means that every moment is an opportunity to reevaluate and pray, "Thy will be done."

The Prayer Life of Muslims

While Muslims may offer spontaneous, personal prayers to God similar to the familiar Christian prayer form, the primary aspect of Muslim devotional practice is a formalized ritual prayer called *salat*.

Salat involves a series of bodily postures and utterances while facing the holy city of Mecca. It begins: "God is most great. I testify that there is no god but God ...." It is recommended that the salat be done in a mosque, a temple, or a church, but it is permissible to pray at home, at work, or outside. Muslims believe their participation joins them with the Prophet Muhammad, who is the Messenger of God. The prayer concludes by turning the head in either direction and saying, "Peace be upon you all the mercy and blessings of God." What an impressive offering Muslims make to Allah by interrupting their livelihood to turn to him five times a day!

My first encounter with this form of Muslim prayer was on an overseas airplane flight some years ago. On my way to the bathroom, I saw a Muslim man in an open space near an exit door unroll a carpetlike cloth and kneel down in prayer. Imagine the sincerity of devotion it would take to perform one's prayers and prostrations in such a public place, surrounded by uninformed, curious, and even judgmental onlookers.

From Allah to Zen

The **salat** is a formal prayer Muslims are required to perform five times daily: early morning, noon, mid-afternoon, sunset, and evening.

Christians and Prayer

In Christianity, prayers of petition are common. Jesus taught his disciples The Lord's Prayer in which the person doing the praying petitions God in different ways: that heaven become manifest on Earth, that God forgive them, that God provide them their daily bread, and that God deliver them from evil and harm. Combining all these petitions in the same prayer that speaks of God's kingdom and glory can be a powerful way to feel close to Spirit.

Intercessory prayer, praying for another person to achieve physical, emotional, or spiritual healing, is also encouraged and valued by Christianity. Every person is viewed as a brother or sister, and in some Christian traditions, people who lived exemplary lives are honored after death as saints. Some Christians can pray for the intercession of a saint, or holy person, to help gain virtues or heal certain conditions.

Heavenly Helpers

In 1960, John Kennedy stated in his inauguration address, "Ask not what your country can do for you, ask what you can do for your country." This powerful statement can be made into a helpful spiritual tool by replacing the word *country* with the word *God.* Are you willing to serve others? Try asking yourself throughout the day, "What can I do for my God?"

Let Thy Will Be Done

We tend to pray for selfish desires, rather than for what would be best. Rather than thinking that you get *what you pray for,* it can be helpful to imagine that you get *where you pray from.* For example, if you pray from a feeling of compassion for others, you'll receive more compassion in your life. If you pray from a feeling of wanting to be closer to God, you'll become closer to God. In this way of looking at things, prayer is simply a magnifier of our deepest longings.

While we normally think of prayer as asking for something, the statement "let thy will be done" is a powerful form of prayer. The mere act of sincerely surrendering to God's will can bring an immediate sense of peace. When we say, "Let thy will be done," we are indirectly stating that we don't know what is best. Yet we are also saying there is an intelligence behind the events that occur, that we recognize it is useless to fight the reality of what *is.*

Surrendering to what *is* may be seen by many people as a passive step, yet it is not. It takes effort and humility to let go of our concepts and desires and fully accept the reality that the universe provides to us. Choosing to accept frees up our energy.

Amazing Grace

Studies have been done in which people tried to make plants grow faster using various types of prayer. In one famous experiment, plants were placed in one of three groups. First, there was the control group in which no prayers were prayed. Second, there was the group of "directive prayer" in which people prayed the plants would grow quickly and become big and strong. Last, there was the group of "nondirective" prayer in which people merely prayed, "Let thy will be done." Ironically, the form of prayer that seemed to consistently have the greatest effect on the growth of plants was, "Let thy will be done."

Making Space for Quiet Time

In our culture, busyness is looked upon as a positive way to live life. We are taught that action, accomplishment, and material gain are the reflection of a good life. We are constantly engaged in activity—working, socializing, cleaning, making more money to accumulate more things, and, of course, taking care of all of our accumulations. We even need to make lists because we cannot possibly remember to do all of the things required to maintain this lifestyle. Leaving space for quiet time is perceived as doing nothing, and doing nothing is usually seen as a waste of time.

Our busyness is paradoxical: When we have a moment with nothing to do we feel uncomfortable. We are afraid of feeling vulnerable in relation to God, yet feeling vulnerable is necessary for God's grace to manifest. Taking time for quiet does not raise our level of anxiety and fear; it only uncovers the fear and anxiety that is already present because of our lack of connection to God. We can return to the lost art of "being" by taking the time to become friends with silence. The practice of prayer is one way to learn to make friends with silence.

Cosmic Potholes

Through the grace of God, inner peace is available to us. Yet through our busyness we are saying, "Not now, I'm too busy." Grace is present, God is present, but are we available? If you don't take time to be with God, God may not take time to be with you.

Amazing Grace

When I was in Jerusalem, there was a line to enter the tomb of Jesus—in which only three people at a time may enter. Finally I walked in and started to pray, but the two other people present began talking about their dinner plans. In frustration, I prayed to be in the tomb alone—in quiet. Suddenly, I *was* alone, and I enjoyed several minutes of intense prayer. When I walked out of the tomb, there was still a long line of people waiting to get in, and three people immediately walked in. I have no explanation as to why people waited to enter the tomb except for the fact that I had prayed to be alone.

Consider examining what you do with your time. Could you cancel some appointments? Could you reduce your work hours? If these steps are too big to make, then make smaller ones, such as reducing unnecessary conversations on the phone. The most sincere prayers arise out of quality quiet time and inward contemplation. Creating space for quiet time is, in an indirect manner, itself a prayer for deeper union with Spirit. It's like creating the right soil in which a healthy prayer life can grow.

To help create more time for prayer and quiet, ask yourself, "Are there things I do that could be accomplished with the help of family or friends?" For example, I live in a household of spiritual seekers, and we share some of our resources. We buy groceries, appliances, furniture, maintenance items, and whatever else we can buy together in order to save money and work fewer hours. Sharing responsibilities with your household, friends, or family is a wonderful way of freeing your life for more quiet time.

How Do I Pray?

There is no "best way" or guaranteed formula for praying. A good way to start is to just begin a conversation with God that comes from your heart.

Little kids instinctively know how to pray when they need help. In a moment of desperation, a child simply cries out, "Help!" Your prayers for help, such as, "Please have mercy on me," or, "Please teach me to be more loving," are more than adequate as long as they are heartfelt and followed by appropriate actions that indicate your sincerity. In Chapter 20, "From Fear to Magic," I talk about how gratitude and giving thanks for each thing in your life can be a powerful form of prayer.

Since prayer is a form of communion with God (or your soul), you can pray in many different ways. For example, you can pray by being fully present in your words and action. Any act that you do with an intention or attitude of reverence can be considered as an offering or prayer to God. You can commune with God or pray by listening to your feelings and getting in touch with what feels right to you. If you follow someone else's form of prayer without listening to your own heart, you will be reciting rather than talking to God. If you seek a holy person to teach you to pray, such as a rabbi, guru, priest, or minister, ask yourself, "Does his suggestion enhance my personal expression?" As you explore the world of prayer, you'll soon discover what seems to assist you in feeling connected to God's love, compassion, and peace.

Rumi, a thirteenth-century mystic credited with beginning the Sufi branch of Islam, recited many spontaneous verses about the longing for God. In the following poem Rumi eloquently speaks of how our longing for God is one of the purest forms of prayer:

"Love Dogs"

One night a man was crying, Allah! Allah!
His lips grew sweet with the praising,
Until a cynic said, "So! I have heard you calling
out, but have you ever gotten any response?"
The man had no answer to that.
He quit praying and fell into a confused sleep.
He dreamed he saw Khidr, the guide of souls,
In a thick, green foliage.
"Why did you stop praising?"
"Because I've never heard anything back."
"This longing you express *is* the return message."
The grief you cry out from draws you toward union.
Your pure sadness that wants help is the secret cup.
Listen to the moan of a dog for its master.
That whining is the connection.
There are love dogs no one knows the names of.
Give your life to be one of them.

Fortunately you already have a map to God. When you get lost, it will lead you back to God. This map is your heart. It is the most precious gift you have on your journey.

The Least You Need to Know

➤ Prayer is being vulnerable before God. One way to become "smaller" before God is to ask questions that expand your concepts or help you to feel remorse for inharmonious actions.

➤ The world religions provide us with many different ways to think of prayer. By trying their ideas, you may find a method that feels right for you.

➤ Taking quiet time away from your busy schedule is a key element for allowing grace to enter your life.

➤ Listening to your feelings and heart, and conversing with God like a child, can be a good place to begin your prayer journey.

Chapter 10

The Significance of Service

In This Chapter

➤ What, exactly, is service?

➤ The naturalness of service

➤ Obstacles to service

➤ How can you serve?

➤ Service and the spiritual path

All spiritual traditions contain some component of service as part of their path. Muslims are encouraged to give alms and donate to the community. Buddhists consider generosity to be the fundamental virtue, and like Hindus, charity and almsgiving is seen as a required step on their path to liberation. In Christianity, serving your brother is recognized as a way to imitate the love of Jesus Christ.

While we all agree that helping each other is a good thing, we sometimes find that we fall short of our aspirations to be a giving person. The first thing we need to do is understand the obstacles within ourselves that keep us from serving others. Once we see our own resistance, we can uncover the naturally compassionate heart within.

What Is Service?

What, exactly, is *service?* Is it the hours we spend volunteering at the convalescent home or homeless shelter once a week? Is it the money we send to a nonprofit organization to feed starving children in a developing nation? Is it a friendly smile to a stranger on the bus? Is service defined by the results, or by the intent of the server?

From Allah to Zen

Service is an action or gesture offered with the intent of helping the person or organization receiving the service.

If service were to be defined in terms of outcome, we would need to judge whether the results of an act were in fact for the best. If you offer your arm to help an elderly person cross the street, it's not difficult to judge the results. But consider another example—building a new road in a remote area of the Third World as part of a Peace Corps project. The finished highway may be straight and smooth, but what about the unforeseen consequences? In addition to a bringing a higher standard of living, the road may bring a faster pace of life, increased materialism, and the rejection of traditional values.

In weighing the results of an action to assess whether it is in fact a service, we may be confronted with situations in which one side or entity benefits at the expense of another. I read an article recently about a man who runs an organization created to protect oceans and marine life. He had approved the killing of goats on Catalina Island in order to save endangered flora and fauna. The photo showed a protester with a sign saying, "Free Willy, but kill Billy?"

Amazing Grace

The wonderful movie by Akira Kurosawa called *Dersu Uzala* portrays a rare and deep relationship that develops between Vladimir Arsenyev, a well-known Soviet explorer, and Dersu Uzala, an indigenous hunter who becomes his guide. After years of friendship Vladimir gives Dersu one of his best hunting rifles, a gesture of his love for Dersu and his sincere desire to help him. Though the intent behind the gift was to help, there are disastrous repercussions for Dersu. Was the giving of the gift a service, in light of what followed?

It gets tricky. Save a spotted owl, but lose a lumber mill. Get a good deal on a shirt from Thailand, but don't look in the sweatshop where it was made, or you may not feel so comfortable. If someone or some population "wins" and another "loses" through an act of service, does humanity or the planet Earth as a whole really benefit?

Another approach is to consider intent as opposed to outcome. To qualify as service an action must originate from the good intentions of the server or servers. Of course, this requires that a person know himself and be free from self-deception. If we decide that service is characterized by the purity of intention in one's heart, then that person must be unable to fool himself into mistaking personal motives or agendas for noble desires to serve.

For me, the idea of defining service in terms of one's intentions is the most workable approach. We'll never be able to know what good or harm will come in the future from our efforts to aid, but if we learn to be honest with ourselves, we can at least know for sure our intentions were to serve.

Service Comes Naturally

Fortunately, serving is an innate capacity. We don't need to learn techniques, add information to our database, or in any way acquire something we don't already have. Caring is instinctive. When our nose itches, our hand "cares" and scratches it. We recognize that our nose and hands are connected, that they are parts of the same whole. When the hand tends to the nose, it is in fact serving itself.

Let's take the example of a mother and her children. While she recognizes her offspring as separate beings, in some ways she senses them as extensions or appendages of herself. Their connection to her is obvious, and caring for them comes naturally to her. Family members in general feel connected, and will help each other when in need. Of course, if we aspire to serve a larger entity than our immediate family, our definition of *family* may have to change.

If you've ever traveled in really poor countries, you may have been impressed, as I have, by the extraordinary generosity of people who have so little.

A couple of years ago, I spent part of a summer camping with friends in the Sierra of northern Chihuahua, Mexico. There weren't any other tourists in the area, so the Tarahumara Indians who lived nearby were curious and came to visit us at our tent. One man invited the four of us to eat lunch at his house the following day. We gladly accepted. We dined on fresh handmade flour-and-corn tortillas, a huge pot of chicken soup filled with large pieces of chicken and many vegetables, and sodas. The meal was so tasty we gorged ourselves.

Amazing Grace

There is an inspirational scene of an Amish barn raising in the movie *Witness*. An entire community gathers to build a barn for one of its members. The women prepare the food, the men are busy with hammers and nails, and the children have tasks according to their capacity. In a single day, the barn is constructed. Why did all those people organize and complete such a monumental job (at no cost!) for someone else? The explanation is in their perception of themselves as one. They are a single community, sharing a common unity.

Cosmic Potholes

Money can buy you comfort, convenience, and the ability to pay your way out of an unpleasant situation. Yet using money to manipulate your circumstances creates the illusion that you are in control of your life. What's more, if money can buy you what you need, you no longer need other people. If you're not careful, prosperity can often lead to increased separateness from other people.

Heavenly Helpers

As an experiment, try taking impeccable care of something for a week. It could be a child, a plant, a pet, or even an object like a car. At the end of the week, notice if you feel closer to what you took care of. Making the connection that "taking care of" leads to caring can be an important insight on the spiritual path.

It wasn't until sometime later that we realized that our host had killed 4 of his 14 chickens to serve us the meal. That's a big percentage of his flock, and this man was living in a two-room house of adobe brick with no electricity or running water. Why did he do it?

While some of us have been blessed by affluence, others have been given the "gift" of poverty. In Western culture, most of us have been given the ability to buy whatever we need, whenever we want it. But we pay a price in our feelings of separateness that stem from the independence our money makes possible. For those without money, an independent existence is not an option. In a small, poor village, one guy has a truck, another has a TV, but no one owns one of everything. The people share what they have. Their connection to each other is real, practical, and tangible. They don't need metaphysical experiences to teach them oneness.

The impulse to help or serve each other is natural, and the more we recognize our common unity, the more we express this tendency. It is also true that the more we express our caring through acts of service, the more we tend to feel our common unity. When you first buy a car, the "two of you" aren't really close yet, but you start taking care of it, checking all the fluids regularly, keeping the tires full, washing and waxing it when it gets dirty. After a while, it's your "baby." All that "taking care of" resulted in your caring.

I'm reminded of the song from *Fiddler on the Roof* in which the fiddler, Tevye, and his wife, Golde, ask each other, "Do you love me?" Their marriage had been prearranged by a matchmaker; they had not been in love with each other on their wedding day. Twenty-five years later, they wanted to know if they had grown to love each other. Golde thinks back on 25 years of cooking meals, mending clothes, and cleaning house for her husband, and Tevye in turn recollects all the work he's done to sustain their family. After so many years of taking care of each other's practical necessities, they conclude that the result is love.

We now come to an important question: If caring feelings are instinctive, and if simple acts of service evoke such feelings, why don't more people help others? The world is clearly in need. There must be obstacles that inhibit us from acting out of our natural caring heart. If we aspire to serve, discovering what these obstacles are, and how they might be removed, becomes vital.

Obstacles to Service

If a person really wants to help, he must be willing to look at himself straight on, and confront the numerous impurities he may find. The garbage one discovers may not smell sweet, but you can't dispose of it until you know it's there. What makes such self-study possible is knowing that all the *obstacles* we encounter were added on to us through our upbringing, our culture, and the peculiar circumstances and events that shaped our lives. Beneath these cloaks to protect us from a seemingly dangerous world, innate goodness and generosity remain unblemished.

Many of the obstacles we run into are the ways we think about ourselves and the world we live in. For example, we may think that we can't help someone because we haven't been trained to deal with her particular needs. In today's society of specialists, it's easy for us to feel we are inadequate compared to an expert who holds the appropriate diploma: "I'm not a therapist. She should talk to a counselor."

In defining ourselves only by our job titles, our roles as spouse, parent, or child, we limit the scope of our helping to the confines of what we already know. If we admit, however, to the existence of an underlying universal consciousness where all answers exist, then only our openness and willingness to serve would be required in order to serve others.

From Allah to Zen

Obstacles, in the context of spiritual growth, are a person's intellectual, emotional, or physical manifestations that keep him from evolving to a higher state of consciousness.

Cosmic Potholes

There are hundreds of reasons not to serve—busyness, self–absorption, rationalizations the mind creates, and so on. If you listen to your mind, it will always provide reasons to avoid selfless service. Be careful of the excuses the mind creates to avoid serving others and opening up your own heart.

Other obstacles we encounter may result more from how we perceive the world visually. For instance, our eyes take note of the differences we see in people—skin color, physical traits, clothing, and so on. Our mind picks up the idea and tells us that others are not like us. "I'm not black." "I'm not physically handicapped." "I don't wear nose rings." We end up feeding our separateness rather than our unity, and thus squelch any service we may have to offer those in the "other" category.

Heavenly Helpers

Don't be discouraged by the prospect of uncovering your worst qualities. They aren't the real you. They are bad habits you acquired along the way. Beneath them there is goodness and generosity. Knowing this will give you the capacity to look at your deficiencies straight on. Seeing the obstacles to your innate beauty is the first step to being rid of them.

From Allah to Zen

Needs can be defined for the spiritual seeker as those conditions that support his spiritual development. These may include food, clothing, shelter, some friends, some money, and some leisure time. Desired possessions or involvements that retard rather than accelerate spiritual growth would be considered **wants.**

We may find that we don't help more because we haven't been givers in the past. Resistance to change is a powerful force. Even if we've been stuck in stinginess, loneliness, or other cold places, it is hard to act differently than we did yesterday. What's more, the familiar is always more attractive than unknown territory. In understanding the normal human reluctance to explore new situations and behaviors, we gain the chance to decide whether we want to stay the same or begin to change.

Another blemish we may observe in looking into the mirror is laziness. We may have become accustomed to doing what we feel like, moment after moment, day after day. When we *do* hear a call for help from others, we may honestly want to respond, but find we can't—especially if helping involves acting in a way that challenges us. Our good intentions may not be powerful enough to override our tendency to follow the path of least resistance.

Sometimes, serving others gets in the way of serving ourselves. We feel that we have to attend to our own *needs* first, and then, if there's time, we can help others. The question becomes, "How much do I need?" The commercial world around us continually tells us we need more. If we were to believe the advertisements, our days would be consumed by acquiring new possessions or refurbishing the ones we already have.

If it's not a matter of adding to our inventory of accumulations, then there's always that endless to-do list. But will checking off items on our list satisfy a real need? Don't we really have enough already? What if our house, our job, and our relationship are already good enough, and the changes and improvements we make aren't actually needs, but diversions?

"What do I need?" rather than "How much do I need?" is an interesting question. On the one hand, much of our busyness serves *wants* that try to pass as *needs*. On the other hand, are our real needs being met? What about our need to know our purpose in life, or our need to feel the presence of God? We have put so much focus on satisfying outer needs that our inner life may be seriously bereft. And how can you fill the bowl of another when your own is empty?

As we continue to examine our obstacles to service, we may discover that what we call service really isn't. An honest appraisal of our behavior reveals that our help, while benefiting others, is motivated by our personal needs. We find we need to feel useful, or good about ourselves, or maybe we are looking for approval or praise from others. Perhaps we offer our service to assuage guilt, or pay back a debt we feel we owe. Maybe we're lonely, looking for intimacy, or need human company to cover up the uneasiness we feel about being alone. Simpler yet, we see that we are just plain restless, and will do anything to avoid boredom.

All of our selfish manipulations wear us out and leave us with little energy left to truly serve the needs of others. By acknowledging our selfish designs, we become less bound by them. In losing some of our self-importance, we make space for something else, something deeper. Through the opening that is created, the natural compassion of the heart finds expression.

How Can I Serve?

Once you become aware of the obstacles to serving others, you come to the question of how exactly you are going to serve. If you look around, it isn't hard to find people in need. It's more a question of where to begin.

In your own city you may find hungry and homeless populations. Organizations may already exist that provide food and shelter for the needy, to which you need only contribute your time and energy. If you live in a small or rural community, you may have to organize a group to serve these needs. In almost every town there are lonely senior citizens in convalescent homes who need simple human companionship and support. If you feel so called, you could solicit adoptions for the local animal shelter or help take care of its dogs and cats. Wherever you live there is undoubtedly an environmental issue that needs fighters for its cause.

You may decide you want to put your energies into alleviating a crisis in some other part of the world. There are numerous international organizations that serve ongoing needs and provide disaster relief. By contacting these agencies you can find out exactly how you can help. If you find that only your financial help is needed, but you want hands-on involvement, don't despair. Keep inquiring. Church groups of various denominations frequently send volunteers overseas to serve local needs. You can find books in the library and bookstores that list countless volunteer possibilities abroad.

Amazing Grace

I had a spiritual teacher who requested I spend time in convalescent homes talking to the residents. At first I hated it. I didn't like the smell, and it was depressing. After many months of repeatedly visiting the same people, I grew to care for some of the folks. I saw that they had a perspective on life that, in my youth, I didn't have. When a favorite resident I visited, Vye, suddenly died, I cried. I realized that I had been transformed by being willing to go past my initial resistance.

Cosmic Potholes

Don't deliberate too much about who or where to start serving. Give it a little thought, do a little research, then proceed. The time you spend thinking takes time away from the people you could be helping.

The most important thing, if you desire to be of service, is to make yourself available to serve somewhere. It probably doesn't make that much difference where you apply yourself. Needs of every sort surround us. If you let God know that you're willing to be used, God will use you.

We may feel pulled to serve people in a much more subtle way than providing food and shelter for the hungry and the homeless. For example, we may have gained a perspective on life that has eased and enlightened our way, that we could pass on to others. The help we have to give may be sharing our understanding.

I'll give you an example from my own life. Self-study had taught me that in every conceivable situation, I was always looking to win in some way or another. It might be the job I sought, the girlfriend I dreamed of, or in littler moments, the hope that the hamburger I ordered would taste just right. When I didn't win, I lost, and that hurt. Big hurt or little hurt, that approach to life caused me a lot of pain because, as the odds have it, half the time I lost.

A spiritual teacher I know offered me a different outlook. He suggested that when I didn't win, I try to learn something about myself. I might learn that my assumptions were erroneous, that my confidence in myself was misplaced. Or maybe I'd learn something about how much weight I put on satisfying a particular want of mine!

Taking on this perspective has changed a lot for me. Because I can find value in a situation regardless of how things turn out, I don't worry about winning and losing so much. My experience of life is more relaxed. For me to pass on this understanding would be a service to someone else.

Heavenly Helpers

Our job is to try and see ourselves as we are, remove the obstacles that keep us locked in self-service, and do our best to help as we see it. The rest we have to leave to the powers that be.

We can also serve when we are alone. In meditation we serve the whole creation by dedicating ourselves to expanding our consciousness. Whether alone or with people, wherever we are and whatever we're doing, we are being of service when we meditate. The more aware we are, the better we recognize our obstacles to serve; seeing our obstacles, the freer we are of them, and the more able we are to serve as needed.

We don't really need to go anywhere or do anything specific to serve. We need only ask the question, "How can I serve, here and now?" As we grow in consciousness, pain in those around us becomes more apparent. Depending on our level of awareness, we will be able to recognize others' needs and respond accordingly.

Sometimes when we begin to serve more, we can get attached to how well the service goes. Are the homeless getting fed fast enough, or is the environmental organization I'm helping doing a good enough job? Soon, if you're not careful, your acts of service can turn into acts of worry. There's an ancient Sufi saying that goes something like, "Trust in Allah, but tie up your camels." To me that means take responsibility for my part, then leave it be. If the universe sees fit to unleash my camels, well, who am I to think that it doesn't serve the cosmic plan? All along the path of service, we get opportunities to let go of our attachment to how "it all works out."

Service and the Path

Service is not simply the actions we perform. It is an attitude—an attitude of exploration, of openness, of humbleness, of giving. It is a spirit that we aspire to. The path to that spirit is a journey of awakening consciousness.

This awakening is at the heart of spiritual growth. Service, then, is more than an end in itself. It provides a context for gaining self-knowledge, and as such, is an integral component of the spiritual path.

Through the process of gaining self-knowledge, and ridding oneself of the obstacles that block our innate goodness, a person becomes kinder, more loving, and better able to serve God. The cleaner the vessel, the less clouded by distortion, the more useful it is as an instrument of God's will. Service is a grace of God, and an opportunity to participate in the evolution of humankind.

The Least You Need to Know

➤ Service is the attempt to alleviate suffering, on any level.

➤ The ability to serve is not something we must learn, but an innate capacity we already have.

➤ In order to better serve, we need to overcome the obstacles that inhibit our helpful impulses.

➤ Acknowledging our resistance to serve can reduce resistance.

➤ Self-study is in itself a service to God.

Chapter 11

The Art of Meditation

> ## In This Chapter
>
> ➤ The purpose, benefits, and power of meditation
>
> ➤ Keys to successful meditation
>
> ➤ Mantra and breath meditations
>
> ➤ Visualizations and contemplation exercises
>
> ➤ The benefits of active and initiation meditations

Meditation has been around, in one form or another, for thousands of years. Every major spiritual tradition extols its importance. Yet it wasn't until Maharishi Mahesh Yogi taught a simple form of meditation to The Beatles that it began catching on in the West.

Nowadays, even Medicaid pays for programs that teach people meditation—not because of its spiritual potential, but because of its health benefits. Hundreds of studies show that people who meditate on a regular basis have lower blood pressure and heart attack risk, less chance of depression, and higher levels of "life satisfaction." Although *meditation* is catching on largely because of its health benefits, its real purpose is to help people quiet their minds and open their hearts.

There are many different types of meditation. For example, there is mantra meditation (such as Transcendental Meditation), visualization, contemplative exercises, active meditations (such as T'ai Chi), breath meditations, and many others. Different types of meditation can be likened to different types of food. Although potato chips and broccoli are both foods, they have different nutritional values. Likewise, some meditations are very simple and easy to do, and some are more difficult, but extremely powerful. When first exploring the world of meditation, it can be a good idea to try several different types to see which appeals to you the most.

In general, it's better to begin a meditation with a technique you find easy to do. As with most skills, meditation becomes easier the more you do it. Try several of the meditation exercises in this chapter and commit to a technique that feels right for you.

Meditation and Your Mind

One of the goals of meditation is to quiet the mind. Yet the human mind does not like to be quiet. In fact, in the Hindu tradition, the mind has been likened to a wild monkey, darting everywhere imaginable. When beginning a meditation practice, you will undoubtedly face resistance. This is normal. Although I've meditated every day for more than 20 years, I still feel an initial resistance to it.

The mind resists partly because meditation is powerful medicine. When done correctly and consistently, meditation can help you over the "diseases" of separateness and distraction. Meditation can give you the experience of inner peace and connection with all of creation. Unfortunately, the human mind thrives on creating ways to distract us from the simplicity of the soul. Therein lies the rub.

While there are many types of meditation, all involve focusing the mind as a means of quieting it. In fact, in many meditation techniques, the goal is to completely stop one's thoughts. When our thoughts slow down or stop, it opens us up to a whole other world of perception and experiences. Yet stopping one's thoughts can be like stopping a fast-moving train.

You'll have better luck meditating if you do it when you're not wound up. Going for a walk, listening to music, or taking a bath can be good ways to prepare to meditate. In addition, many of the methods sprinkled throughout this book for becoming more "now focused" are great ways to prepare for meditation.

From Allah to Zen

Meditation derives from the Indian Sanskrit word *medha*, which roughly means "doing the wisdom." At its core, it is any form of concentration or technique whose purpose is to quiet the mind, open the heart, and connect with a source bigger than one's normal sense of self.

Cosmic Potholes

Some people, upon seeing that they can't quiet their mind when meditating, give up in defeat. Yet, the goal of meditation should not be to be successful at quieting your mind. The goal should just be to do it. The process of *trying* to quiet your mind is a statement to God and yourself that you are a sincere person seeking Grace. If you keep at it, eventually it'll become easier.

Once you're ready to meditate, find a comfortable, quiet place. Make sure you won't be disturbed by a ringing phone or noisy kids. Find a comfortable chair or sit in such a way that your spine remains fairly straight. You're ready to begin.

Transcendental Meditation

In the 1960s, after The Beatles learned Transcendental Meditation (TM for short), thousands of Westerners began learning how to meditate. TM centers sprouted up in every major city, and for a fee, people were instructed in this simple technique. Well over a million people have since learned the TM technique, and hundreds of studies have been done to prove its impressive array of physical and emotional benefits.

One reason for TM's popularity is that it's easy to do, and many people find it immediately enjoyable. A person using the TM technique repeats a special Sanskrit word known as a *mantra*. Studies show that by slowly repeating this sound, a person achieves a very deep level of rest.

Herbert Benson, a research doctor at Harvard, studied people who practiced the TM technique. He was impressed by the changes meditators reported in their lives, as well as the physiological changes he measured in his lab. However, after studying people who practiced TM for many years, Dr. Benson concluded that it didn't much matter what mantra a person used. Although the TM organization insisted that the mantra specifically chosen by TM instructors were critical for the best results, Benson wrote that virtually any soothing sound, repeated in the way that the TM teachers instructed, would create a profound "relaxation response." Dr. Benson suggested that people use the word "one" as a mantra, and save themselves the hefty price of the TM course.

Having been instructed in the TM technique, I agree with Dr. Benson that there is little advantage to getting your own special mantra handpicked by a TM teacher. The main benefit to taking the TM course is the ongoing support it offers. In addition,

Heavenly Helpers

To overcome resistance to meditation, try making it part of your daily routine—such as doing it before you go to work each day. By being consistent with your practice, you make it easier to overcome your initial resistance to quiet your mind.

From Allah to Zen

A **mantra** is a sound, or combination of sounds, in Sanskrit that are believed to have a specific, soothing effect on the nervous system when used as an object of concentration. It derives from *man*, meaning "to think" and *trai*, meaning "to protect or free from the bondage of the phenomenal world."

when you spend a lot of money to learn to meditate, there's a tendency to stay with it—even though it can be a challenge to fit it into a busy lifestyle. On the other hand, when you read the basic technique from a book, you don't have the support and commitment level of people who have invested their money in TM instruction.

That being said, I'm going to reveal the basic technique here, and you can decide for yourself whether you're committed to doing it consistently. As with most spiritual growth disciplines, it gets easier with practice, and the more time and effort you put forth, the greater the benefits you receive.

Meditating the TM Way

In the TM technique or any form of mantra meditation, you first need to find a quiet place where you won't be disturbed. Sit in a chair, with your spine comfortably straight, close your eyes, and take a couple of slow, deep breaths.

After about 30 seconds, begin to slowly say the mantra to yourself (not out loud). For the time being, we'll assume you're using the word "one" as your mantra. Repeat the mantra to yourself at a comfortable pace. Whenever you realize you're thinking other thoughts, immediately (but gently) go back to slowly repeating the mantra: "one … one … one … one …." Don't be concerned with coordinating the mantra with your breath—simply think the mantra at a pace that feels comfortable to you.

After 20 minutes, or however long you've set aside to meditate, stop repeating the mantra, take a couple of deep breaths, and when you're ready, slowly open your eyes. That's it!

Amazing Grace

If you desire, you can choose your own mantra. It should either be one, two, or three syllables long, and have a soothing sound to it. For people who like to use two-syllable mantras, I often suggest the words "one love." Other common mantras include "Allah," "Jehovah," "Rama," "Hahmsaw, and "ohmmm."

If you're like most people, you'll spend a lot of time thinking thoughts instead of repeating the mantra. That's okay. The one important rule to remember is that, as soon as you realize you're thinking something other than the word "one," immediately refocus on the mantra. Your thought process might go like this:

"One … one … one … this is boring … oops … one … one … I wonder how much time has gone by … one … one … one … one … one … I don't know if this is really doing any good. I should be preparing for that meeting I have tomorrow. Oh no, I didn't even remember to get that woman's e-mail address. I need to … oh … one … one … one … one … one."

By going from mantra to thoughts and back to the mantra, you release stress and eventually enter a more refined level of consciousness. After 20 or so minutes, you'll likely feel very relaxed, much more at peace, and physically refreshed. It's 20 minutes well spent.

Cosmic Potholes

If you get a mantra from a teacher, make sure you hear it correctly. When I learned the TM technique at age 16, I was instructed by an attractive young woman. As she bent over to whisper the mantra in my ear, I couldn't help but look down her blouse. Since I was distracted, I thought she said my mantra was "mama." At the time, my mom and I weren't on good terms, and the thought of repeating "mama" over and over in my head struck me with terror. My instructor, seeing that I was distracted, whispered my mantra again. I was happily relieved that my mantra was *not* the word "mama."

Consistency: The Key

To get the greatest benefits from Transcendental Meditation, it's important to meditate consistently. Maharishi Mahesh Yogi suggested people meditate for 20 minutes in the morning and 20 minutes in the evening. My belief is that any amount of meditation is better than none, and that consistency is more important than how long you do it.

Although there are literally hundreds of different forms of meditation, I decided to include instruction based on the TM technique because it's so easy to do. The *best* form of meditation is whatever type you'll consistently practice. If you know of a powerful method but never use it, it's of little value. The TM form of mantra meditation has helped millions of people throughout the ages experience a deeper level of peace, harmony, and spiritual connection. If you make a commitment to practice it, it can have a major impact on the quality of your life.

From Allah to Zen

Vipassana means "insight." It refers to a meditation technique that the Buddha himself taught. In this method, a person briefly labels his or her thoughts, feelings, and sensations as they are observed.

Contemplating Your Navel

Besides a mantra, the other most commonly used focus during meditation is the breath. Since you take your breath with you wherever you go, it's a very convenient thing to focus on.

Cosmic Potholes

When you find a mantra that feels right to you, stay with it. Don't change your mantra for the sake of variety. Over time, you develop a relationship with your mantra and you learn to use it to ever deeper states of peace and joy.

In Buddhist traditions, meditators typically focus on the rising and falling of their abdomen. To help focus on their breath, they are sometimes instructed to clasp their hands gently by their navel, and silently note "rising" when they inhale, and "falling" when they exhale. An alternative to this simple technique is to focus on the sensation of air passing through one's nasal passages, thinking "in" and "out" with the flow each breath.

In a popular form of meditation, known as *Vipassana* or Insight, the practitioner also uses the breath, but not as the sole focus. In Vipassana, a person is instructed to impartially note what he or she is aware of in each moment. For example, if while you're meditating you start thinking of your dinner plans, you would simply note, "thinking about dinner." If you become aware of your back hurting, you might note, "back has throbbing sensation." In between the labeling of your various thoughts, feelings, and sensations, you turn your attention back to your breath. A moment-to-moment experience of Vipassana meditation might look like this:

> *Feeling the breath going up and down .... Thinking about problems at work Note: Thinking about work .... Criticizing yourself for thinking so much. Note: Being self-critical .... Return to the breath going up and down .... Hear the cars passing on street. Note: Listening to cars .... Feel an itch near right elbow. Note: Elbow itches .... Return to the breath going up and down ....*

The idea is to follow your awareness, making impartial observations of where your attention goes by briefly labeling your thoughts, feelings, and sensations. The breath is used as an "anchor" in between the mental notes or labels you make, helping you to go back to something that is always in the present. This form of meditation helps you to experience that your thoughts and feelings are just parts of you, but not the *real* you.

Visualization Meditations

In researching why most spiritually oriented folks don't meditate, I found out that they claim it is either too difficult to do, or they don't have the time. With this information, I set out to develop a form of meditation that could be done in five minutes or less, and yet would be so powerful that it could move many people to tears of love and gratitude.

After a couple of years trying various combinations of methods, I developed something I call the Pure Love Meditation. In the workshops I lead, I've found that more than 50 percent of the people who do this form of meditation become teary-eyed. For something so brief and easy to do, it has a lot of impact.

The Pure Love Meditation

The Pure Love Meditation combines three simple aspects that work together to quiet your mind and open your heart. The first part is to get comfortable in a chair and play music that helps you feel peaceful, relaxed, loving. Next, take a deep breath, hold it for about five seconds, and then exhale with a long, slow sighing sound. Repeat three or four times as the music plays, each time ending with a long sighing sound.

By now you should feel more relaxed, a bit "softer" inside. At this point it's time to focus on some person or animal you feel great love and affection for. It can be a child, a parent, a former lover, your current partner, your pet—virtually anyone or anything. The important thing is that you have a strong heart connection with this being.

Picture this person or animal clearly in your mind, and imagine him or her giving you a look that melts your heart. Think about the things you most love and appreciate about this being. You can even imagine giving a warm, heartfelt hug to the one you love. With each breath, let your heart be filled with the love and affection you feel. Imagine your two souls being connected by the caring you have for each other. Once the music ends, continue to feel the glow in your heart.

Pure Love Variations

Although most people find they can go deeper into this experience if they do it while listening to some favorite music, some people prefer to do it in silence. You might try it both ways and see which one you enjoy more.

For another variation, you can use this technique for just 30 seconds or a minute by simply taking a deep breath and *then* thinking of the one you love. It can be surprising to discover that diving into an experience of love for just a brief time can dramatically change the way you feel. Studies done at the Institute of HeartMath have shown that focusing on feelings of love and appreciation for even a single minute can reduce stress hormones for several hours.

From Allah to Zen

Visualization meditation *is* any form of meditation in which a person uses an internal image to help quiet their mind and/or open their heart.

Heavenly Helpers

Many people have found they can deepen their feeling of connection by thinking the words "I love you" as they picture the one they are sending love to. I have found that when I picture my partner and call her by one of the many endearing nicknames I have for her, I feel my love for her even more.

The Pure Love Meditation is not only a way to feel love, but also a way to tap into the reservoir of peace within. Normally during the day we get caught up in worries and concerns, and lose sight of the bigger picture. By focusing on love, you center your energy in your heart, and the thoughts and worries of your head begin to dissipate.

Incidentally, practicing the Pure Love Meditation can help you get in touch with your intuitive guidance. As the mind quiets and the heart opens, it's easier to distinguish true guidance from ego-based thoughts. As you practice this meditation, you'll find that it not only becomes increasingly easy to tune into the love and peace that's always inside you, but that it becomes easier to seek answers within yourself.

Meditation for People Who Can't Sit Still

In our frenzied world, many people find it nearly impossible to sit still and meditate. Rather than shrug the whole thing off, there are some simple meditations that involve only a minute or two of sitting still. If you can't sit still even that long, there are longer, more active meditations you could try. Whether you are restless or enjoy the idea of active or shorter meditations, these methods can be a handy addition to your internal tool bag.

Amazing Grace

Several years ago, I did a live interview on CNN's *Talk Back Live*, which has a global audience of millions. I was extremely nervous. Three minutes before we went live, I asked myself, "What do I need to know or do to feel more peaceful now?" I received an answer, and my body and mind began to relax. By the time the cameras were rolling, I was fully at ease, and the interview went very well.

Questions and Answers

To begin with, a very simple form of meditation is to contemplate the answer(s) to a particular question. As your mind thinks about and feels the answer to a specific question, a deeper level of awareness or a positive feeling can result. Over many years of trial and error, I have found there are three questions that are particularly effective in quickly changing a person's feelings and deepening his level of awareness. They are …

➤ What do I need to know or do to feel more peaceful now?

➤ What could I feel grateful for?

➤ Whom do I love or who loves me?

Each of these questions can be like a flashlight that helps you see past your inner darkness to the heaven within. It takes only a minute or two of focusing on any of these inquiries to change what you perceive and how you feel.

To tune into the magic they offer, begin by taking a slow, deep breath, and then repeat the question a couple of times. At first you'll probably come up with intellectual answers that don't seem very connected to your feelings. With practice you'll learn to feel or intuit the real answers.

For example, if you find yourself feeling overwhelmed, you might ask yourself, "What do I need to know or do to feel more peaceful now?" As you think of several answers, you'll notice your thoughts will begin to move in a different direction. If you receive the answer that the way to feel more peaceful is to let go of the tension in your body, then that's what you can do. By focusing on how your body feels tense, you can begin to let go and feel a deepening sense of peace. In just a couple of minutes you can feel immensely better.

For the second and third questions, the important thing is to think of *specific* answers. They need not be big, dramatic examples—they only need to be things that are emotionally meaningful to you.

For instance, when asking yourself, "What could I feel grateful for?" you could feel thankful for literally hundreds of things. You could feel gratitude for being healthy, for having food when much of the world goes hungry, for friends, or even for the use of your telephone. By focusing on how fortunate you are, you can learn to tune into the feeling of gratitude whenever you desire, and quickly feel more at peace.

The question, "Whom do I love and who loves me?" can be a wonderful way to dive into your heart and experience the grace of love. By remembering a specific time you felt loved by someone, or a particular time you felt *in love* with someone, it's possible to tune into the warmth within your heart. With practice, you can take "minilove breaks" throughout the day that open your heart with love in just a minute of meditation and contemplation.

Staying Active

Besides quick meditations, people who can't sit still for long often enjoy *active meditations*. Active meditations can range from T'ai Chi movements and yoga postures to intensive cathartic processes. In Chapter 13, "Using Negativity as Rocket Fuel," I talk about some of the more common body-centered practices that are traditionally used for spiritual growth. You can create your own method of meditation by practicing various forms of movement.

The spiritual teacher known as Osho created many forms of active meditation. He felt that Westerners were too mentally oriented, and that they needed active forms of meditation to learn to relax their minds.

From Allah to Zen

Active meditation is any meditation that involves slow or vigorous movement of the body. Its methods include dancing, shaking, twirling, slow bodily movements, certain martial arts, or movement-oriented yoga postures.

One example of his many techniques is called kundalini meditation. There are four distinct parts to kundalini meditation, of which the first three are performed to music. In part one, practitioners shake their entire body as vigorously as possible. During part two, they dance. In part three, the goal is to sit and watch one's thoughts pass by like clouds in the sky. Finally, in part four, one sits or lies down, the goal simply to *be*.

What differentiates active meditation from dance or other forms of movement is its intended purpose: to dive deeper into your being. In active meditation, you focus on your body as a way to overcome the obstacles to being fully present in the moment. As you feel your body, and as you release the tensions held in your body, the mind relaxes into its home of pure awareness.

Initiation Meditations

Some of the most powerful forms of meditation are secret, transmitted directly from spiritual teacher to student. To learn such forms of meditation requires a lot more effort and commitment on the part of the student. First you must find a teacher or group that possesses this special knowledge. Then you must complete certain required steps before you can receive their sacred teachings. In Appendix B, "Surfing to Enlightenment," I denote with an asterisk those spiritual teachers and groups that teach meditations requiring a special initiation process.

You might be wondering, "Why go through the trouble of learning a meditation that requires a special initiation?" The advantage of such initiations is that you can learn about objects of concentration that can help you to meditate at a higher level. A mantra or your breath are merely things to concentrate on. Neither of them can actually "pull you up" because they are not directly connected to God. In certain initiation meditations, you can learn about focusing on an inner sound, light, or vibration that *is* directly connected to God. The advantage of this is that, in my opinion, such initiation meditations can help you to go "higher" than other forms of meditation. In addition, when learning about meditations that require a special initiation, you usually need to be involved with a group of like-minded seekers. Group support can be very helpful for your spiritual development.

No matter what meditation method you try, the key to success is consistency, sincerity, and persistence. As you've heard, the kingdom of heaven is within. Meditation is perhaps the most time-tested way of connecting with heaven while still on Earth.

Heavenly Helpers

If you want to be initiated into a specific meditation, I suggest you call or visit several groups. Ask what their requirements are, and try to get a feel for them. The more information you have, the more likely you'll choose a teacher or group that's right for you.

The Least You Need to Know

➤ Meditation can quiet your mind, open your heart, improve your health, and help you to connect with Spirit.

➤ In mantra meditations such as TM, you can easily achieve a very peaceful state by focusing on a particular sound.

➤ In breath meditations, you can become more present by noting the rising and falling of your breath or your passing thoughts.

➤ Those who have a hard time sitting still can benefit from brief meditations that use visualizations or questions or meditations that involve movement.

➤ Meditations that involve an initiation process can be especially powerful but must be taught by an authorized teacher.

Chapter 12

Body-Centered Practices

In This Chapter

➤ Hatha and other forms of yoga

➤ Qigong as a physical and spiritual healing method

➤ The many types of martial arts

➤ The purpose and benefits of T'ai Chi

➤ How breathing exercises can enliven your soul

➤ The joy of whirling like a dervish

When it comes to spiritual practices, there are three basic avenues: the mind or intellect, the emotions, and the body. In order for us to soar to heavenly heights, we need to develop all three aspects. Although our emotions and minds are constantly "worked out," our bodies frequently are not.

In a culture in which one third of the population is considered obese, we need to have more awareness and respect for the temples of our souls. Most people eat poorly, are physically stressed, rarely exercise, and have little sense of what it means to develop an energetically balanced and healthy body. Having never experienced the joy of total health, they don't realize how much more peaceful and centered a well-toned body could feel.

Fortunately, many profound methods for using one's body as a vehicle for spiritual work are readily available. For thousands of years, spiritual traditions have created and practiced methods of using the body to raise one's awareness. Body-centered spiritual practices can be all-encompassing, or used in addition to other forms of spiritual work. In the last 40 years, many body-centered methods have gone from the fringes of society to the boardrooms of corporate America.

Many people in the West live in a state of numbness. If on a scale of 1 to 10, 10 being the optimum amount of receptivity and sensation your body could experience, where would you rate yourself? In this culture, most people would rate in the one, two, or three range. What if, to experience your inner *bliss,* your sensitivity level needed to be at least a six? The various body-centered practices discussed in this chapter can help you refine your body, and develop a new relationship with it. Once you are more aware of and at ease with your body, you may find that Spirit is a more frequent guest.

Yoga for Beginners

Yoga, a 4,000-year-old art from India, is now a household word in the West. Yoga means union. The ultimate purpose of yoga is to unite with the God-energy inside of us. According to Eastern philosophy, to unite with this creative force enables us to step off the cycle of death and rebirth. The only true freedom is to be able to leave the temporary earthly life behind and live in a higher state of being. The human body is the vehicle with which to experience these higher states. In order for this ultimate goal of union to be attained, one must devote his or her life to it, and be under the care of an enlightened master.

There are many different kinds of yoga. The yoga we are most acquainted with is called *hatha yoga,* which involves postures and breath work. The poses can take us out of the thinking mind to a quiet, deep place inside. They also stimulate the organs and the lymph system and relax the nervous system.

From Allah to Zen

Hatha has been translated to mean "health." We must have health to have union. We must have a healthy body to prepare for spiritual illumination. The *ha* means "sun"; the *tha* means "moon." Hatha is the union of the sun and the moon. This union of the positive and negative creates a new force, a force that is needed to grow spiritually.

By the way, those guys who walk on hot coals and stick needles through their arms are not yogis. They are called *fakirs* and focus their attention on supernatural acts. Yoga is a gentle and natural process between you and your body. You may have seen yoga classes where the students are sweating, gasping, and straining. I may take some flack for this one, but I call that aerobics. A classic yoga session should focus on deep and attentive meditation. This meditative state, engendered by the poses, is the door to the union with the Creator.

In the Bhagavad-Gita, the most important book of yoga philosophy, Sri Krishna comments on what a true yogi is like. He states …

A lamp does not flicker in a place where no winds blow; so it is with a yogi, who controls his mind, intellect, and self, being absorbed in the spirit within him. When the restlessness of the mind, intellect and self is stilled through the practice of

Yoga, the yogi, by the grace of the Spirit within himself, finds fulfillment … He has found the treasure above all others. There is nothing higher than this. He who has achieved it, shall not be moved by the greatest sorrow.

Some other types of yoga are …

➤ **Bhakti-yoga.** The yoga of surrender, or devotional yoga.

➤ **Raja yoga.** The yoga of control over the will.

➤ **Yantra** and **mantra yoga.** The yoga that focuses on geometrical diagrams of mystical significance or sounds and words of occult power.

➤ **Karma yoga.** The yoga of service and good works in life.

➤ **Jnana yoga.** The yoga of self-knowledge.

Cosmic Potholes

If you look at a yoga book and see a yogi walking on his hands with his legs in the shape of a pretzel, don't be deterred! You don't have to accomplish any more than you are naturally able to do. You will benefit from any yoga postures.

Nowadays, people practice hatha yoga for many reasons other than spiritual enlightenment, including pain relief, strengthening, flexibility, weight loss, gracefulness, stress reduction, and healing. Yoga practitioners (yogis) say that the poses and breathing increase the life force in the body. With more life force it is easier to stop addictive behaviors. So whether you want to get off the karmic wheel of death and rebirth or you want to stop chewing your fingernails, yoga might be for you.

Qigong and the Body Electric

Qigong, the grandparent of modern-day acupuncture, is a practice of movements and meditations that influence the flow of vital force in the body. *Qi* stands for that vital force, also called consciousness, or the eternal energy that all is created from. *Gong* means "work, skill, and practice." With diligent work a qigong practitioner can absorb and channel the vital energy of the universe to become or stay healthy, heal others, and grow spiritually.

Qigong originated in China. It is first reflected in the *I Ching,* or *The Book of Changes,* written in approximately the twelfth century B.C.E. Around the third century B.C.E., Buddhism came to China from India, and shared its secrets with those who practiced the art of qigong. This period is called the Religious Period, when the focus of qigong was spiritual enlightenment rather than just bodily health. Finally, in 1911, with the overthrow of the Quing dynasty, qigong as an art of spiritual and bodily health became available to the world. The training began to mix with Japanese and Indian styles. Secrets that had been locked up in monasteries are still being released, making it a very exciting time for alternative healing, martial arts, and those interested in spiritual growth.

Amazing Grace

Qigong masters have become known for performing supernatural feats. I had the opportunity to be treated by the famous qigong Master Zhou. I watched as he popped a balloon from five feet away. He dried a wet washcloth with the heat from his hands. He held his empty hand over one of my knees and told me to tell him when it started to burn. Sure enough, he generated so much heat that I had to ask him to move it! I know people who say they have felt the wave of the qigong master's hands from across the room as if he or she were touching them.

Qigong has been called acupuncture without needles. As with qigong, acupuncture maintains the view that the body contains 12 meridians and 8 vessels, with tributaries, that flow like rivers of energy. These rivers of energy feed the organs, tissues, and muscles, and keep them healthy. When there is a shortage of energy or a block in the flow, there is disease. The movements, meditations, and visualizations of qigong keep the flow of energy and oxygen at an optimum level. They can also direct the flow to the parts of the body that have become unhealthy. The body, with a balanced flow of energy, can heal itself.

The medical effects of qigong are starting to be documented in this country. In China, research is so extensive that there are hospitals devoted only to qigong treatment. One recent abstract documents that people who have been doing qigong for more than two years are in better health than control groups. Even four months of qigong practice significantly improved the health of people in the studies.

Another abstract documented positive changes of type A individuals. Type As are likely to be workaholics with symptoms like high blood pressure. With qigong practice these people showed improvement with an increased ability to relax.

A portion of qigong focuses on the martial arts. Qigong martial arts are called soft styles. The victor, traditionally, is the challenger who wins without needing to strike. He or she can neutralize the *qi* or power of the opponent simply by understanding it so well.

There are hundreds of different styles of what is known as external qigong. One that you might be familiar with is T'ai Chi. Others are the famous animal forms like the Soaring Crane and the Wild Goose. The sight of someone performing an animal form is beautiful. There is no question what animal it is, and the effect can be mesmerizing. This hypnotic effect, no doubt, relates to qi as it is being called into the being of the practitioner. One woman describes this phenomenon in a qigong newsletter. "For me what separates qigong from other exercise is the qi feeling. The feeling comes quite early in the training and is a great motivator."

Martial Arts

Cool, calm, collected—and *lethal*. Those words describe famous martial arts heroes like Bruce Lee, Chuck Norris, Steven Seagal, and David "Kung Fu" Carradine. But the relationship of martial arts to spiritual awareness may be more accurately represented by the Karate Kid wiping the car over and over. His teacher, Mr. Miaggi, demanded discipline, respect, and patience.

Some schools of martial arts focus on fighting techniques, being tough, and competing. Other schools —with a more spiritual bent—focus on how straight you park your shoes at the door, and how respectful you are to the teacher.

Martial arts are from 3,500 to 5,000 years old. Cave paintings in Egypt and Babylon depict human figures in martial arts poses, presumably defending themselves from animals.

Martial arts, as we now know them, may have begun with a famous Indian Buddhist monk named Bodidharma. Bodidharma traveled from India to China in the year C.E. 526, presumably with knowledge of Kataripayit, an ancient Indian fighting technique. In an effort to strengthen the physically weak monks at the Shaolin Temple, in Central China, Bodidharma created the first fighting techniques. These techniques mixed religious practices with strengthening exercises. Kung Fu, a catch-all term for many of the Chinese martial arts, developed from these early beginnings.

Heavenly Helpers

Anyone can buy a black belt and put up a sign on the door. If you're shopping for a martial arts school, do your homework. Check on the teacher's background. Note whether the students are respectful toward the teacher when he or she leaves the room. After that, give the practice a year. Less than that and you will have an incomplete picture.

Periods of history followed when weapons were outlawed and martial arts were the only means of defense. The Japanese term *karate,* in fact, means "empty hands," or "to defend without weapons." It can be further translated to mean "empty self."

From Allah to Zen

Empty self is a term used in certain Eastern traditions that refers to a state of consciousness in which a person is fully present in the eternal now moment. In this state of heightened awareness, a person is best able to respond to his or her environment in an appropriate manner.

By the mid–nineteenth century the warrior classes were faced with having to fit into a society that had no need of their services. The training continued, but its purpose became self-development and spiritual growth. In the early twentieth century, the father of modern karate, Gichin Funakoshi, wrote that karate "strives neither for victory or defeat, but for the perfection of the character of its practitioners."

Martial arts became popular in the United States after World War II when some of the troops in Okinawa learned it and brought it to the West. The first dojo, a martial arts school, was opened in Phoenix, Arizona, in 1946, by a former U.S. sailor. In 1964, judo became an official sport at the Olympics. Training began in earnest in the 1960s when Chuck Norris began winning titles. The popularity of martial arts was secured with Bruce Lee's last film, *Enter the Dragon,* a huge box office success. Millions of people are now studying hundreds of different martial arts styles.

If a student asks, "How long does it take to get a black belt?" then maybe he or she is not interested in the spiritual aspects of martial arts. A better question to ask is, "Why do I want to learn a martial art?" This question can help pinpoint your intention, which is the basis of beginning a spiritual path. In some martial arts, such as Aikido, fighting is the opposite of the goal. A famous Aikido master once said, "Aikido is the art of reconciliation. Whosoever has the desire to fight has already broken his connection to the universe. We study how to resolve conflict, not how to start it."

The study of any martial art is what you make of it. It can be a form of physical exercise, mental focus, a fighting technique, or a spiritual discipline leading to a form of service. It depends on what your goal is, and what the aim is of the school or teacher you work with. As a spiritual path, martial arts can help bring your mind, body, and emotions into a state of one-pointed stillness. From such a quiet inner place, the doorway to higher states of awareness becomes visible.

Is T'ai Chi for Me?

T'ai Chi began as a martial arts practice, supposedly originating from an enlightened teacher named Chang San-feng. Over time, it became associated with the Taoist (pronounced *dowist*) philosophy, and it evolved in three distinct but related directions: as a fighting art, as a self-healing tool, and as a method of spiritual growth and energetic enhancement. Today, millions of Chinese practice it on a daily basis, and it has become increasingly popular in the West.

In its most traditional form, T'ai Chi consists of 108 separate movements that are connected in a particular order. Nowadays, there are several different styles of T'ai Chi. Many of the different styles of T'ai Chi offer a shortened version for beginners, usually consisting of 20 to 40 movements.

Practitioners of T'ai Chi look like they are doing a dance in very slow motion. The purpose of the precise, slow bodily movements is to harmonize the energy of the body with the energy of the cosmos. By focusing on each movement of the body, the T'ai Chi practitioner becomes more balanced, relaxed, and connected to the energy of the universe.

Because T'ai Chi is known for enhancing health and integrating movement and meditation, many people find it to be a wonderful spiritual practice. Although it can take a while to learn, once the movements are memorized, there is a poetic feeling to performing its routine. Some people fall in love with it, while others find it very difficult and frustrating to do. By taking a class or practicing along with a video, you can get a sense of whether T'ai Chi is right for you.

While T'ai Chi consists of very precise movements, in recent years some teachers have emphasized the "spirit" of the movements over the exact form. Indeed, you can get a taste of what T'ai Chi is like simply by moving your body in a slow, meditative manner, following whatever feels good. Through practice and exploration, you can discover ways of moving your body that feel expansive, grounding, or energizing. Once you know some of the basic T'ai Chi movements, you can improvise your own to feel a poetic connection to the energy all around you.

The Bridge of Breath

Pranayama is one of the eight forms of yoga as put forth in the ancient texts known as Patanjali's Yoga Sutras. The word *prana* means "breath," and *ayama* means "to extend, stretch, or control." Therefore, pranayama means "the prolongation of breath and its restraint."

Heavenly Helpers

If you want to learn T'ai Chi, there are many good videos that demonstrate the various techniques. I recommend Chungliang Al Huang's various videos, which you can order by calling 217-337-6113. While a video is helpful, learning from a teacher is even better. You may be able to find a T'ai Chi instructor by looking under T'ai Chi or Martial Arts in your phone book.

Amazing Grace

During the Cultural Revolution in China in the 1960s, all forms of qigong and most forms of T'ai Chi were outlawed. For a period of time, only a single form of T'ai Chi was certified to be allowed by the ruling party. Yet today, T'ai Chi is openly practiced in large groups by millions of Chinese.

In yoga theology, prana is seen not only as what we breathe, but as the energy that permeates the entire universe as well. It is energy that is simultaneously physical, mental, spiritual, and cosmic. In pranayama exercises, a practitioner prolongs his inhalation, holds his breath, and then exhales with the intention of surrendering his ego to the larger self.

While there are literally hundreds of different breathing or pranayama exercises you can learn, for simplicity's sake, I'll explain my personal favorite. The beauty of the power breath is that it takes only 90 seconds to do, and yet its energizing effect can last for an hour. In addition, it can drastically change how you feel, propelling you from a lethargic feeling all the way to euphoria.

To do the power breath, sit up in a chair with your spine straight. Make a soft fist out of each hand, and place the back of your hands so they're near your shoulders. Have a clock or stopwatch in front of you so you can easily check when a full minute has passed.

Cosmic Potholes

Don't do the power breath or other breathing exercise soon after a meal. It will just make you nauseous. In addition, before doing the exercise, it's a good idea to blow your nose so it's easier to breathe. And third, a minute is longer than you think. If you can set an alarm to go off at the appropriate time, you won't have to constantly look at the time.

To begin the breath, inhale powerfully through your nose while lifting your arms straight over your shoulders. When you exhale, bring your hands back next to your shoulders as you powerfully let out air through your nose. That's it. Repeat this form of "aerobic breathing" as quickly and as intensely as you possibly can for a full 60 seconds. If you need to slow down due to light-headedness, take a regular deep breath—then proceed once again at a comfortable pace. The more powerfully and rapidly you do each breath, the more effect you'll likely feel.

Once you've done this breath for the full minute (which will seem like a very long time), take one last deep breath and hold it. You can put your hands in a comfortable position on your lap. Hold your breath for at least 20 seconds, and longer if you can. Then, exhale with a long, slow sighing sound. Aaahhhhh-hhhhh! Feel the energy throughout your body. Pretty amazing, isn't it?

Besides the immediate physical and psychological effects of this breath, it's also incredibly good for you. The power breath is a quick way to oxygenate the blood and help your body get rid of toxins. You may find that it's initially hard to do with any amount of speed or intensity, but if you do it every day for a month, you'll notice a tremendous difference. You'll feel more energy, and you'll feel healthier and more relaxed.

The Wonders of Whirling

The art of whirling as a way to connect with the cosmos began with the famous Sufi teacher and poet, Mevlana Jalaluddin Rumi, in the thirteenth century. People who use this practice are called dervishes. As part of the whirling practice, dervishes typically follow an elaborate preparation ritual. Once ready, the dervishes extend their arms, the right palm face up, and the left palm face down. As they silently recite "Allah, Allah ..." repeatedly, they begin to turn from right to left.

When whirling, dervishes imagine receiving energy from above through their right hand. This energy passes through their body and is transmitted down into the Earth through their left hand. When possible, dervishes revolve around a master teacher, known as a sheikh. The sheikh represents the sun, and the dervishes represent the planets turning around him.

Part of the reason they whirl, aside from the fact that it leads to an altered state of consciousness, is that spinning is considered a fundamental condition of our existence. Since everything from electrons to planets seem to whirl around a center, by spinning around a teacher, dervishes participate in the shared revolving of all of existence.

Having taken a weekend workshop in whirling, and practiced it on several occasions, I can tell you that this can be a fascinating technique. My experience was that, as long as I could surrender to the whirling, and not worry about anything, I could enter a very blissful state. Yet once I would have a thought such as, "Am I going to run into someone?" all hell would break loose. Instead of twirling with ease, I would begin to look like a spinning top that was out of control. Whirling can give a person an immediate experience of how his thoughts can wreak havoc on his life.

Although whirling may look easy, to do it right requires a high degree of skill. Unfortunately, unlike people who are trained in it, I never learned how to avoid feeling incredibly dizzy and nauseous afterward! Those who practice it regularly experience much bliss, rather than dizziness, from the method. It is also very beautiful to watch. Since dervishes are part of the Sufi school, and Sufis are a branch of Islam, calling a mosque is a good way to find out more information about whirling.

Amazing Grace

Legend has it that the practice of whirling began when Rumi's teacher, Shams of Tabriz, either died or was killed. In his profound grief, Rumi began twirling around a pole in a local mosque. While he would spin around this pole, he began to spontaneously recite beautiful poetry. Rumi's students wrote his poetry down, and preserved it. Today, 700 years later, Rumi is the best-selling poet in America!

The Least You Need to Know

➤ By increasing your connection to your body, you can increase your receptivity to health and Spirit.

➤ There are many types of yogas, but the most common in the West is hatha yoga, which aims to make the body strong and healthy.

➤ Qigong is a method of increasing the flow of energy or "qi" in the body for health and spiritual purposes.

➤ Martial arts and T'ai Chi can be used for varying purposes, depending upon the focus of the practitioner and school.

➤ Breath exercises (pranayama) and whirling are powerful ways to use the body to experience higher states of energy and ecstasy.

Part 4

Using Negativity to Develop

Negative emotions, events, and aspects of ourselves can actually be used to accelerate our spiritual progress! That's good news because there is rarely a shortage of negativity around us or inside of us. In this part, you'll learn how to make use of your negative feelings, difficult circumstances, and even difficult relationships to grow spiritually.

Ultimately, a sincere spiritual seeker must take responsibility for the negativity he or she experiences. To do this, it's helpful to learn the causes of our negative reactions in precise detail, as well as how to transform these reactions into spiritual "food." If you can get good at watching or transforming the negativity around you, you'll have plenty of "fuel" to dive into the "kingdom of heaven within."

Chapter 13

Using Negativity as Rocket Fuel

In This Chapter

➤ Using negativity to grow spiritually

➤ How people avoid learning from the lessons life throws their way

➤ How negative emotions talk to us

➤ How negative feelings reveal your shortcomings

➤ Using bad feelings as an alarm clock

To blast off on the journey to inner space, you need plenty of rocket fuel. "Rocket fuel" in this context is what drives you to stay persistent in your spiritual practices.

In my opinion, the best fuel for the inner journey is your negative emotions. The desire to avoid feeling bad is often what gets people to begin the spiritual journey in the first place. If you can learn to *make use* of your negativity, you'll always have plenty of energy and motivation to propel yourself forward. After all, there is always plenty of negativity to be had, and it can be gratifying to convert some of it into learning, fascination, and motivation.

When things are going wonderfully in our lives, it's hard to be motivated to do inner work. We don't like to be distracted from our good feelings. Yet, most people would be willing to let go of some of their negativity. Negative emotions are incredibly valuable on the spiritual search because they can help pinpoint something in your self that is off-kilter.

Cosmic Potholes

Because negativity can be motivating on the spiritual journey, some people mistake feeling bad with doing "spiritual work." Actually, feeling bad is not an indication of growth. In fact, it's easier to learn important lessons from small problems and small negativity, rather than big things. When we are inundated with negativity, all our effort goes toward feeling better. Whereas with small things, some of our attention can more easily go toward the lesson inherent in the situation.

In addition, negativity can act like an "alarm clock," waking you up to the possibility of using a spiritual method or learning something new. Finally, negativity can feel like lead weights on your back, and it's difficult to be a light-filled, happy person with lead weights on your back. By letting go of some of the excess baggage you carry around, you'll likely experience better results.

How to Not Learn from Life

As a therapist, I get to see an endless variety of ways that people avoid learning from the situations in their lives. I think all the devices humans use to avoid learning can be categorized into three basic methods: denial, distraction, and blame.

Let's look at denial first. No, let's not. It's probably not really a problem, so let's just forget about it. That's denial in a nutshell. We convince ourselves that something isn't a problem, even when it is: "My drinking isn't that bad," or, "All couples argue a lot—it's natural." By denying that we have a problem, we avoid even the possibility of looking at what might be creating trouble for us. The problem with denial, as with all protective measures, is that it doesn't solve anything. The issue doesn't disappear, because we refuse to acknowledge it.

A second method for not learning from the situations in your life is to distract yourself from the pain you feel. As a culture, we use this in full force. We have TV, radio, movies, food, alcohol, drugs, work, tabloids, and on and on. By focusing on such things, the pain we feel goes away—temporarily.

Unfortunately, the root of the problem does not go away. Like a weed that hasn't been pulled out from the roots, whatever it is we're trying to avoid quickly grows back. Many people in our culture spend all their free moments trying to run away from their own negativity, hoping to cover up all the empty spaces in their lives. Eventually, it's a losing battle. Reality has a way of seeping in despite our nonstop efforts to stop it.

The third, and perhaps most problematic defense mechanism is blame. Blame is a big problem because it's so prevalent and invisible to the people who use it. In our externally oriented culture, there's a lot of agreement that if we feel some kind of pain, it's because of something "out there." For example, if our relationship is going bad, it's because our partner is being a jerk. If our work is not going well, it's because the job is boring. If we're not happy, it's because we're not making enough money.

While the external world certainly has an effect on our emotions, the people and situations of our life are not the root cause of our suffering—we are, through our neurotic tendencies or deficiencies. The problem is, through the vehicle of blame, we hide these parts of ourselves from ourselves, which enables them to continue.

What You Resist Tends to Persist

Just as there are certain physical laws, such as gravity, there are certain spiritual laws. You may not like these laws, but as with gravity, there's little you can do about them.

One of these laws is "What you resist tends to persist." On a practical level, this statement means that if there is something you're trying to avoid through blame, denial, or distraction, it will likely continue to be a problem until you face it head on. In fact, the longer you avoid it, the more problematic it becomes.

Negative emotions exist to warn us that something is wrong. Sometimes the something wrong is in the external world, such as when our life is threatened by a mugger. Yet, most of the time, what's

Heavenly Helpers

To see how much you use distraction to cover up your negativity, simply go on a "media fast" for a couple of days. Watch no TV or movies, and avoid all radio, music, or reading. Try just sitting by yourself, doing nothing. Notice what you feel. Do you feel anxious, fearful, bored, resentful, sad? These are the feelings you normally avoid by keeping yourself occupied.

Amazing Grace

As a psychotherapist, I often teach people to go "into" their negative feelings as a way to transform them. Trying to avoid feeling sad, anxious, or hurt can often prolong the feelings. Instead, I have clients "open up" and focus on the feeling they've been resisting. Ironically, this embracing of their negative feelings usually leads to the feeling changing, neutralizing, or even becoming a positive feeling.

139

wrong can be traced back to some shortcoming within us. By being receptive to the lessons negative emotions try to teach us, we can avoid a lot of unnecessary pain and accelerate our spiritual growth.

Holes in the Balloon

Our shortcomings are like holes in a balloon. Even a small hole in a balloon will cause all the air to leak out. When you think about it, it's unfair. The balloon is 99 percent intact, yet because of one small hole it's useless. The same is often true with our desire to find happiness. Almost everything can be going well, but a single short-coming or problem can wreak havoc in our lives. The good news is that, if we're willing to trace our pain to our personal shortcomings, miracles can happen. In this light, negative emotions can be seen as God's way to get our attention so we'll become aware of the holes in our balloon.

Let me give you an example to show you some of the principles I've been talking about. I had a psychotherapy client named Bill several years ago. Bill originally came to me complaining of stress because "some jerk" was trying to sue him. At first I took Bill's side, but as the weeks of therapy went by, I could see that Bill had a way of being misleading with me, as well as with himself. I tried to point out to Bill that this was a possible reason he was being sued, since I knew he was being sued for having misled a person about a business agreement. Unfortunately, he would have none of it. Soon he stopped coming to me.

Cosmic Potholes

When you start to see that your shortcomings play a part in the negative things that happen in your life, it can be depressing and disturbing. Be gentle and compassionate with yourself. At least you're now seeing the truth. As your awareness grows, know that you are letting more "light" in. Getting down on yourself does little good.

Two years later, Bill came to me in a panic because he was now being sued for a much larger amount. Once again I tried to help him see how his shortcomings might have contributed to his "bad luck" in business. He still didn't listen. Finally, a year later, when faced with possible imprisonment for fraud, he began to see his own part in the experiences he was having.

Bill's story is a classic example of the spiritual law that "What you resist tends to persist." If you don't listen to the small lessons the universe sends your way, the lessons become bigger until you do start listening. The same could be said of our negative emotions. If you don't listen to and receive the lessons that small negative emotions have for you, they will get bigger until they do get your attention. That's why blame, denial, and distraction are ultimately so self-defeating. They are like a cosmic credit card, delaying the time that you'll have to pay for your actions until later—when you'll owe the same amount plus a lot of interest.

The Signposts

To avoid the huge problems, it's a good idea to learn the lessons you're supposed to learn when they're still small. The best way I know of doing this is to use your negative emotions as a signpost of what your shortcomings are.

Here's an example: Let's say you frequently get irritated at your mate when they are late for dinner. The most likely thing you do is to simply get mad and blame them for being inconsiderate. That's the easy thing to do. The harder thing to do is to learn about how a fault in you is contributing to the suffering you feel. How can you do that? Well, you can ask yourself the question, "What shortcoming in me might be helping to contribute to this situation?" This question can help point you in the direction away from blame and toward the "holes in your balloon."

Once you ask yourself this question, try to think of several answers. In the example of a partner who is often late, your answers to the question, "What shortcoming in me might be helping to contribute to this situation?" might include …

➤ I'm afraid to sincerely tell him how much it hurts me, and instead I just pretend like I don't mind.

➤ When I finally do tell him how much it bothers me, I explode in a rage, which leads to his getting defensive rather than really hearing what I'm saying.

➤ I am unable or unwilling to feel compassion for the stresses he has at work. I refuse to feel compassion for how it's difficult for him to say no to his boss.

➤ I like being self-righteous and proving others wrong, even if my relationship pays a price.

➤ I lack the communication skills that would allow him to hear me without getting defensive.

➤ I set very high standards for others, and am not flexible in adjusting to how others actually are—which leads to my being frequently disappointed.

Heavenly Helpers

To know how you might be causing a problem or difficult situation in your life, ask yourself, "What shortcoming in me might be creating or contributing to this situation?" If you draw a blank, ask a trusted friend for his feedback. Sometimes the people who know you well can see better than you how your faults contribute to the difficulty in your life.

Some readers will object to the above and insist that the partner who is late is the only one to blame. For the person who wants to become a purer, happier person, exploring how he may have contributed assists him in spotting the holes in his balloon. It can help him be inspired to work on himself through learning to communicate better or becoming more compassionate, for example.

Unless a person notices his own shortcomings—and desires to make a change—it is hard to find the motivation to do spiritual work. The motivation to do spiritual work is, in my experience, mostly driven by seeing how screwed up we are. Therefore, when you notice such shortcomings, celebrate them! Seeing your shortcomings—how you cause yourself and others unnecessary pain—is the fuel that will help you to persist in your journey to inner space.

Amazing Grace

The song "Amazing Grace" was written by John Newton, in collaboration with William Cowper. Newton was a master of a slave ship. In a moment of connection with God, he saw the errors of his ways, and penned "Amazing grace how sweet the sound that saved a wretch like me. I once was lost, but now am found, was blind but now I see." Once his eyes were opened, Newton stopped slave trading and devoted his life to evangelical Christianity.

What's the Point?

Once you see that negative emotions can point to shortcomings in yourself, it becomes important to interpret them correctly. Although blaming your mate may seem like a relatively "correct" interpretation of what's happening, the problem is that blame does not lead to personal growth. If it did, we'd all be enlightened.

Fortunately, with a little practice, you can learn to interpret your negative feelings in a way that helps you to grow spiritually. In general, we have negative feelings for one of two reasons. Either we have desires or expectations that are not being met (and are often unrealistic), or we lack certain skills or abilities. Usually, it's a combination of the two. Whatever the reason for our negative feelings, in every case such emotions can be traced to a specific internal obstacle.

In the following chart, you'll see a list of negative emotions, the message or lesson each points to, and the skill or ability you'll need to develop to overcome them. If you have one of these feelings, see if the corresponding lessons help you interpret what's going on. Then determine whether you need to focus on a certain skill or ability to make this negative feeling less prominent in your life.

Negative Emotion	Message/Lesson That May Fit	Skill/Ability You May Need
Anger	You have unrealistic expectations.	Communicate your needs better and/or let go.
Hurt	You have an expectation or hope that's unrealistic.	You may need to be flexible in your communication.
Guilt	You are violating your own standard, or holding on to one that is outdated.	Update your standards to fit who you are now; stick to your values.

Negative Emotion	Message/Lesson That May Fit	Skill/Ability You May Need
Depressed	You're focused on the past or the future and not on what you can do that's meaningful now.	Decide what's important to you now and act on it. Avoid self-pity or being a martyr.
Insecure	You let fear and embarrassment stop you.	Let go of the need for others' approval. Learn to act even if you're afraid.
Fear	Be better prepared, or break things down into smaller steps.	Practice what you fear or let go of unrealistic worry. Need for faith.
Frustration	Your expectations are too high.	Communicate needs better and/or let go more. Set more realistic goals or timelines. Be more flexible with goals.
Self-dislike	Your expectations are not in line with who you are, or you're off-course.	Create more realistic expectations of your abilities or have more compassion.

This is not a complete list of negative emotions, and the lessons or deficiencies they point to, but it may help you to discover something about yourself and take the first step in understanding what is really going on.

Keep in mind that although this list describes how negative feelings point to deficiencies in our self, it doesn't mean that bad feelings always tell us something is wrong with us. For example, if someone you care about is hurt or dies, sadness is certainly appropriate! Yet, so many of our bad feelings are the exaggerated reactions to imagined needs, or problems that result from the blame, denial, and distraction within us.

As I started to see how much I contributed to the negative feelings in my own life, it motivated me to do spiritual practices. I became more committed to daily meditation and becoming aware of my faults. It also made me more humble and receptive to help from friends, spiritual mentors, and God. I used to be afraid of looking at and seeing how much negativity I lived in, but I finally realized that what is, is. By listening to, accepting, and not distracting myself from my negative feelings, I've been better able to feel my connection to myself, to other people, and to God.

Heavenly Helpers

All human beings share the experiences of hurt, fear, anger, frustration, jealousy, and self-dislike. When feeling such pain, try to become aware of how such feelings actually unite humanity in a shared experience. Then, it's not so much "your pain," but rather "our pain." From such a perspective, it's easier to feel compassion for yourself and others.

143

I've also sometimes experienced difficult times as a form of grace. It's often been during difficult times that I've been forced to find a deeper connection to people and God than I would have otherwise explored. Nowadays, when times are rough, a little voice in my head says, "In the past, times like these have led to a lot of growth. Hang in there." Perhaps the same attitude can be of help to you.

Getting a Wake-Up Call

Besides pointing to obstacles in yourself, negative feelings can serve as a wake-up call to turn to a specific spiritual practice. Many traditions use bad feelings as a catalyst to turn to a certain spiritual technique. For example, in Catholicism, feelings of guilt might lead a person to go to confession. In Buddhism, people are often guided to focus on the breath when fear and worry take hold of their mind.

Negative Alarm Clocks

Negative feelings make good alarm clocks for several reasons. First, they tend to be prevalent, so they can lead to a plethora of wake-up calls. Second, negative feelings can be detrimental to one's peace of mind, so interrupting their momentum can be beneficial for one's inner peace. Third, negative feelings are usually due to some unwanted tendency of the mind. Responding to them with a spiritual practice of some kind is like applying medicine at just the right location.

Throughout this book, there are numerous spiritual techniques you can use to become aware of and ultimately transmute negativity into a neutral feeling or learning experience. Chapters 3, "Diving into Now," 11, "The Art of Meditation," and 16, "Turning Lead into Gold," are full of simple meditations and exercises to help you transmute your negativity. You need to be careful with how you use such methods. If you use them to *mask* your negativity, you are misusing them. If you just want to distract yourself from what you're feeling (and admit it, we all do it), then it's better to use TV or ice cream. Once you feel like you've learned what you can from your bad feelings, and all you're doing is indulging in them, a spiritual method can help you overcome negativity. You don't get any points in heaven for unnecessary *suffering*.

After a while, most people find that they have a weakness for certain negative emotions. For example, I apparently have a fondness for frustration. I spend a lot of my life feeling frustrated. Since I like to think of myself as a groovy spiritual guy, it took me a long time to admit that I was seeped in frustration and impatience much of the time.

From Allah to Zen

Suffering is the tendency to dwell on or resist a specific situation that is causing pain in one's life. Unlike pain, which is inevitable, suffering is optional, since it is primarily a function of one's mind resisting the pain or unpleasantness of life.

To defeat my frustration, I had to get past my denial, blame, and distraction, which was no easy task. I became receptive to the feedback I received from friends and family that indicated I was often perceived as impatient and frustrated by life. Then I had to look at the lesson frustration was trying to teach me—that my need to achieve was too high. Finally, I surmised the deficiencies I had which led to my being so mired in frustration and impatience. I asked my intuition, "What shortcomings in me are leading to my feeling frequently frustrated?" I began to gain insight from such questions. Once I was aware of all those things, to my surprise, I still spent a lot of time being frustrated! It's been a long, frustrating journey to deal with my frustration.

Sometimes just being aware of the thoughts that lead to a certain feeling does not lessen its impact on your life. You may have gone over the lesson and been aware of the negative thoughts 100 times, and still it eats away at your mind and emotions. At that point, you should try to use such feelings as an alarm clock.

Heavenly Helpers

When you want to avoid indulging in a harmful negative emotion, it's helpful to come up with a precise strategy. To think, "I'll just relax when I notice I'm worrying," won't do as much good as thinking, "I'll follow my breath for 10 seconds every time I notice I'm distressed over money." The best strategies include the specific method, the trigger for using it, and even the precise time length for using it.

Whenever you notice you're indulging in the same feelings and thoughts that get you nowhere, create a preordained strategy for dealing with it. The negative feeling becomes your alarm clock for turning to that preordained strategy. For example, you might meditate by following your breath, or praying, or focusing on the method of "outer presence" discussed in Chapter 3.

After seeing that I still was lost in frustration despite all the insights I had about it, I decided to use my frustration as a spiritual alarm clock. Since I've surmised that frustration is trying to teach me that my need to achieve is too high, I've tried to use it as a reminder to relax and let go of my goal-oriented behavior. Sometimes, I just sit and take a few deep breaths. Another method I have found helpful is to ask myself the question, "What could potentially be good about this?" When I'm lost in negativity, this question helps me to focus on the value I could ultimately gain from going through a difficult experience.

The Alarm Clock in Action

Recently a printer managed to do a print job on a book of mine incorrectly 14 times in a row. What should have taken two days ended up taking two months. Guess how I felt? Yep, frustrated. To avoid indulging in my impatience, anger, and self-pity, and to keep from pulling my hair out, I asked myself the two questions I've mentioned in this chapter that I've come to revere for the spiritual learning and peace of mind they impart:

➤ What shortcoming in me may have contributed to this experience?

➤ What could potentially be good about this?

In answering the first question, about my shortcomings, I realized that my self-righteous insistence that people be competent was causing me a lot of pain. I also realized that I was too cheap to pay for a good printer, and that I was not taking responsibility for deciding to hire a marginal printer.

In answering the second question, about the potential good that could result, I came up with many answers. First, I saw how this experience was another opportunity for me to let go of my driven behavior and unrealistic expectations. Second, I could see that in each of the 14 mistakes, I was able to practice a method of letting go—and therefore become better at it. Third, I was able to see the need I have to learn compassion for people who are not always competent in their line of work.

As you use your negative emotions to learn about yourself and trigger the use of spiritual methods, you can greatly accelerate your spiritual growth. Separating yourself from the world and trying to create a haven for peace may look like spiritual growth, but really it's a fraud. If your peace of mind depends on things going your way, you're just playing the game that everyone else is playing—the game of control. We need to learn to find peace even when the tire goes flat, the printer can't get the job right, or the kids are complaining. Until you have a permanent foot in the world of spirit, let your negative emotions help point you to the lessons you need to learn and the baggage you need to let go of.

The Least You Need to Know

➤ Negative feelings can alert a person to lessons he needs to learn and to deficiencies that could slow him down on the spiritual journey.

➤ Many people fail to learn from their lives because they use the defenses of denial, distraction, and blame to avoid seeing the lessons they teach.

➤ "What you resist tends to persist," so it's best to learn from your life before it causes you more unnecessary suffering.

➤ Asking questions such as "What shortcoming in me may be contributing to this situation?" can help focus your mind in a way that leads to peace and learning.

➤ When negativity arises, you can use it as an alarm clock to practice a spiritual method.

Chapter 14

The Yoga of Relationships

In This Chapter

➤ How relationships can accelerate your spiritual awakening

➤ How relationships bring up our shadow side

➤ How to go beyond judgment and blame to compassion and love

➤ Why honesty and vulnerability help awaken a connection with both people and Spirit

---

I've heard it said by many spiritual teachers that relationships are the "yoga" of the West. *Yoga* is a Sanskrit term that means "union." Yoga refers to any practice that helps a seeker unite with God. While in the Western world relationships are not generally considered to be a way to unite with God, they certainly can be used to do so. In fact, intimate relationships can offer an accelerated path to spiritual awakening—if you know how to use them for that purpose.

Most people don't use romantic relationships for spiritual awakening because they don't know how to do so, or because the prospect of doing so is too scary. Normally, intimate relationships help us to feel safe and adequate in the world. Because they're so important to us, they bring out our tendency to control, hide, and manipulate. The essence of spirituality is letting go of our tendencies to control, hide, and manipulate.

Letting go is scary when so much is at stake. For people who are willing to be radically honest in their intimate relationship, much growth is possible. But beware—using your relationship as a vehicle for spiritual awakening can be both intense and difficult.

Amazing Grace

I know a wonderful couple, Joyce and Barry Vissell, who use their relationship as a vehicle for knowing God, and teach others to do likewise. They've written many books about their path and methods. In workshops with them, they create a safe place to allow couples to bring up all the "stuff" that gets in the way of deeper intimacy and vulnerability. It can be a scary process, but by the end of a weekend workshop, it's amazing how much healing has taken place, and how much more love can be felt in the room.

Making Shadows Visible

When we say "I love you" to someone, what we're really saying is "You help me get to the place in myself where I am one with the feeling of love." Our partner is our connection to help us feel the love that's already within us.

Cosmic Potholes

Because your partner can't possibly be as reliable (or as eternal) as God, it's important to avoid totally relying on just one person for your connection to love and happiness. It's better to have some of your emotional needs satisfied by friends and family. This will make you less needy, and better equipped for your spiritual journey.

Unfortunately, because we crave the feeling of love so much, we tend to become addicted to the person associated with it—just as people get addicted to drugs. Then, if our connection to love—our partner—starts acting in ways we don't like, we get upset. That's why it's been said that soon after falling in love, everything unlike love starts to show up. You soon find yourself getting annoyed at how your partner eats, or enraged when he or she says something you don't like.

The love we feel for a partner is similar to the love we can feel for God. God and love are often equated with light. Although bright light feels warm and makes everything glow, it also makes shadows more noticeable. When we're not in a relationship, the shadowy parts of ourselves are unseen. However, in the light of an intimate relationship, the shadow side of ourselves shows in all its glory.

As our shadow side becomes more noticeable, with the right attitude it's possible for the layers of fear to start to melt away. A couple who can reveal their hidden fears to each other will often feel a deepening sense of love and connection to each other *and* to God.

The Path of Radical Honesty

To use a relationship to become closer to God, a couple must be honest with each other. That may sound simple, but it isn't. We all keep an almost infinite number of fears and secrets to ourselves. We're afraid that if we were truly honest with each other, our relationship would quickly fall apart. In fact, that is often the case. So rather than risk being alone, we decide that a distant relationship is better than nothing at all. However, to use a relationship to unite with the source of love, our myriad of protective mechanisms must be revealed. We must become vulnerable—and that is frightening for most people.

Since I'm a psychotherapist known for working in a spiritual context, I often see couples who say they want to use their relationship as a vehicle for awakening. Yet when I reveal the basic technique for doing so—total honesty—few are willing to use it.

For example, recently I counseled a couple named Jim and Linda. When they reported they wanted to use their relationship for growth, I told them to try the following method: Reveal anything that's true for you that you've been afraid to say to your partner. If there is something you haven't told him that you'd be uncomfortable telling him, tell him now.

Jim haltingly revealed that he had had an affair with a woman during the previous year. Linda, who had been trying to convince Jim and I that she really wanted the truth, did not react well. After the name calling, the demands for a divorce, and the screaming, Jim and I were convinced that she preferred a little less honesty.

Like anything difficult, honesty in a relationship takes time to develop. If you go from being totally secretive to being totally honest overnight, it's often too much of a shock. If you slowly but consistently reveal difficult things about yourself, and your partner continues to accept you, it'll give you encouragement to keep moving in that direction.

Heavenly Helpers

Try asking your partner how much honesty, on a scale of 1 to 10, he would like from you. If he says he wants total honesty, try saying whatever you're afraid to say and see how he reacts. If he reacts well, keep it up. If he doesn't react well, try being a little less revealing. Find the level that seems to work in your relationship.

Cosmic Potholes

Some people use honesty as a weapon to hurt their partner, rather than as a way to become more intimate with them. When attempting to be more honest, make sure you are doing it with a loving intention in mind, and only doing it if you feel you and your partner are ready for it. Otherwise, you can break the trust you've established in your relationship.

149

Everyone wants intimacy. Fortunately, the instructions for finding intimacy are hidden within the word itself: "in to me, see." A couple creates intimacy by revealing things to each other. Of course, this can be hard to do because we fear rejection. We've all been hurt, and we don't want to repeat the experience. Rather than risk rejection, we hide our vulnerable side.

Many couples end up blaming each other for the problems in a relationship, instead of revealing their fears to each other. Although being vulnerable brings us closer to the light of love and God, it also brings us closer to our fears. Most couples avoid such an experience by blaming their partner rather than revealing their fears.

Being Right vs. Being Loved

Along with being more honest, another way to awaken spirituality in a relationship is to let go of blame and the need to always be right. In my book *Communication Miracles for Couples,* I talk about how our egos love to make us right and our partners wrong. After blaming our partner for all our troubles, we secretly hope he'll say something like, "Thank you for telling me that. I've been wrong all along and didn't even realize it. I'm very happy you showed me the errors of my ways."

Of course, since many people would rather die than say such a thing, a lot of couples spend their time being right—rather than being loved. The funny thing is, admitting to how you contributed to a problem is what tends to restore the love and intimacy in a relationship. In a disagreement with your partner, you often have the clear-cut choice of insisting on being right, or of letting go of that choice and restoring your sense of connection.

From Allah to Zen

Remorse is deep anguish and regret for past misdeeds. Although it is sometimes defined as guilt, guilt often has the connotation of being something imposed on someone by others. Remorse, in contrast, occurs when a person clearly sees and feels the painful ramifications of his actions on himself and others.

Since spirituality is largely a process of dismantling the ego, admitting you've been wrong can be a valuable method of spiritual growth. And if you're like me, there are many opportunities for apologizing when you've been stubborn, selfish, or just plain impossible to deal with.

I consider feeling true *remorse* and apologizing for selfish things I do to be a definite help to my spiritual development. After all, I don't like hurting other people, and they don't like it either! When it becomes obvious to me that my behavior is hurtful to others, I try to feel the pain of that. By not making excuses for what I've done, and allowing myself to feel remorse for my behavior, I find I'm less likely to do the same thing again.

Although there is a long history of preachers telling us how sinful we are, such proclamations rarely lead people to feel true remorse. Instead, they just make us feel generally guilty. If you can clearly see how something you do causes you or someone you love to feel hurt, then you can begin to feel what I call "beneficial remorse."

Beneficial remorse is different than just feeling guilty or bad about yourself. Rather, it is a clear understanding that something specific you've done has been harmful or distasteful. By allowing yourself to be vulnerable in this way, you become open to outside help. Sometimes that help comes from a partner who appreciates your vulnerability and gives you a hug. Other times you may feel you're getting help by feeling a deeper connection to Spirit. After all, letting go of your need to be right is like removing a cloud that was blocking God's love from reaching you.

There are no easy ways to admit that you've been wrong or hurtful to others. It's always hard to do. Having the right technique can mean the difference between its being possible and being impossible to do.

Amazing Grace

Because my book *Communication Miracle for Couples* became a best-seller, I get a lot of letters from people who tell me how love was restored when they admitted to how they've contributed to problems in their relationship. It's as if the simple act of going beyond having to be right allows love to enter back into a relationship. In my own relationship, I always find it difficult to admit when I've been wrong, but it's so incredibly helpful and rewarding when I do.

When I notice I'm being stubborn and attempting to prove my partner wrong, I try to complete the following sentence: "The way I see I'm contributing to this problem is ..." I just keep trying to complete that sentence. Although it's hard to do at first, after a while it feels like a wall of isolation being quickly dismantled. When I manage to say how my "stuff" is helping to cause a difficult situation, it often leads to my partner admitting to her own contribution to the problem. Soon, as if by magic, we have gone from being angry with each other to being fully at peace once again.

Overcoming Separateness

Attempting to overcome the separateness you feel with your friends or partner is good practice for overcoming the separateness you feel toward Spirit. Since people are like a wave in the ocean of God's energy, as you feel less separate from people, you'll automatically feel closer to God.

While honesty and vulnerability are the basic techniques for lessening one's separateness with people, it can help to have some specific methods to use. One thing you can do is simply complete the sentences "I feel ..." and "What I want is ..."

We normally try to hide what we feel and what we want, and expressing this is at the core of what honesty is all about. As you share this information, you'll feel vulnerable. If the person you're talking to can hear you without reacting badly, you'll likely feel a much deeper sense of intimacy with him or her. Try it with your friends or partner and see what happens.

Another method to help you feel closer to people (and therefore God) is to answer questions that reveal things about yourself. In workshops I lead I have people partner up and answer the following 10 questions. They take turns answering each question before going on to the next one. I encourage them to answer the questions at whatever level of self-disclosure they wish. If a conversation naturally arises from the given questions or answers, that's perfectly okay. Here are the 10 questions:

1. When are you the happiest?

2. What is your greatest strength?

Cosmic Potholes

Saying what you're feeling can be used to make yourself more vulnerable (which is good), or to place the blame on your friend or partner (which isn't helpful). When revealing your feelings, try to talk about your own shortcomings—rather than your partner's. This will make it easier for others to hear you and feel close to you.

3. What is your greatest weakness?

4. What was the most difficult time in your life?

5. How do you keep yourself from being close to me?

6. What do you consider to be your greatest accomplishment?

7. What are you avoiding right now?

8. How do you think I see you?

9. What was your first impression of me?

10. What do you like best about me?

Answering these questions with an intimate partner, or even someone you just met, can be a powerful way to quickly reach a state of spiritual intimacy. Once you've experienced how powerful this can be, it might motivate you to reveal other things about yourself that can lead to deeper levels of intimacy.

Expanding Love Through Awareness

Another aspect of the yoga of relationships is knowing what your partner (or friend) needs. Just because one partner may need a lot of sex to feel good about a relationship does not mean it helps the other partner feel loved. It's common for people to think their partner has the same desires and needs they do. This is rarely the case.

I learned this lesson many years ago. I had been in the habit of giving my partner a lot of shoulder massages—mostly because that's what I wanted from her. One day as I gave her a massage she annoyingly said, "Would you cut that out?" I was shocked. I told her I was just doing it because I loved her. She retorted, "Well I don't feel very loved; after all, you never tell me that you love me." She was right. I rarely said those words because I thought that talk was cheap, and the way to show you love someone was to give her a shoulder massage.

After a long discussion my partner revealed that she had been sexually molested when she was young by an uncle who used to give her a lot of "massages." She took my massages as a sign of impending doom. Lost in my own world, I hadn't noticed that she often cringed when I gave her a massage. Realizing I had been unaware of her needs, I asked her a very important question: *What is it I do that helps you to feel safe and loved?* Her answers to that question totally changed the way I related to her, and made our relationship much more intimate.

In my counseling office, I rarely have couples come in and say, "We understand each other perfectly—so we want a divorce." Instead, most of the feelings of separation couples experience come from a lack of awareness and understanding. As you become aware of your own needs, and express them in a vulnerable and nonblaming manner, you open up the possibility of progressing to deeper levels of love. Saying what you feel and what you want is a simple exercise for expressing your needs. In a recent counseling session, Sarah, a client of mine, expressed her feelings and needs to her husband in this way:

➤ I feel afraid you're going to have an affair when you go on your business trips.

➤ I want you to call and connect with me each night when you're away.

Amazing Grace

In my workshops where I have random people partner up and answer the 10 "spiritual intimacy" questions, I have received some surprising reports. After doing the exercise, some people have said they never felt closer to anyone in their entire life! Answering those 10 questions with someone can be very powerful indeed.

Heavenly Helpers

Being aware of how we each have different needs, and caring enough to give a person what he really longs for, can add a lot of intimacy to any relationship. Try asking your mate, "What is it I do that helps you to feel really cared for by me?" After you hear his answers, he can ask the same question of you.

153

Heavenly Helpers

Asking your partner or friends questions about what they're thinking, what they're wanting, and what they're feeling can be a great way to become more aware of their needs, and a great way to enhance the intimacy in your relationships. People generally react well to such questions because they indicate that you care.

➤ I feel hurt when you turn on the TV when you first come home from the office.

➤ I want you to hug me when you first come home.

Once Sarah expressed more of what was going on with her, it opened up the communication in the relationship. Now that her husband was more aware of her needs, it gave him a chance to satisfy most of them.

By being attentive to the specific needs of your partner (or friends), you also help to expand the amount of love and trust you have in your life. One way to be aware of their needs is to ask questions. Even the single question I previously mentioned, "What is it I do that helps you to feel safe and loved?" can be a bridge to a deeper connection to your mate and friends.

Overcoming Judgment

A final way to turn your relationships into a spiritual discipline is to overcome judgment. Overcoming judgment means practicing forgiveness, and practicing forgiveness means developing compassion. Let's look at this relationship.

If you've ever watched your mind, you may have noticed that it is a judgment machine. It loves to find any angle in which to separate ourselves from others so we can judge them. It likes to hold grudges for real or imagined wrongs. Self-righteousness is easy and makes us feel safe and powerful, whereas forgiveness is hard, and makes us feel vulnerable.

The first step in overcoming judgment is to practice forgiveness. When we judge others and hold grudges against them, it is really ourselves who get hurt. When you close down your heart, your connection to Spirit is lessened. The farther you get from your heart, the farther you get from Spirit.

How do we learn to forgive? By realizing that people generally do the best they can based on their personal history. Keeping this in mind makes it easier to let go of our negative feelings toward others. Of course, this is easier to say than to do.

In my own desire to practice forgiveness, I have found that asking myself two questions can help me to immediately change my focus toward a more compassionate direction. They are ...

➤ How is what he is doing similar to something that I do?

➤ What pain must this person have experienced in the past that makes him act so desperately now?

Amazing Grace

When I asked one spiritual teacher how to practice forgiveness, he said the key is to pretend that you hired that person to act like a jerk toward you. Then, when he does something stupid or harmful, you tell yourself he is helping you to grow more compassionate. When looked at this way, all the difficult people in your life are really just trying to help you become more loving and less judgmental!

The first question helps me to see that I, too, do stupid and inconsiderate things at times. This realization helps me to feel compassion—or at least a lot less self-righteous. Recently, I was feeling very angry at a friend for not remembering my birthday. Then I realized I had forgotten to return a call to my mother. Seeing that I sometimes forget to act considerately to people I love helped me to let go of my grievance.

The second question helps me to focus on the pain of the person I'm judging. People do not generally act out of malevolence. Rather, people do things based on a combination of their genetics and experiences from their past. If you knew (or imagined) that the person who angrily cut you off on the freeway just lost his job or was going through a divorce, it would be easier to feel forgiving!

Part of the reason we hold grudges and judge people is that we take ourselves too seriously. As I mentioned in Chapter 4, "The World According to Awareness," our sense of our own importance ensures that we'll be easily offended. Don Juan, the Yacqui sorcerer made famous in Carlos Casteneda's books, has this to say about how we react to people:

> Self-importance is man's greatest enemy. What weakens him is feeling offended by the deeds and misdeeds of his fellow men. Self-importance requires that one spend most of one's life offended by something or someone.

Ultimately, forgiveness, letting go of judgments, and developing compassion are some of the most useful spiritual skills you'll ever learn. For better or for worse, there are plenty of opportunities to practice these skills. Many people throughout your life will be more than happy to hurt, annoy, or be bothersome around you. If you use such people to practice techniques of forgiveness, letting go, and compassion, you'll be helping to heal both yourself and others.

155

The Least You Need to Know

➤ Relationships help us to see our shadow side, which can then be used to expand our awareness.

➤ Through extreme honesty, a couple can overcome their separateness and feel more connected to Spirit.

➤ Blame, judgment, and self-righteousness are signs that you have a block to your partner's and God's love.

➤ Admitting mistakes, feeling remorse, and being honest and vulnerable help you to let go of separateness.

➤ Serving your partner by being aware of his specific needs will help you experience more love.

Chapter 15

Selves of Lead

In This Chapter

➤ The obstacles to feeling peace

➤ How noticing your selves of lead can help make you more free

➤ Using your negativity to trigger the state of pure awareness

➤ Bad feelings can be good for awakening

The famous psychologist Carl Jung once said, "One does not become enlightened by imagining figures of light, but by making the darkness conscious." Becoming "conscious" means having your pure awareness, or soul, occasionally watch over what you do. As your spiritual awareness grows, you may find that your mind can be quite entertaining to watch. As you watch, you begin to notice certain *selves,* and you become better able to not get so lost in them. Many of our selves are like needy little children. They weigh us down unnecessarily, which makes it a lot harder to contact God and experience peace, love, or bliss. It's like trying to jump high into the air with a bag of bricks on your back.

You don't need to be a totally together person to experience God or mysticism. Thank God—none of us would ever get there! It definitely helps if you can recognize the selves that frequently keep you from your spiritual essence, or keep you too busy to be receptive to listening to your inner world. When you notice certain habitual selves come up, in the moment you observe them, you are not identified with them. You are temporarily in the state of pure awareness—which is what spirituality is largely about.

From Allah to Zen

Selves are subpersonalities within us that have their own unique perspective, thoughts, and agenda for our lives. When a certain self is in charge of our behavior, we become unaware of other perspectives that might help us act more in harmony with our other selves, or our environment.

Amazing Grace

The word *sin* as translated from ancient Aramaic originally was an archery term that meant "to miss the bull's-eye or mark." At one time it simply helped spiritual seekers identify that they were doing something that was steering them away from their spiritual goals. Unfortunately, in recent times, the word *sin* has taken on a more condemning tone.

What follows is a description of seven selves that frequently give me and other people trouble. It's not that they are evil, bad, or sinful; but they are fearful, heavy little creatures. When they get hold of my mind and body, they take me away from enjoying the present moment—which is usually a prerequisite for awakening one's spirituality. When you learn to view such selves from your internal witness or soul, they seem more like cute little kids that can no longer bother you.

As I've gotten to know these selves, they have begun to let go of being in charge of my life so much. By describing them to you, I hope you'll be able to relate to them and have a good laugh. In addition, I hope my descriptions help awaken you to know when you're in a similar self. The more you make the darkness conscious, the easier it is to stay in the high of inner peace.

The Hurried Task Completer

I see this self so much that I've begun to affectionately refer to it as "Mr. Goals." This self thinks that life is a series of tasks to complete as quickly as possible in order to get to the "good stuff." Unfortunately, like a hungry dog that doesn't know when to stop eating, Mr. Goals tries to hurry through just about everything. Perhaps it's reasonable for a person to hurry through doing the dishes. Perhaps it's reasonable to hurry through brushing one's teeth, shaving, or cleaning one's house. Yet, when Mr. Goals gets me to hurry through eating a delicious meal—well, it's gone too far.

A close cousin to Mr. Goals is a self I refer to as the Task Completer Scanner (TCS). This self's job is to scan for additional tasks to complete. Whenever I get anywhere near close to the end of my to-do list, the Task Completer Scanner offers up a bunch of new things that I absolutely *must* do.

I think these two selves are hired by some cosmic conspiracy, headed by the devil himself, to make sure that I and all other human beings have as few moments of peace as possible. They definitely work in cahoots with each other. For example, the other day I was hurrying (as usual) through walking the dog when the bizarre thought occurred to me to actually slow down my driven, paranoid pace and enjoy the walk. However, I only managed to get about three relaxed steps completed before the archenemy of leisurely walks shouted, "You can't walk slowly, you have to do blah, and blah-blah, and blah-blah-blah ..." By the time I hit my front door, I was practically in a full sprint.

I'd write more about this self, but I want to get this writing over with as soon as possible. Perhaps you even want to get this reading over with as soon as possible. Why? Because you have more important things to do—like the dishes, errands, or just keeping busy. This is one self that definitely pushes God away.

The Blaming Excuse Creator

The Blaming Excuse Maker, or "BEC," is so prevalent in our society that it almost goes unnoticed. If you watch yourself or others carefully, you'll see that we blame almost anything and everything for the difficulty in our lives. Bored? That's because there's nothing on TV. Don't like your job? That's because your boss is an idiot. Depressed? That's because your lover is treating you poorly.

For whatever negative emotion we feel, the Blaming Excuse Creator has a ready list of culprits. Unfortunately, the reality of our own indulgences, negative thoughts, and inadequacies never strike us as part of the problem. That's BEC's job—to make sure we never even suspect that the problem is us.

As a psychotherapist, people pay me to listen to their "story." I used to listen to clients' blaming, excuse-making stories and then, in a display of extreme naïveté, show them how the situation they described was actually their own fault. That went over about as well as a lead balloon. Initially, I thought people would be grateful to have the *actual* cause of their problem pointed out. When I realized that none of my clients ever called for a second appointment, I began to think that maybe I was doing something wrong. Over the years I've become an expert in sneaking certain ideas and insights past the big, mean, paranoid BEC self. It's a nasty job, but somebody's got to do it.

Cosmic Potholes

When people start to see how much they blame other people or situations, it can sometimes make them nauseous, whereby they start blaming themselves. This can lead to self pity and depression. The spiritual journey can be difficult at times. When seeing undesirable traits in yourself, it's always important to keep a sense of humor and perspective.

You can recognize you're in the Blaming Excuse Maker self when you hear yourself whine, or get defensive when someone points out an obvious truth about you. The problem with this self is that it weighs a ton. It keeps people from seeing harmful habits by rationalizing them all away. By going beyond the protective measures of this self, a person can often discover he is carrying extra baggage that keeps him from soaring into the higher realms.

The Anxious Stimulation Filler

I've noticed that many of our more neurotic selves are actually supported and encouraged by friends, family, and even health-care practitioners. For example, I have a self I call the Anxious Stimulation Filler, and affectionately refer to as Mr. Busybody. It's a common self in the modern age. It has a need to always be busy, even when there is no need to do anything whatsoever.

Amazing Grace

The average American now sees more than 400 advertisements per day, whereas only 100 years ago the average American saw practically none. All this extra stimulation from TV, radio, the Internet, magazines, and billboards makes it more difficult to be internally oriented. That's why, when we spend time in simple natural surroundings, away from all this stimulation, we start to feel more peaceful.

In a futile attempt to drown out our internal dialogue, Mr. Busybody is always reaching to give us more stimulation. Its motto is "More, more, more." It's in a constant struggle with reality to distract us from unwanted thoughts and feelings. Rather than listen to our out-of-control internal dialogue, Mr. Busybody reaches for the remote, a magazine, or the phone. It's so effective at its job that many of us can actually go hours, and even days, without taking time to quietly contemplate our lives and simply relax into the moment.

Last week I vowed to fight this self. My goal was to not fill up the quiet moments in my life with additional stimulation. I was definitely outgunned. As I drove off in my car in the morning, Mr. Busybody grabbed my hand and forced me to turn on the radio. Realizing I had violated my agreement, I turned the radio off. Five seconds later, I started humming a song. Once I managed to stop humming, I became committed to reading every billboard I passed. When I finally made it to my doctor's office, I sat down quietly for an impressive four seconds before I saw my hand pick up the obligatory magazine from the rack.

I was clearly losing this war.

Some people may ask, "What's the harm in filling up your quiet moments with additional stimulation?" It's a good question. After a day of occasionally not filling up every moment with something new, I began to feel very peaceful. I felt like I was having a relaxing day in nature, despite the fact that I was completing my list of errands while driving around in a big city. I realized that a single self such as the Anxious Stimulation Filler can consistently eat away at the possibility of feeling a deeper peace during daily life.

I still battle with this self a lot, but at least there's a battle going on. While it may be years before I win this war, each time I refrain from picking up a magazine I don't want to read, or watching a TV show that I don't like, I know I'm taking a step toward a deeper peace.

The Looking Stupid Avoider

Watch a three-year-old during a typical day. Then watch an adult for the same length of time. What do you see? Other than the fact that they're both human, there is very little similarity. The three-year-old is likely to be exploring, having fun, acting silly, saying what she wants, saying what she doesn't want, and being vitally alive. The adult is likely to be looking tense, lost in a world of thoughts about various problems, plans, and relationship stresses. The adult is likely to be trying to hide his or her wants, not having fun, trying to act cool, and looking only half alive.

Why such a difference? It's partly due to a self I call the Looking Stupid Avoider. Because this self is committed to avoiding all embarrassment, I refer to it as Little Miss Modest.

Little Miss Modest has a job to do. Its job is to scan each and every environment we're in and convince us that the best move is to be as invisible as possible. If we can't be invisible, then the next best idea is to do what's expected of us. Never—under any circumstances—does this self allow you or me to simply be ourselves and act spontaneously. Such behavior could lead to looking stupid for a moment, and that is a risk that cannot be tolerated!

For the most part, Little Miss Modest works—it does protect us from being embarrassed, looking silly, and getting "eye rolls" from other people. But the price we pay is that we no longer are as spontaneous and full of energy as when we were kids.

Many years ago, I set out to overcome this self that kept me imprisoned. I figured an easy way to look stupid was to go up to attractive women and ask her out. By experiencing 10 rejections, I would know what it felt like and my fear of looking stupid or getting rejected would lessen.

As I approached the first woman, sweat was literally dripping from my forehead. My knees began shaking, and as I said "Hello," my voice cracked. When the woman turned and saw me shaking and sweating, she worriedly asked, "Are you all right? Do you

Cosmic Potholes

The desire to avoid looking stupid can often lead people to living mechanical, safe, and very controlled lives. Some people mistake this safety for the feeling of peace. Yet true peace is not dependent on situations being fully under control. If you ever want to experience inner peace, you have to be willing to look stupid—and be okay with it.

Heavenly Helpers

By making slight stupidity or embarrassment a goal, a person can often overcome his fears of trying new behaviors. This can lead him to experience new joys that he previously avoided. Perhaps you can make a goal to consciously try to look slightly stupid once this week. With practice, the fear of looking stupid becomes less, and you become more free to be fully yourself.

need me to call an ambulance?" She thought I was having an epileptic seizure. I assured her she didn't need to call an ambulance, and that I'd soon be okay. A brief, awkward conversation ensued before I finally mumbled, "Would you like to go out together sometime?" In a kind voice she responded that she had a boyfriend, but that she was flattered that I had asked.

As we parted ways, I took an index card from my pocket and marked down one rejection. Then, as I thought, "Only nine more to go," I began to breathe again.

Fortunately, each time I got rejected and felt the full force of the Looking Stupid Avoider trying to imprison me, it became easier to overcome. Eventually, I was feeling totally at ease while I asked women out, and they frequently responded by giving me their phone number. Without the full weight of Little Miss Modest on my back and in my brain, I was having a great time starting conversations with complete strangers. In fact, after a while I had so many dates that I had to begin acting like a jerk in order to fill my quota of 10 rejections.

But more important than having an active love life was overcoming the constriction I usually felt within. I realized that life beyond the fear of looking stupid could be fun, magical, unpredictable, and exciting—as it was when I was a kid.

The Idle Worrier

A spiritual teacher once said to me that a person needs to think about himself for only about 15 minutes per day. Unfortunately, that means most of us do a lot of extra worrying.

Experts say that the average human being has about 50,000 thoughts per day, and that 95 percent of them are the same thoughts as the day before. If you've ever tried to quiet your mind, you know how much the mind loves to think about anything and everything. Most of all, it loves to worry. It loves to anticipate problems, solve problems, create problems, and relish in the shear anxiety that problems can generate. If there is a rare instance when a person doesn't have any juicy problems to think about, the Idle Worrier will think about other people's problems. Anything to stay busy.

Since there is so much to think about in modern life, it's easy to believe that all our worrying is actually necessary. I was able to see through this illusion while on a 10-day meditation retreat in Thailand. For 16 hours per day, we were supposed to simply quiet our mind—by following our breath. Everything was taken care of for us, from the meals we ate to our sleeping arrangements.

Since I couldn't make a phone call or even talk to another person for 10 days, there was literally nothing to worry about. Of course, my Idle Worrier self didn't let that reality interfere with its mission to keep me ever occupied. Since there was nothing "important" to worry about, I would think about the most ridiculous things imaginable. I'd worry about whether a fly would land on me, I'd worry about whether there was going to be enough to eat for lunch, I'd even worry about the fact that I worried too much. At a time when the Idle Worrier could have been taking a vacation, it was working overtime instead.

In the years since discovering the useless nature of the Idle Worrier self, I've studied its diabolical methods of capturing my attention. First it scouts out an area to focus on. It scans the various aspects of one's life, such as work, relationships, money, and so on, and then chooses a subject that has some good idle-worrying potential. Then it teases us by imagining the worse possible outcome for the situation it chooses.

For example, if the subject is money, it'll say something like, "What if all your investments go south, and an earthquake devastates your home?" It loves "What if?" type questions because the possibilities for worrying are virtually endless. By imagining worst-case scenarios, it builds up worry momentum like a train building up steam. Then when we try to do something like meditate, we have to deal with a locomotive of thoughts barreling down on us at 300 miles per hour.

To the Idle Worrier, peace of mind or mystical experience means unemployment and death. I can understand why it would not want to die, so I've made an offer to this self that I hope it can't refuse. I'll let it live as long as it takes periodic vacations. My Idle Worrier self has agreed to think about it, and think about it, and think about it ….

The Righteous Winner

The Righteous Winner is the self that gets you to argue even when you know you're wrong or you know it'll do no good. To this self, only one thing is important—showing someone else that they are wrong. To accomplish this aim, the Righteous Winner acts like a prosecuting attorney, presenting evidence that "proves" the other person is totally off base. Then, it presents why you are, by chance, 100 percent in the right.

Heavenly Helpers

One strategy for handling excessive worry is to have a "worry hour" each week. When you catch yourself worrying needlessly, simply stop yourself and say, "I'll think about that on Sunday at two o'clock, if it's still a concern." You'll find that many "urgent" worries are totally unnecessary to think about, and that once Sunday (or whenever) comes around, they are no longer a concern.

Cosmic Potholes

If you are the type of person who really *is* often right about something, it's even harder to give up the righteous winner self. You will often have the choice of insisting you are indeed right, or letting it go and restoring your connection to the people or person you are dealing with. Choose wisely.

Amazing Grace

One of the times I was on *Oprah*, a woman in the audience angrily and righteously told everyone they were all going to go to hell unless they followed Jesus. When I told her Jesus preached the importance of loving everyone, and that she didn't sound loving, she started screaming. Security people had to escort her off the stage. A case of the Righteous Winner self gone amuck.

What's fascinating about this self is how it can continue to do its thing in the face of so much opposition. After all, when was the last time, upon showing someone how wrong he was, he said, "Oh, *now* I see what you've been saying! I've been wrong all this time and didn't even *realize* it. Thank you for showing me the errors of my ways." Although words of this sort would be sweet for the Righteous Winner self, it'll probably never hear them.

The Righteous Winner shows its ugly head mostly in intimate relationships. The main difference between this self and a Rottweiler is that a Rottweiler eventually lets go. This self won't. As a marriage counselor, I see it all the time in the couples I work with. Each person presents his case to me as to why his partner is to blame for everything from daily arguments to ozone depletion. Of course, this self believes that by making its partner wrong, it will be vindicated and love and intimacy will be restored.

The fact that such an approach has never worked in the history of humanity does not keep this hard-nosed lawyer of a self from making its best effort.

After I hear both partners present their best evidence, I usually say, "You've both been found guilty of being self-righteous. The penalty is you will feel no love, intimacy, or peace of mind until you stop trying to prove how right you are." With these two sentences I can usually get two people who are angry at each other united again—in their anger toward me. (Now you know why I became a writer to support myself.)

There is an excitement to being in the Righteous Winner self. Our dream is that our mate or someone of authority will say, "Yep, you're absolutely right." Of course, since everyone has the same dream, we're all trying to get the other guy to say "Yep, you're absolutely right" first. Unfortunately, God wired humans so that when people act self-righteous toward you, it automatically turns you against them and makes you want to show them how wrong they are. This is a self that definitely does not improve your love life.

The Know-It-All Judger

Years ago, I thought of myself as a rather nonjudgmental person. I thought people who judged others were jerks. I would become indignant when others passed judgment on how someone else should be or act. Then I realized I was judging all the people I thought were too judgmental. For a moment I felt remorse for being such a hypocrite. To avoid being one of "them," I thought, "Well at least I judge people for only the right reasons." When I heard myself concoct this train wreck of an excuse, I knew I had found the enemy—and of course, it was in me.

The Know-It-All Judger, or "Judge" for short, loves to feel superior to other people. It relishes the opportunity to put another person down so that we can feel better about ourselves. As we pass by someone who smokes, the Judge might think, "Well at least I don't smoke cigarettes." Meanwhile, we miss noticing that we're busy biting our nails and downing a third cup of coffee. Besides getting to feel safe, smug, and important whenever the Judge does his thing, we get to feel like we're not at all like the person we're condemning. This is ironic considering that the Judge usually is triggered by people who do things similar to what we do.

You may have noticed that people involved in spiritual pursuits are some of the most judgmental folks you'll ever meet. Spiritual fanatics (such as myself) have a literal smorgasbord of things to condemn people for. After many years of working on being a better, more loving and accepting person, I now feel qualified to judge just about everyone! Oops, that's probably not a good idea.

My favorite person to judge is myself. Although there are only 10 commandments in the Bible, somehow my mind came to believe that there were actually more than 1,000. Therefore, whenever I break one of these imagined cosmic laws, the Judge goes wild. In the last three hours alone I broke the following commandments:

1. Thou shalt not be late, even if it's only by two minutes.
2. Thou shalt not eat fast because to do so proves you are unspiritual.
3. Thou shalt not judge thyself for judging thyself.
4. Thou shalt not yawn when someone is talking to you.
5. Thou shalt not have the emotions and thoughts you are currently having.
6. Thou shalt not watch TV, or if you do, thou shalt not enjoy it like the people you so love to make fun of.

I don't know how the Know-It-All Judger managed to create more than 1,000 commandments that it feels obligated to enforce, but it can be as tough as a New York cop. When other people break one of our fabricated laws, it does not compassionately point out the errors of their ways. Instead, it behaves as if it had the authority to be cop, judge, and jury all rolled up in one.

Heavenly Helpers

Sometimes people can get lost in an endless cycle of judging themselves for judging themselves and others. One way out of this cycle is to begin *watching* and *appreciating how skilled* you are at judging others. You can think, "Look at how easily and precisely I can find fault in myself and others. I'm good at this." Sometimes it takes a little insanity to overcome insanity.

Fortunately, my spiritual teacher gave me a way to help overcome this self. He suggested that whenever I judge others, ask myself the question, "How is what this person is doing similar to something I do?" It's a great tool. Yet it interferes with one's ability to feel superior to others, and it can be hard to give that up when you've practiced it for so long.

There are countless others of these "lead" selves that weigh us down, keep us too busy, make us feel superior, and just keep us feeling separate from others. The seven described here can be a starting point for witnessing your own thoughts—and not getting too caught up in them. May your soul enjoy watching the endless parade of passing selves, and recognize that the *real* you is the one doing the watching.

The Least You Need to Know

➤ We become more free by looking at the parts of ourselves that interfere with being fully present, loving, and peaceful.

➤ The tendency toward hurrying, blaming, worrying, and feeling self-righteous are common examples of ways people avoid connecting with Spirit.

➤ When we fill up each moment with stimulation, avoid embarrassment at all costs, and judge others or ourselves, we engage in behaviors that take us away from inner peace.

➤ By labeling, witnessing, laughing at, and not identifying so fully with the parts of ourselves that take us away from Spirit, it's possible to become lighter and more free.

Chapter 16

Turning Lead into Gold

In This Chapter

➤ The art of disidentification from leaden selves

➤ Anticipating the arrival of leaden selves

➤ Inoculating oneself from the negative effects of a self

➤ How to transform lead into gold

During the Middle Ages the science of alchemy arose as the supposed art of turning lead into gold. Turning lead into gold is a useful metaphor for describing the art of turning our heavy, burdensome selves into lighter, more positive ones.

In the last chapter we learned to see and identify some of our "selves." It's helpful to remember that we are *reacting machines,* and selves are the result of those reactions. Let's take the example (we've all experienced it) of sitting at a traffic light. It's our turn to go and some dimwit flies through his red light and almost kills us. Common reactions are, "He should be arrested," "Where are the cops when we need them?" "What a moron!" "That guy needs his license yanked." And so on.

We need to see that in this instance we have reacted in a machinelike way. As long as we "react" rather than "act," we are invoking one of the leaden selves within. The "gold" is impartial or pure awareness, the freedom to choose. The purely aware self in turn can channel God's energy into the positive selves each person has within.

Lightening the Lead Through Disidentification

That guy who went through the red light evoked negative selves and states in you. According to many philosophies, "states" are transitory. If at that moment you could objectively observe the state or feeling of blame in yourself, you would experience a moment of disidentification from that state. The process might look like this:

> What a jerk! He should be arrested! Here I go again, blaming everything outside of me for my present state. What was it that caused this mechanical reaction? I felt out of control. I don't like feeling out of control. I am afraid when I am out of control.

This person has now disidentified from the blaming self and has gotten closer to the real emotions that are living through him—that the guy running the red light reminded him of the fear he feels at being out of control.

From the previous exercise you can learn that "it" represents many different selves, reactions, and emotions. To see ourselves as "it" also reminds us of our humble place in the world. This exercise can also show us our own self-importance, which blocks us from really seeing the world as it is. As long as we are reacting machines (sounds rough but bear with me), we cannot take the next step in the spiritual climb. As we see and watch how we consistently react to the different situations in our life, we can begin to have more freedom in how we act.

After some study we can start to get to know the selves as they assume their positions, sensations, and tone of voice in our bodies. That presents an opportunity that stems from seeing what triggers their arrival. If every time I walk into the kitchen I find myself in front of an open refrigerator, I can see that the kitchen is triggering The Anxious Snacker self. Before I was able to see that self, I couldn't attempt something different. Now that I've labeled that self, I can choose to not open the refrigerator door. I can take a step toward spiritual growth. When I say no to the automatic behavior, the alchemy of turning myself from lead to gold begins.

From Allah to Zen

Reacting machines is a term that signifies that, most of the time, human beings react to external situations in a predictable, machinelike manner. Only through becoming more aware of the way selves are triggered by external events can a person become free to choose his reaction(s) to life situations.

Heavenly Helpers

To help you disidentify with your selves, try to refer to yourself as "it." "*It* got very mad at the person who ran the stoplight. *It* realized that *it* was afraid. *It* is driving to the store to complete *its* errands. *It* is hungry." If "it" is too impersonal to start with, try using your name instead: "Jonathan got mad at the guy who cut him off."

The refrigerator is one of 1,000 places where there is automatic behavior in our lives. Look for opportunities throughout your day to see mechanical behavior. Do you always greet your co-worker the same way? Shop for the same foods? Which sock do you put on first? Which ear do you hold the phone up to? Do you hear yourself repeating the same story over and over? Do you wait until the gas tank is almost empty, or do you always fill up the car when it is only half-empty?

What is your mechanical behavior? Anticipate the arrival of each mechanical self. Watch it for a while, then ambush it. Do a miraculous thing. Put your sock on the other foot first.

Inoculating Yourself from a Self's Effect

You probably recognize this next person. Let's call him Fred (maybe it's you). "How's it going Fred?" Fred gives you a pained, burdened look. "Everything would be fine if it weren't for the …" Now we can fill in the blank: "the stock market," "the weather," "the house payment," "the dental bill," "the relationship problem," and so on. But the story of this overburdened, glass-half-empty person is just that: a story. And as soon as Fred and the rest of us start to see the repetition of our particular stories, we have a chance to grow.

Fred can hear that burdened voice, notice his shoulders slouching forward, and say, "Aha, here it is again." This time there will be something in Fred watching the repeat behavior. He can start to see it as a broken record, a mechanical act triggered by certain occurrences—like someone saying, "How's it going, Fred?"

Amazing Grace

There's a well-known story called "My Autobiography in Five Short Chapters," by Portia Nelson. Here's a paraphrased version: Chapter 1: I walk down the street. There is a deep hole in the sidewalk. I fall in. It isn't my fault. It takes forever to find a way out. Chapter 2: I walk down the same street, I fall into the hole. It still isn't my fault. Chapter 3: I walk down the same street. I see the hole. I still fall in. It's my fault. I get out immediately. Chapter 4: I walk down the same street. I walk around the hole. Chapter 5: I walk down another street.

This story spells out the stages we go through on the road to change. At first we are unaware and blame, then we see our choices but still do our old behavior, and finally we act differently.

Sound a little like a science fiction movie? The good news is that there is a possibility of a different ending. Fred could catch that "story" of the self that slouches. He can now make a choice whether to go forward with it for the umpteenth time or take a different path, a "higher" path. By doing something different, he (and you, too) is opening the door to a "higher" possibility instead of following the road over and over.

Watching a Self Until It Disappears

Here is a true instance of the dramatic metamorphoses that can happen as you watch a self. My friend Carla told me this story:

> I came home tired from my business trip and found the house a mess. My husband and my recently divorced, sexy girlfriend were laughing over a beer. My daughter had not done her homework or had any dinner. I wanted to throw down my bags and commit crimes of passion and lunacy. I excused myself, went into the guest room, locked the door, and threw myself on the bed in a rage. Then a voice, which I would call a part of me that is interested in my spiritual life, said "How can you make use of this situation?"

> Sensations were streaming through my system. I followed them. I sensed as they rose up from my abdominal area, flooded into my chest, and then rolled down my arms into tightened fists. My jaw was clenched tight. Determined to watch my reaction, I remembered not to buy into the thoughts as they tried to sneak into my mind. I watched various thoughts go through my head, loud thoughts like, "What is *she* doing here? Does *she* come here often when I am away?" I said no to listening to those thoughts and instead watched the stream of sensation.

> To focus on this task, I remembered to ask myself questions: "Is the sensation changing? Is it more on the right side of my body or my left? Are my legs as mobilized to kick as my arms are mobilized to punch? How is my breathing? Are the sensations all upward or do some of them stream back down again?" I tried to latch on to any question to keep me focused on the goal of feeling my body sensations.

> After about 15 minutes, the intensity of the sensations lessened. My fists let go and my hands began relaxing. The tightening in my stomach subsided. I noticed an energized feeling of calm. A new voice started to speak. "Your friend came by to see *you*. She is lonely. The

Cosmic Potholes

Begin the process of learning to watch a self disappear with small situations. Don't start with a volatile situation, when you are more identified with your self-righteousness and anger. You should practice it many times with small things before you try it on "bigger" selves and more negative situations.

homework will get done." It was a voice of neutrality, a voice that sees things from a different perspective. I sat up and experienced myself breathing normally. My back and shoulders were now relaxed. I was able to notice the room, the colors, the furniture. I felt present and alive. I knew I had shifted from a very negative state.

The voice that this woman heard is one that we all can access if we're not at the mercy of our own reactions. She was able to use a potentially ugly and volatile situation to her advantage. Instead of exploding with mechanical reactions, she was able to stop and experience the sensations of "reaction." She was actually able to gain energy and perspective and become more present in her life. She was able to watch a self disappear as it led her to another, more positive one.

This experience of presence is echoed in the famous quote by James Thurber: "Let us not look back in anger, nor forward in fear, but around us in awareness."

Work on Small Things

It is easier to try this method in small situations rather than larger, more volatile ones. Suppose you are standing in line at the bank or grocery store, feeling impatient, looking around and saying to yourself, "Why the hell don't they add a checkout person or another teller?" Now is the time to try to make a negative self disappear. Ask yourself, "What is impatience? Does impatience have a sensation in the body? (It does, by the way.) Does it have a posture? Is it hunched over or is it puffed up? Do I want to growl or whimper?" If the line is *really* long, then tackle the next part of the experiment and *follow* the sensations as my friend Carla did. See what happens. Life can be quite sensational when you think of it as an ongoing exploration.

Daily inconveniences, like the long bank line, are actually a subtle gift if you can recognize them as a chance to study yourself. A long bank line is an opportunity to take a step on the path of surrender. There will be a day when you will be standing in the line and something besides impatience will well up in you. It could be gratitude for the day. It could be a minute to take a deep breath and relax into the present moment. Ultimately, you might look around and see what is needed, what work the Creator might be asking of you. It might be a smile to someone, letting someone go ahead of you, or just being in a relaxed state that others can sense.

The other day I was in long bank line and I remembered the above. I looked around and saw many tense faces. I said to the woman ahead of me in a light voice, "Well, this gives us all a chance to stop rushing around and relax a little." She looked surprised but answered, "If it weren't for these silly shoes I guess I could enjoy it." She pointed to her tight-fitting high heels. We laughed and started a conversation and soon two people behind me joined in. I left the bank in a better state than when I went in. I felt rewarded for taking the chance of doing what I thought was needed, despite my fear of being rejected.

Do Sweat the Small Stuff

To transform lead into gold, we need to take good care of ourselves so there will be enough of what the late author Carlos Castaneda calls "free energy" for the transformation. Castaneda once explained that the average man spends all his allotted energy in the drama of daily living, and does not save enough energy for inner alchemy. In order to "save," we must keep company with fellow alchemists. Fellow seekers are those folks who encourage our spiritual aspirations and who will tell us the truth if we are messing up with things like unhealthful foods or lifestyles or cynical talk. You can read more about groups and fellow alchemists in Chapter 22, "Back to School: Students, Teachers, and Groups."

Amazing Grace

Carlos Castaneda was a doctoral student studying anthropology at UCLA in the early 1960s when he met a Yacqui Indian "sorcerer" in Arizona that he nicknamed "Don Juan." Through several best-selling books, Castaneda documented Don Juan's teachings and way of seeing the world. His first book about Don Juan was actually used as his doctoral dissertation. In his later books, Castaneda became fully absorbed in Don Juan's teachings, and became a sorcerer himself. Castaneda died a mysterious death in 1999.

Another aspect of turning lead into gold is to successfully deal with the resistance our friends and family may have to our spiritual pursuits. These are some of the things people may say to us to deter us from our aim:

➤ "Gee, you're changing. You aren't the old friend you used to be."

➤ "God is a crutch."

➤ "What do you want to get to know yourself for? You're getting too self-involved. Just send a check to United Way instead."

➤ "Watch your money."

➤ "I don't need to do all the things you're doing. I am already at peace."

It can be hard to deal with the resistance friends and family have to our spiritual goals, but it's just one more opportunity to practice patience and compassion.

As a therapist, I see many clients struggling with what I see as spiritual issues and opportunities. For example, Susan is someone who aspires to spiritual goals, but is meek in her daily life. Recently she said to me, "I am finally catching little ways that I keep myself from having a direct experience of my life. When I catch myself and act in a more direct way, I feel a strength that is new to me. The other day I was about to ask my partner what movie he would like to see. I already knew what movie I wanted to see so, instead, I said 'I want to go to this movie. Do you want to come?' In that moment I felt I had climbed a small mountain."

Drew asks for what he wants but has trouble being vulnerable. "My situation with co-workers had become so strained that I was afraid I would have to quit my job. I decided I had nothing to lose and shared with them that my mother was dying and I was incredibly sad and confused. Ever since then, people changed their tune and have been supportive and friendly to me. It was like my sharing broke through to a deeper place in all of us."

Cosmic Potholes

Keep watch for the blocks that will be put in your way by people who do not share your aim. Some of those people will be persuasive and your fellow climbers can help you stay focused.

Each day we face small mountains. Each one gives us a possibility of taking the higher road, the one that leads up the spiritual mountain. The examples of my clients Susan and Drew show that, as we become aware of our patterns, we have more opportunities to turn our mechanical ways—our lead —into gold.

There are so many decisions to make each day: "What should I eat?" "Shall I answer my calls?" "Shall I do this errand?" "Shall I volunteer for that?" Try asking yourself, "Is this the high road?" Or consider yourself and the others involved and ask, "Will this action assist my climb up the spiritual mountain?"

Feeding Selves Deliberately

Susan and Drew are growing "new" selves whenever they choose a new behavior. Susan, by changing her language and asking for what she wants, will build a self that is direct, focused, and strong. That self can help her to meditate and make better choices in other areas of her life, too. She can resolve to make it stronger by feeding it deliberately with the "I want" exercise.

Feeding selves deliberately doesn't mean doing only the difficult things that are in front of us. Think about the concepts of different spiritual traditions. We hear of heaven, the great joy and bliss of the afterlife. We hear of the Buddhist concept of peace and serenity caused by nonattachment. Different native religions contain the idea of walking the "path with heart," where all of nature reflects the beauty of the Creator. With these ideas in mind, we can choose to grow selves that delight in what is around us, selves that see the beauty in all things.

Heavenly Helpers

Psychologists suggest the "I want" exercise to help a meek, passive person shift to being a director in his or her life. Say "I want _____." Fill in the blank at least 10 times a day. Be sure to say at least one of them to someone else.

Amazing Grace

Don't play it safe! Take more risks. Nadine Stare, at age 85, writes, "I'd like to make more mistakes next time. I'd relax ... I would be sillier than I was this trip ... You see, I'm one of those people who lived sensibly and sanely hour after hour, day after day ... If I had my life to live over, I would start barefoot earlier in the spring and stay that way later in the fall. I would go to more dances. I would ride more merry-go-rounds. I would pick more daisies."

Carlos Castaneda writes in *Journey to Ixtlàn,* "For an average man the world is weird because if he's not bored with it, he's at odds with it. For a warrior, the world is weird because it is stupendous, awesome, mysterious, unfathomable. A warrior must assume responsibility for being here, in this marvelous world, in this marvelous time." In other words we need to focus on our blessings, not on our curses!

Start by going outside. Drop the thinking mind (as much as possible). See and hear at least 20 wondrous, beautiful miracles outside your front door. If anyone asks what you are doing, say you are going to work out some flabby spiritual muscles. You are going to strengthen a part of you that must be strong for the journey. This part must be able to see a miracle in every living thing. It must be able to laugh, be grateful, and humble at the awesomeness of our everyday lives.

Relax into the Gold

A Buddhist teacher recently told me that if we could fully relax, we would be able to see the world as it is and not as we think it is. Thinking about everything overlays a film of separation between us and what we are looking at. Because of that separation, we are unable to perceive the miracle that we live in.

Instead, spiritual seekers look for miracles, healings, and special effects. The miracle is already here. To see instead of look, to accept, to be ever curious, to remember our aim at all times and not be deterred—these are all part of the alchemy. Lead is where most of us now live.

Spiritual traditions and teachers, ancient and present, tell us that gold is available to all. By seeing negative selves and taking small steps to encourage positive selves, it is possible to turn lead into gold.

The Least You Need to Know

➤ You can recognize your "mechanical" behavior and change it.

➤ You can transform a negative state by sensing it until it disappears.

➤ You can use ordinary life situations, like standing in a bank line, for transformation.

➤ You can deliberately feed selves that you will need for the journey along the spiritual path.

➤ By relaxing and marveling at the miracle of being here, you are taking steps on your spiritual path!

Part 5

Experiencing the Sacred in Daily Life

It's easy for many people to feel "spiritual" in church. Yet, how about while you drive in traffic, cook a meal, or clean your house? Holy books rarely talk about methods for getting closer to God while performing mundane activities. In this part, I'll discuss spiritual principles and methods that can be used in relationship to work, money, facing small fears, and appreciating daily life.

In the last 50 years, the pace of human life has greatly accelerated. Whereas it used to be easy to take time to connect with nature, meditate, and relax, nowadays most people are rushed for time. Therefore, new methods are needed that help people connect with Spirit even while engaged in a busy life. Some methods presented in this section take only seconds to do, but can definitely help you experience the sacred in daily life.

Chapter 17

The Alchemy of Money

> ### In This Chapter
>
> ➤ Using money as an aid in the spiritual path
>
> ➤ Five money traps to avoid
>
> ➤ How a simple life can be a road to riches
>
> ➤ Four ways to avoid the wrong use of money
>
> ➤ Money experiments that lead to spiritual growth

Spiritually oriented people make two common mistakes when it comes to dealing with money. The most common mistake is to think that money isn't important and that it's unspiritual. The second mistake is to think that God has made having prosperity and abundance a birthright.

The truth is, in the modern world, money can have a large impact on your life—even your spiritual life. Just because you're a seeker with a pure heart doesn't mean the universe owes you anything. The pursuit of money and how to spend it are topics ripe with spiritual lessons and opportunities. Since money is such an integral part of our lives, a sincere seeker needs to know how to make use of it to grow spiritually.

I came from a family that had a fair amount of money, but it clearly did not make my parents happy. Therefore, I shunned the world of money, and for a while lived in an old van while I meditated many hours a day. One day I asked my intuition, "What is the next step I need to take for my spiritual growth?" It's a great question to ask yourself.

Amazing Grace

Asking, "What's the next step I need to take for my spiritual growth?" has changed my life, as well as the lives of many others. By listening to the intuitive answer to that question, I have been "guided" to write books, make videotapes, end mediocre relationships, visit certain spiritual teachers, and even make certain investments. In my workshops I often suggest this question to participants, and I get letters from people telling me about miraculous guidance they received from repeatedly and sincerely asking this question.

To my surprise, I received the answer that I should make a video on Tantra—which is an Eastern form of "spiritualized" sexuality. Unfortunately, there were a few problems. After some research I found out the video would cost about $45,000 to make, and I had no money. In addition, I knew nothing about video, business, or marketing. My girlfriend even chimed in that I knew nothing about sex! Nonetheless, since I felt divinely inspired to follow my intuition, I set out to do the project.

It turns out that the video became an international best-seller. So began my attempts to integrate the worlds of money, work, and spirit.

The Mission of Money

I've noticed that many spiritually oriented people give money a bad rap. They think it's unspiritual. I used to be like that. I've come to see that money is just a form of energy. It can be used to help others, allow yourself time to meditate, or fry your brain with dangerous drugs. It's all a matter of how you make it and how you use it.

While living in my van, I thought of having money as just a form of selfishness, so I avoided it (and it avoided me!). Once I had the purpose of making an expensive video, I set out to change my feelings about money. First I wrote a list of all the ways having money might help me to grow spiritually. My list included ideas such as traveling to Israel, taking courses on meditation, and helping out with charitable projects. Once I could see in writing how having additional money could affect my inner life, I was motivated to make it.

To help me stay on track and remember why I was pursuing money, I wrote a "money mission statement." Basically, this was a single sentence describing the purpose of money in my life. I would read it a couple of times a day, and it helped me feel good about the activities I was doing. My money mission statement read, "The purpose of money in my life is to give me access to the best information and the finest spiritual resources available so I might help myself and others be more loving and more effective in making this world a better place." Although on the outside I looked like just another businessman, from the inside I began to feel aligned with a higher purpose.

You're welcome to write your own brief description of the purpose of money in your life. By reading it frequently, you can start to think about earning money in a more spiritual context.

As you associate money with things that are truly important to you, you may find yourself more motivated to make it. Once I felt like I was doing projects for my own and others' spiritual well-being, it became easy to read books about finances, to market myself, and to do a host of other things I would never have done before. After all, there were starving children in India who were dependent on whether or not I had money to send them!

Heavenly Helpers

Write a list of how having an extra $10, $50, or $100,000 could help you to grow spiritually and have more peace in your life. Be specific. Would you go to workshops, retreats, or travel to India? The more you associate money with spiritual opportunities, the easier it'll be to make money, and the more likely you'll use it wisely when you get it.

Money Traps

Many people fear the world of making money—and for good reason. Like any whirlpool of energy, it's easy to get lost in it and forget about one's higher purpose. From watching how people get off course with how they use money, I've delineated five different "money traps." Let's look at these negative tendencies so you can better recognize when you fall into them, and therefore pull yourself out more quickly.

For each money trap, there is also an antidote—a way to relate to money that can lead you out of the muck and into higher consciousness. By first understanding the traps, and then their antidotes, you can learn the art of using money to bring you closer to your spiritual essence. That's what money *alchemy* is all about.

From Allah to Zen

Alchemy is a term that refers to the medieval art of turning base metals, such as lead, into gold. However, in a spiritual context it refers to the art of turning mundane pursuits, such as money and sex, into a means of spiritual growth or awakening.

Not Enough

The first money trap people fall into is thinking they never have enough. Western culture has provided us with a singular mantra: "If only." We go around thinking, "If only I had a better relationship," or, "If only I had a nicer house, then I'd be happy." The mind is infinitely creative. No matter how rich you get, you can always think of new "if onlys" that you need to feel like you have enough.

In fact, middle-class folk live better today than kings lived just 100 years ago. But we still think we need more. Even though the average annual income for people on Earth is about $700, there are people making $100,000 a year who feel poor and deprived! Our capitalist society encourages this feeling so we'll buy more products. It's an easy trap to get stuck in.

Attachment

Money trap number two is getting too attached to the money you have or the things it can buy. Many people think that the Bible states that "Money is the root of all evil," but that's not the case. In fact it says that "The *love* of (the *attachment* to) money is the root of all evil." That's a big difference. Unfortunately, when people have a lot of money, they usually get very protective and fearful of losing it. Without the fear of losing it, money can be a very helpful accelerator for doing good in the world. Signs that you're overly attached to the money you have include worrying about it and spending too much time at work.

From Allah to Zen

An **attachment** is an emotional desire for something or someone that, if not fulfilled, leads to suffering. Attachment is different than a mere "preference," in that a preference does not lead to suffering if not fulfilled.

Selfishness and Arrogance

Selfishness is the third money trap, and the fourth is arrogance. Once we have more money than we need, it's easy to start thinking of how to use it to gratify our every whim. We buy a bigger house, or a nicer car, and soon we feel even more separate from everyone around us.

Having money can also make people feel better than everyone else. No one likes a rich, arrogant snob. Selfishness and arrogance create separation, and if you're not careful, having more money can lead to these undesirable tendencies.

Laziness

The fifth and last money trap is laziness. When people make more money than they need, they sometimes become slothful. Instead of continuing to put forth their talents into the world, they buy a projection TV and a yacht. Unfortunately, the spiritual path requires a certain amount of discipline. If you become used to the life of total leisure, it becomes difficult to do the hard work that is often required.

Money Miracles

As I mentioned earlier, for each money trap, there is an antidote approach for dealing with it. For example, for the problem of thinking you never have enough money, the antidote is cultivating gratitude for whatever you have. In a world where half the people alive have never even made a phone call, it should be easy to feel grateful for all that we have. Yet it isn't. It takes discipline to be grateful for the prosperity we enjoy.

Cosmic Potholes

Unless you have an exact plan for how you'd spend extra money, you will likely end up falling into the various money traps. Through endless advertising, our society subtly influences us to spend money on things that have little or no meaningful value to the quality of our lives. Therefore, it's important to decide, before you get extra money, exactly how you could use it to help you spiritually.

Instead of focusing on the airplane you don't have, try to feel grateful for the hundreds of items and opportunities you do have. After all, isn't it miraculous that you can go to a supermarket that has 20,000 different items in it, and in a few minutes easily pick up everything you need to live on? Think about it—it's quite a wonder. I'm sure our stone-age cousins would be quite impressed. By feeling grateful for what you have, you can get out of "if only" thinking and into an appreciation of all that the universe provides.

The second and third money traps are attachment and selfishness. To go beyond these fear-based reactions, you need to cultivate the remedy of letting go. Letting go means being willing to give away what you have if it would serve you spiritually. I don't mean giving everything away, but instead, listening to your heart and giving what you can. When we fail to give what we can, we're like a lagoon with no outlet for its water. Eventually, the water turns into a swamp and starts to stink. Only by letting go and letting your natural generosity shine can you experience the joy of connection to the human family. No gadget can compare to feeling connected to your fellow human beings.

The fourth money trap is arrogance, and its natural antidote is humility. Rather than think of the money you have as yours, it can be helpful to think that it's on loan from God. God is taking notes on how well you handle the slice of wealth given to you. In this light, your job is to use your money with a sense of responsibility for the whole. Of course, part of the whole is you and your family. But if you are awake to the needs all around you, then part of your responsibility is to help others.

One way I try to be a humble steward of the money I'm given is to seek intuitive guidance on how to spend it. Asking your intuition how to spend your extra money is a great way to let go of the arrogance of the mind and tap into the humility of the heart.

Amazing Grace

Since my family always had money, and I felt better than others because of it, when I was 26 I decided to try to live for eight weeks without any money at all. I knocked on doors for food and a place to stay, and asked supermarkets if they had anything they could give to me. It was actually a very beautiful experience; I felt both grateful and humbled by people's generosity. Once I saw that I could actually get by with no money, it made me less afraid of losing the money I had or of not having enough.

The final money trap is laziness. In order to get over being lazy, all one needs is a passionate sense of purpose. While you might think that if you had a billion bucks you'd become a lazy slob, that's not likely true. Bill Gates and Ted Turner certainly have enough, but they still work hard. Why? Because they feel passionate about their work. They know that having a sense of purpose is more important than having a lot of money.

Without a clear sense of purpose, money is just green pieces of paper with pictures of dead people on it. With a sense of purpose, money is a miraculous means of creating harmony for both yourself and the world you're part of. You can overcome any laziness you have by remembering your mission. Having a clear sense of purpose will help you feel wealthy faster than any get-rich-scheme ever could.

The Road Less Traveled—to Riches

In Western society, there is very little attention paid to the "alternate" road to wealth. The road less traveled to riches is simply to be content with having less stuff, and living a simple life.

In truth, we don't need much stuff. Most of the stuff we buy is just to distract us from our pain, keep us busy, or give us indulgences that we don't really need. By living a simple life, you may find that you feel peaceful, loving, and wealthy—even if you don't have much money.

When I lived in my van, I used a local health club's shower and sauna. While in the sauna one day, a man was talking to me about his life. He was complaining that he couldn't make ends meet on $40,000 any more. I found this hard to believe, since I was making about $4,000 a year at the time, and was actually *saving* money. I tried to feel compassion for this troubled gentleman as he told me about his kids in college, his mortgage, and so on. I began to really feel for him until he said, "You just can't make ends meet on $40,000 *a month* anymore." I learned that day that no amount of wealth can make up for a feeling of spiritual poverty.

We've been led to believe that the easiest way to feel wealthy is to make a lot of money. I don't think this is true. I think the easiest way to wealth is to reduce your needs, desires, and indulgences. The Buddha said that the cause of our suffering is desire. By working to reduce your desires, it's possible to grow spiritually and have less need to work long hours.

It's true that the best things in life are free. *Voluntary simplicity* is a spiritual discipline that can be very rewarding, as well as incredibly helpful to staying true to your deeper longings.

Tithing and Other Experiments

Tithing has traditionally been known as the practice of giving 10 percent of your money to your church or spiritual organization. Historically, the church was a very important part of community life, and everyone was called to help support what was seen as a spiritual necessity. Nowadays few people seem to feel truly nourished by their church, and therefore not many people give 10 percent of their income to it.

From Allah to Zen

Voluntary simplicity is both a political and a spiritual movement that began in the 1980s in reaction to the materialism of Western culture. Practitioners attempt to simplify their needs, possessions, and activities as much as possible in order to live more peaceful and harmonious lives.

Heavenly Helpers

To help you cut down on unneeded indulgences, throughout the day you can ask yourself, "Do I really need to have this?" For example, at dinner you can ask yourself, "Do I really need dessert?" If so, have it. While shopping, ask, "Do I really need another outfit?" Sometimes such things won't be important to you, and you can skip them. By doing so, you'll save money, simplify your life, and become less indulgent.

Although the role churches play in our lives is generally smaller, the practice of tithing can still be a beneficial one for spiritual growth. As with many spiritual techniques created a long time ago, I believe the practice has to be updated to fit in with modern times.

Cosmic Potholes

With telemarketing and endless junk mail asking for our money, it can be easy to feel overwhelmed and decide to do nothing with it. It can also be easy to give to charities that really don't mean much to you, but then they keep asking, and more frequently. Instead, decide on what you can afford to give, and who or what charity you most want to support.

Heavenly Helpers

Decide on an amount you'd be willing to set aside as "God's money" each month, even if it's only a small amount. Then periodically listen within for how you can use this money to spread joy and kindness to people you love and people in need.

Since tithing originally represented giving back to God (via the church), I figured it would be an interesting idea to allocate 10 percent of my income as "God's money." I started putting this money in a separate bank account and then, periodically, I asked God (via my intuition) where this money should go. I have found this to be a liberating practice. Previously, it was hard for me to give to spiritual organizations, friends in need, and worthy charities. After all, it meant less for me (and I'm pretty cheap). But once it was God's money, and not really mine, it became a joy to listen for instructions on what to do with it.

About once a month I get quiet and ask which of various friends, charities, or organizations it feels right to send money to. Besides making the practice of giving more fun, it has also opened me up to giving to my friends and total strangers. Every now and then, I take some money from my "God account" and treat a friend or person in need to a pleasant surprise. Besides helping them out, it has helped me experience the joy of giving in a very direct way.

Besides tithing, there are many other money experiments you can try to see what effect they have on your life. For example, I used to worry about money a lot. Then I decided I would not worry or think about money at all except for on Sunday afternoons between 2 and 2:30 P.M. Every time I'd have a thought about money, I'd say to myself, "If it's still a concern, I can think about that on Sunday afternoon." It worked! By Sunday afternoon, most of the things that seemed so urgent during the week were no longer a concern. I reduced my thoughts about money by approximately 90 percent.

Another money experiment I enjoyed was spending 10 percent of my income for one year on spiritual growth workshops and retreats. If spiritual growth is important to you, then it makes sense to allocate a certain amount of time and money to it. Unfortunately, most people don't. Look at your checkbook. By seeing what you spend money on, you can get an honest glimpse at what your true priorities are. How much of your money goes to spiritual growth activities? It can have a major impact on your spiritual evolution to devote a consistent percentage of your income to things that nourish your soul.

As with any experiment, a money experiment is something you do for a period of time to see how well it works for you. After committing to any of the experiments I've described, observe the results. If tithing or not worrying about money for a couple of months works for you, keep the experiment going. If you find it makes you even more uptight about money, try a new experiment.

Many people find their relationship with money is analogous to their relationship with God. As you try new ways to align your income to the world of Spirit, you'll notice a positive change in your level of well-being.

The Least You Need to Know

➤ Money—depending on how you use it—is simply a form of energy that can be used to accelerate or hinder your spiritual growth.

➤ Spiritual problems to avoid with money include thinking there's never enough, attachment, selfishness, arrogance, and laziness.

➤ Attributes to cultivate about money include gratitude for what you have, the ability to let go, humility, and a strong sense of purpose.

➤ Through living a simple life, you can have more time for spiritual practices and experience less stress.

➤ Tithing and other money experiments can help you worry less and become more generous with your money.

Chapter 18

Work as a Spiritual Path

In This Chapter

➤ Determining a right livelihood for you

➤ Doing a job in a way that helps you spiritually

➤ Using your work to better see your internal obstacles

➤ Turning your work into an offering or service to God

You get up, you go to work. You come home exhausted. You watch TV, you go to bed. You get up, go to work, watch TV, go to bed. The cycle repeats itself, devoid of excitement and meaning. That's how a lot of people relate to their work and to life.

Our job as spiritual beings is to figure out how to express our unique essence in all parts of our life, including our work. Holy books from various traditions have little to say about how to turn your work into part of your spiritual path. This makes it more important than ever to explore what it means to bring spiritual principles into what one does for money.

The average person spends about 42 hours a week at some kind of work. That translates into a lot of time. If you could somehow turn all the time you spend at work into a spiritual growth activity, you would greatly accelerate your progress. In this chapter, I'll discuss a lot of different ideas about how to do that. If one of these ideas feels right to you, then explore it for yourself. When it comes to turning work into a spiritual activity, our culture offers largely uncharted waters. It's up to you and me to figure out what works and what doesn't.

Right Livelihood

Twenty-five centuries ago, the Buddha put forth the importance of right livelihood as part of his Eightfold Path to enlightenment. As espoused by the Buddha, right livelihood is the practice of avoiding occupations or jobs that can cause harm to other beings.

While this may sound easy, it can be more difficult than you think. It's pretty obvious that a seeker might want to avoid being an arms dealer, but what about an exterminator? Is it okay to kill termites for a living? Is it okay to work for a pharmaceutical company that uses monkeys as test subjects for experimental drugs? Each person must answer these questions for themselves.

When it comes to money and work, our culture is pretty warped. Many occupations are geared toward increasing our greed, lust, and need for mindless entertainment. A seeker interested in right livelihood has to consider the price he (and the world) pays for pursuing such jobs. After all, if you contribute to an industry bent on increasing humanity's baser instincts, it will likely take a toll on your soul. In a culture in which most people will do anything if enough money is offered, we have to remember that some things *are* more important than a good income.

Amazing Grace

When I was offered the job of writing this book, the publisher (Macmillan) initially wanted it done in three months. I told them that in order to keep my sanity while writing this book, I'd need six months. They said that was too long, and that they'd have to find someone else. I felt disappointed, but I felt good about sticking to my commitment to maintain a more relaxed, peaceful lifestyle. Three days later the publisher called back and said, "Would you be willing to write the book if we gave you five and a half months?" With a sense of relief and joy, I said, "Okay."

Another way to look at the concept of right livelihood is to consider the price people pay for different types of occupations. Most people would say it's harder to connect with Spirit when their lives are full of stress, rushing around, and activity. By their very nature, however, many jobs are full of stress, deadline pressure, and constant demands. A spiritual seeker would probably do well to avoid such occupations. Many people find that a simple job and a simple lifestyle are conducive to a life of service and spiritual connection.

Working on Your Self

Perhaps more important than *what* job you do is *how* you do your job. The quality of caring and consciousness you bring to your daily interactions affects you, your co-workers, and your customers.

I know a man, Bill, who owns a copy shop. Every time I enter his shop, I feel personally welcomed and cared for. He asks me about what is happening in my life, and he listens with real interest and concern. One day, when I complimented Bill on his service, he replied, "As I see it, my job is help people in any way I can. Besides, it makes me feel better to really connect with folks." Although he doesn't claim to be a religious person, Bill exemplifies what it might look like to bring spiritual values into the workplace.

Besides kindness and service, there are other traits that a spiritual seeker might try to emulate in the workplace. For example, one could cultivate the quality of *equanimity.* In these fast-paced times, it's easy for people to get caught up in the dizzying speed of most jobs. A commitment to peacefulness, even while in a hurricane of activity, is a powerful, albeit difficult, spiritual practice.

Many seekers I know make sure they meditate or do yoga during their lunch breaks. Instead of coffee breaks, they listen to peaceful music or sit at their desk and focus on their breath. When I worked at a halfway house for people with schizophrenia, I found that by meditating periodically throughout the day, my peacefulness had a positive effect on the residents. You may find that the same thing happens at your place of work.

Learning on the Job— About Yourself

Another way to use your work to work on yourself is to learn from what goes on at your job. Like a relationship, the interactions and activities that happen at work can show you valuable things about yourself. If you can avoid the defense mechanisms

From Allah to Zen

Equanimity is the ability to feel relaxed and at ease, even in difficult circumstances. Equanimity is a trait that spiritually "advanced" people usually have, largely due to the sense of presence they experience in their daily lives.

Heavenly Helpers

To know if a job is right for you, get quiet inside and ask your intuition, "Does this line of work feel right for me?" Listen for what feels like the most truthful answer. If the answer is no, you don't have to quit right away. See if you can gradually make the transition to work that feels more suitable to you.

Cosmic Potholes

When doing spiritual practices at work, it's easy to get a "holier than thou" reputation. Try to avoid calling attention to whatever you do, and certainly refrain from proselytizing to your co-workers. The best advertisement for the value of what you do is your kindness and equanimity. If co-workers are sincerely interested in what you're doing, they'll ask.

Heavenly Helpers

To better know what personal obstacles might be in the way of your enjoying a job you feel good about, try asking a couple of trusted friends. They may be able to see something that you're blind to. Listen to them carefully, even if you don't like what you hear.

of blame, denial, and distraction, you'll see that each day offers many opportunities to see your internal obstacles.

For example, you'll see that there are some people you don't get along with, some you shy away from, and certain parts of your job you consistently avoid. Rather than accepting these situations as being unfortunate, you could view them as opportunities to learn valuable skills and spiritual traits.

I'll give you an example of how this works. Although I like writing, I used to hate marketing my books. I would avoid it as much as possible. I always felt embarrassed talking about how valuable my books were. Seeing that marketing brought up negativity in me, I asked myself why. I concluded that I was afraid of rejection, and I had an arrogant attitude that said "a writer shouldn't have to market himself." Of course, these obstacles were reflected in how many books I sold. I vowed to go against these personal restrictions, and I began to do a lot of book signings and radio interviews. Besides greatly helping book sales, by going against what used to stop me, I've become less afraid of rejection.

Facing Your Fears

For many years, my former partner, Helena, was a legal secretary. Although the money was okay, she didn't find her job fulfilling. What she really wanted to do was be a massage therapist. Unfortunately, we lived in Santa Barbara, California, where it seemed that almost *everyone* was a licensed massage therapist. Nevertheless, I encouraged Helena to do what she loved, and told her that if she were willing to face the challenge of working on her weaknesses, she could make a living doing massage. For years she resisted. She said there was too much competition. I pointed out that if she were willing to work on herself, she could overcome the many challenges she'd face while changing her career.

Finally, Helena couldn't stand her job as a legal secretary anymore. She quit, and decided to work for a temporary agency as she built up her massage practice. She immediately faced her fears of not having enough money. She also came up against her resistance to promoting herself. Helena, by nature, was a quiet person. Yet now the need for money was challenging her to face her fears.

Fortunately, she was up to the challenge. She began walking into offices and offering people free 10-minute massages. Not only did this act of service make her and others feel good, it also led to acquiring some massage clients. As she received feedback about what worked and what didn't in her advertising and promotion, she secured more clients. Now she enjoys a strong massage practice.

Helena is now able to make money doing what she loves because she listened to the lessons money and work were trying to teach her. She realized it was only her fear and a lack of creative marketing that prevented her from doing what she really wanted to do. Once she faced her fears of failure, self-promotion, and not having enough money, the universe rewarded her with a job she loves. As long as she wasn't facing her fears, she couldn't take the next step.

That's the way the world works. When people have trouble in their work or finances, there is always a lesson for them to receive. The question is, are they willing to receive it?

What are the things at work that give you trouble? What or whom do you consistently avoid, and why? As you answer these questions, you may see that you're being given a message that points to a personal shortcoming. You can avoid the message and blame the situation (like most people do), or you can learn from it. If you want to use it as an opportunity, ask yourself, "What could I do to grow in this situation?" Then, listen to your intuition. Act on it. You may notice amazing things happen as you become willing to use situations at work as part of your spiritual growth.

Amazing Grace

Several years ago, I asked a trusted friend about the shortcomings he saw in me that prevented my having greater success in my speaking career. He said that I never wear nice clothes. He went through my wardrobe and threw out everything he didn't like. I was barely left with my underwear. Then, with his guidance, I bought a whole new wardrobe. In the three years since doing this, I've had more professional speaking success than in the previous 20 years. It convinced me that when you're willing to humble yourself, ask for help, and work on your shortcomings, magic happens.

Making Your Vocation Your Vacation

Remember the hot-and-cold game you used to play as a kid? Someone would hide an object, such as a pen, and you would try to find it. Whenever you got closer to where it was hidden, they'd say you're getting warmer. When you veered from its hiding place, they'd say you're getting colder. Eventually, you'd get "red hot" and would find the hidden object.

Getting Hotter, Getting Colder

I believe God is really playing the *hot-and-cold game* with each of us. We're all trying to find the perfect job—work that is both highly enjoyable and profitable. God is continually sending us messages about whether we're getting nearer or farther from this goal.

From Allah to Zen

The **hot-and-cold game** is a method of discerning whether you're getting closer to or farther away from your goal. By listening to internal and external feedback, you can better determine whether you are on the right course.

There are two ways such messages are communicated. First, when we enjoy our work, or find it particularly rewarding, that's a message that we're getting warmer. Such an internal experience means we are doing something right. When we feel our work is unrewarding or boring, that means we're getting cooler. It's time to reevaluate the direction in which we're going.

The second way we receive messages about how we're doing is by the external feedback we get. If you invent a widget and someone offers you a lot of money for it, that's a good indication you're on the right path. On the other hand, if you never sell what you create, that can be an indication you're off course. By listening to the inner and outer messages the universe sends your way, you can learn to steer yourself to the treasure that awaits you—work you enjoy and find profitable.

The Moses Model

When I began my career, I used a different technique for trying to figure out what I should do. I thought that if I meditated enough, God would speak to me in a booming voice and tell me exactly what career I was supposed to pursue. I call this the "Moses model" for finding your life's work. Many spiritually inclined people believe that God will one day speak to them in a distinct manner and say, "You need to go this way!" After all, that's what he did with Moses, so why not with you and me?

Actually, God didn't do that with Moses. Moses had to stumble along for many years on his own before he received direct and clear guidance from Spirit. I believe that we have to do the same thing. Only after a long time of listening to the hot-and-cold feedback we get from the universe does it become fully clear what would be most in line with our soul to do.

After many years of discerning when I've been warmer or cooler, it *has* become clear what my unique purpose is. Yet I have traveled an often-crooked line toward my goal of discovering my life's work. I have had to endure dozens of messages that, in effect, said, "You're freezing."

Fortunately, like a connect-the-dots drawing that's been filled in, the picture of what I am to do has become strikingly clear. Each time I acted and got the message that I was off course, I became wiser. I learned perseverance and compassion. Each time I acted and got the feedback that I was *on* course, I became wealthier and more able to contribute to others. Through this feedback process, God teaches us to be strong, flexible, persistent, and humble.

Some people are secretly angry with God for not being directly guided about what they should do. They don't want to take action when they're uncertain, or make a few wrong turns along the way. Yet, I believe we *need* to go through the hot-and-cold-game process to become a stronger, more spiritual person. It's only through overcoming difficulties that we become spiritually strong, just as it is only through lifting weights that we become physically powerful. In my own life, I have seen how going through the hot-and-cold process has made me more capable, smarter, and better able to handle the many challenges of the material world.

God Is My Boss

In the Hindu and other traditions, there is a concept known as *Karma* yoga. In Karma yoga, one seeks to do things to serve God, without any attachment to how they turn out. Since one's actions are not performed for self-gratification, a person doing Karma yoga frees him- or herself from creating future problems. As a result of not being attached to outcomes, a person can become completely involved in whatever he or she is doing.

People can do the same work and have very different experiences, depending upon their attitude and the reason they do their job. If you do a job you hate just for the money, you'll have a different experience than you would doing a job that you see serves your beloved Lord. Mother Teresa used to say, "I serve my Lord in all his distressing disguises." When she held a vomiting leper, instead of feeling disgust, she felt she was taking care of Jesus.

From Allah to Zen

Karma refers to the cosmic law of cause and effect. In the traditions in which it is used, it is believed that everything you do has an effect on the universe that will echo back to you in some way. In Karma yoga, through selfless action and service, one tries to become free of the binding effects of past karma.

Amazing Grace

When St. Peter's cathedral was being built, a scribe went to see how it was going. He interviewed three men moving bricks onto a wall. He asked the first man, "What are you doing?" The man replied, "Can't you see, I'm moving bricks onto this wall? Get out of my way!" He asked the second man about his activities. The man replied, "I'm moving these bricks so I can feed my two daughters and wonderful wife." When he asked the third man what he was doing, he replied, "I have the honor to serve God by moving these bricks. With each brick I lay, I help to build a cathedral that will help millions of seekers worship our Lord."

For most people, it is quite a stretch to view one's work as an offering to God. By starting with small things, you may be able to get a sense of what that experience would be like. If you're a parent, you've probably felt a sense of devotion toward your kids—a strong desire to serve them the best you can. What if you could translate that same sense of responsibility and love to your boss, co-workers, or customers? Would that make your job feel different?

Cosmic Potholes

When attempting to act without attachment to how things go, the tendency is to become sloppy or apathetic. Our attachment and desire to look good is usually what drives us. A true Karma yogi acts passionately and impeccably in every situation—despite a lack of future attachment.

Giving to God

I remember a distinct time in which I felt the freedom and joy of acting like a Karma yogi. I had been trying to sell my book *The Experience of God* to a publisher, with no luck. Fortunately, my girlfriend helped me over my self-imposed hurdle. After hearing me obsess about how all the efforts I had put into *my* book were seemingly going to waste, she suggested I surrender the book back to God, at least for five minutes.

This had never occurred to me. It seemed reasonable to let go of my worry and attachment to the book for five minutes. I prayed to let go for five minutes and soon felt a wonderful sense of release. Since it felt so good, I decided to "give the book back to God" for good.

During the next month, I sent the book out to publishers, but with no concern for whether it got published. After all, it was God's book, not mine. Lo and behold, after a couple of weeks, a publisher called who wanted the book. From this experience, I learned that when we become too attached to a particular result, it seems to block the flow of grace. Holding on to how we think things *should* be is tantamount to telling Spirit we know what's best—and don't butt into our lives. When we let go, it seems to complete a "cosmic circuit" that allows peace to prevail and miracles to happen.

Letting Go

I should point out that letting go does not mean you are passive, nor does taking massive action mean you are attached. The experience of attachment or letting go is really an internal one. In Islam they have a saying: "Trust in Allah, but tie up your camels." People's external actions may or may not indicate their degree of letting go. Nevertheless, they *feel* completely different. Attachment feels like a contraction of one's being and a fear of the future. It leads to worry and anxiety. On the other hand, letting go and serving in the moment leads to a feeling of peace, openness, and expansion.

In Chapter 2, "Keys to the Kingdom," I mentioned that, upon coming close to death, many people report hearing the question, "How well did you use your gifts to contribute to other people and the world?" It would seem that once we handle the basics in life, we are called to serve more than just our own needs. As you act to serve a hurting and needy humanity, the help you offer can bring you closer to the core of God's love.

The Least You Need to Know

➤ Right livelihood involves finding work that doesn't harm people and doesn't add to humanity's troubles.

➤ The peace, kindness, and humility with which you do a job are some ways to bring your spirituality into the workplace.

➤ By being aware of the fears and irritations you have at work, you can better see what holds you back spiritually.

➤ By listening to the "hot-and-cold" messages you receive from the universe, you can better know what is right for you.

➤ As you learn to serve others without attachment to how things turn out, you can discover the secrets of Karma yoga—the yoga of coming closer to God through action.

Chapter 19

Aligning with the Divine

In This Chapter

➤ Tuning into peace in a busy lifestyle

➤ The importance of gratitude in connecting with the sacred

➤ How to find inspiration in yourself and others

➤ The value of surrounding yourself with beauty and art

➤ The perfect world

Experiencing the sacred in daily life is no easy task. While there are numerous disciplines for seeking God apart from daily life, such as meditation, few people know of ways to experience the sacred while driving a car or watching TV.

In the days when most holy books were written, cars, TV, phones, and computers didn't exist. Teachers in those days didn't need to invent methods for aligning with the divine during a busy lifestyle. Nowadays, most of our lives are spent in fast-paced activity. The methods in this chapter are simple enough to be used even while on the phone or while stuck in traffic.

To feel connected to the sacred in daily life, it can help to think of Spirit as a very high vibration. Normally, our frenetic pace keeps us feeling separate from each other, as well as from Spirit. While spiritual practices help to increase our awareness temporarily, we soon lose our "high" when faced with the material world.

Through the ideas and methods that follow, you may find that you can keep your awareness at a high level while engaged in your normal daily activities.

Thank God for Gratitude

In the New Testament (Colossians 3:12), Paul instructs people that "… whatever you do, whether in word or deed, do it all … giving thanks to God the Father …" Hidden in these words is a truly remarkable way to feel closer to God during one's daily activities.

You don't have to be a Christian to make use of this method. When I interviewed 40 notable spiritual leaders for my first book, the method I heard for feeling closer to God more than any other was that of practicing gratitude. As one person put it, "Gratitude opens your heart, and opening your heart is a wonderful and easy way for God to slip in."

Thanking, Not Asking

In Western culture, we often think of prayer as *asking* God for something. Yet, in many spiritual traditions, prayer is primarily considered a way of *thanking* God for the blessings in one's life.

Many years ago, I received an important lesson about "thankfulness prayer" from a Native American medicine man named Bear. As a condition of being interviewed about his life, Bear requested that we meet at a location sacred to his tribe. Once there, he suggested that both of us begin by offering up a prayer to the Great Spirit.

Heavenly Helpers

When practicing the "thank-you" technique throughout my day, I sometimes place my hand on my heart while trying to feel grateful for whatever I'm focusing on. This helps me to feel my heart, and reminds me of the importance of really *feeling* the gratitude—rather than just saying the right words.

My simple prayer was that our time together be well spent, and that it would serve our becoming closer to God. Bear began his prayer in his native tongue, as I listened patiently. After 10 minutes of listening to the sounds of his tribal language, I began getting impatient. After 30 minutes of listening to his prayer, I was secretly irritated. While I grew restless, Bear looked like he was soaring as high as the eagles that flew overhead. Finally, after 50 minutes, Bear finished his prayer.

Trying to hide my irritation, I began my interview by asking Bear, "What *did* you pray for?" Bear's calm reply was, "In my tribe, we don't pray *for* anything. We give thanks for all that the Great Spirit has given us. In my prayers, I simply thanked Spirit for everything I can see around me. I gave thanks to each and every tree I can see from here, each rock, each squirrel, the sun, the clouds, my legs, my arms, each bird that flew by, each breath I took, until I was finally in full alignment with the Great Spirit." It was clear to me that this man really *knew* how to pray.

Thank-You Prayer

From Bear's inspiration and the wisdom of many others I've interviewed, I began trying this new method of prayer. To make this method practical in my daily life, I began by simply saying, "Thank you God for (whatever is in my awareness)." Sometimes I would "prime the pump" by first thanking God for things that are *easy* for me to feel grateful for. For example, I might say, "Thank you for my health. Thank you for the warmth of the sun on my shoulders. Thank you for my wonderful dog, Rama." Once I truly felt a sense of gratitude in my heart, I would use *thank you* as a mantra for whatever I was currently aware of.

For instance, if I was driving somewhere I might say, "Thank you for my car, thank you for my tape player, thank you for this beautiful music, thank you for this nicely paved road, thank you for the man who just cut me off, thank you for the anger that he stirred up in me, thank you for the opportunity to practice forgiveness."

The secret of this technique is to see *all* things as gifts given to us by God to enjoy or learn from. Normally, we take virtually everything for granted, and rarely stop to appreciate the wonderful things we are given. Although we are given so much, without the "thank you" technique, all the amenities of modern day life can go unappreciated.

Once you have used this method for a while, you can even use it to begin to value things that are unpleasant. In the example above, getting cut off by an aggressive driver was not my idea of a good time. Yet, if I'm doing my "thank you" mantra, I'm more likely to see how such an event can serve me. From a higher state of mind, I can see that this driver is helping me to learn patience, compassion, and forgiveness—three things I'm not very good at. Fortunately, there are many drivers and people who are willing to help me learn this lesson! Thank you, God, for all that help!

Like any mantra or phrase that a person repeats, saying thank you can build up a momentum of its own as you use it throughout the day. However, it's important that it not become a mechanical mental exercise. With each thank you that is thought, it's essential to feel a sense of appreciation in your heart for the gift you've been given.

Besides helping you tune into an ecstatic feeling of gratitude, this method can also help you become more aware and present in the eternal now. Normally, we spend a lot of our time needlessly worrying about abstract problems. By giving thanks for what's right in front of us, our worries can disappear and be replaced with an expanded awareness of what is occurring at the moment.

Cosmic Potholes

As with anything you repeatedly do, it's easy for this method to become mechanical instead of heartfelt. Therefore, don't just think "thank you" like you might other thoughts, but rather make sure each time you say it, there is a true feeling of gratitude in your heart.

201

Once you've used the thank-you method for awhile, it's possible to experience an advanced form of this technique. Instead of thinking the words, "Thank you for ...," you can simply notice whatever you're experiencing in the moment and *silently feel* your gratitude to God for this experience in your life. To do this, it helps to be very focused in the present moment, and feel connected to your source. Even after only a few minutes of feeling the gratitude for each step you take and each breath you breathe, you may feel an inner ecstasy welling up from within.

Flowers Through the Concrete

Have you ever seen a flower or some grass rise up between slabs of concrete? When you think about it, it's a wonder of nature. Despite all the odds against it, occasionally a flower miraculously edges its way up between massive concrete blocks or asphalt.

Amazing Grace

I once read a magazine article in which two people shared totally different experiences of knowing Iraqi leader Saddam Hussein. One person talked about him as a ruthless murderer, but the other shared how he'd seen him act compassionately and kindly on many occasions. Although it didn't make me feel warmly toward this man who has done so much harm, it did make me realize that anyone can occasionally manifest acts of beauty.

In a similar way, despite the harshness of the material world and our tendency toward selfish and lazy behavior, humans occasionally display divine qualities. When that happens, it's like an inner flower in us that refuses to be weighed down or denied despite the many forces working against it.

I present this analogy as a way to encourage you to tune into a surprising amount of beauty all around you. As your consciousness grows and you become aware of the preponderance of your own and others' shortcomings, it's easy to become cynical. That's why it's important to make sure you're always on the lookout for the "flowers" or small acts of beauty that people sporadically manifest. Even people who irritate you can, on occasion, do truly beautiful things. If you look for such beauty in others, you may find yourself getting a dose of inspiration several times a day.

Looking for beauty in yourself can also be a fun and spiritually uplifting pursuit. Many people have a harder time recognizing the beauty in themselves than they do the ugliness. Somehow, it makes us feel vulnerable to realize that the divine uses us to manifest acts of kindness and beauty. Yet it does happen. Rather than slough it off, it can be a good practice to savor the moments when you find yourself or others manifesting a "flower."

Beauty Is Soul Deep

Besides appreciating the beauty in people, it can be inspiring to wake up to the magnificence in the world around you. There is the beauty of art, literature, nature, architecture, and music. Usually, a person is born with a predilection to appreciate certain forms of beauty more than others. You may marvel at Bach and Beethoven, but feel nothing for Picasso and Pollack. Whatever you naturally appreciate, make sure you expose yourself to it throughout your life. These days it's all too easy to get caught up in trivial matters and forget the importance of a daily helping of beauty and inspiration.

Once you regularly treat yourself to things that inspire your notion of beauty, you can try expanding your sense of appreciation to new arenas. For example, if you normally don't like abstract painting or ballet, you might try to develop a taste for it. People often get stuck in appreciating only a small portion of what's available to enjoy.

A couple of years ago, I had a friend who became interested in *feng shui,* a Chinese art that is concerned with how an environment feels and is constructed. She hired an expensive feng shui consultant who moved things around her house, and put up various mirrors and crystals to "increase the flow of energy." My first reaction to all of this was that my friend had gone off the deep end. After seeing and feeling how much more beautiful her house was after the changes, I realized there might be something to what she was doing.

In general, if an art form has been around a long time, there is probably some magic in it. By *magic* I mean that many people have been enlivened by it. Therefore, if you don't like the opera, it means that there is something you're missing, not that it's a waste of time. By gradually exposing yourself to new forms of art, you may find that your idea of what is beautiful and inspiring begins to grow.

Heavenly Helpers

To better recognize moments where people manifest divine qualities, begin by looking for little things. A parent wiping the tears from a hurt child, someone picking up a piece of litter, or a kind word from a friend are all small moments of selfless caring. If you look for small things rather than big things, you'll notice more of them.

From Allah to Zen

Feng shui literally means "the way of wind and water" or "the natural forces of the universe." It was developed by the ancient Chinese as a way to live in harmony with the environment. Nowadays, it is popularly known as a way to arrange items in one's house to bring in positive energy and dispel negative or blocked energy.

One reason people rarely enlarge their artistic "vocabulary" is that, at first, it's difficult. If abstract painting does not turn you on, going to a showing of abstract work is not particularly fun. Many years ago I had a girlfriend who was an abstract painter. One day we wandered the halls of a museum together. Whereas she would look at a painting with tears flowing down her face, I would look at the same painting and think, "Any six-year-old could do that simply by throwing paint on a canvas." Despite my initial cynicism, I knew I was missing something, and it was difficult to feel my inadequacy in this area.

Heavenly Helpers

To learn to appreciate areas of artistic expression and beauty that you haven't enjoyed in the past, find someone who is an expert and learn from him. An expert could be anyone who greatly enjoys the art form you know little about. Ask him what he enjoys about it and why. Try to see the world through his eyes. Let his enthusiasm be contagious.

As I saw more abstract painting, I gradually began to like some of it. It's as if a dormant part of my brain started to develop. I began to see beauty, emotion, and symmetry where I had previously seen globs of paint. It was a thrilling experience, like opening up to a world that had previously been invisible to me. It was a lot like the original feeling I had of opening up to the world of Spirit.

Ultimately, we all want a deeper part of ourselves to be stimulated more. If various forms of painting, music, literature, and nature help you get in touch with your soul, then you will often be inspired. Fortunately, I have found the reverse to also be true. As you get more in touch with your soul, more forms of art will mean something to you. Many things in life go unappreciated unless you're living from a deeper part of yourself. One of the rewards of the spiritual journey is an enhanced appreciation of all forms of artistic expression (see Chapters 27, "Sex, Drugs, and Rock 'n' Roll," and 28, "Final Words of Wisdom").

Everything's Perfect

Another way to align with the divine is to tune into the level of reality in which everything is considered perfect. From the vantage point of the human mind and heart, clearly everything is not perfect. There are starving children, nuclear missiles, violent cities, and endless suffering. As we try to alleviate the suffering, it's easy to get lost in it. The world of distress can become our whole reality, while the inner world of perfect peace falls by the wayside.

To avoid getting overwhelmed by the suffering around us, it's important to balance ourselves with a radical point of view: Everything's perfect. Everything is simply what it is. Ultimately, it's only our value judgments of how things *should* be that causes us to see and experience suffering. From another view of reality, it's possible to see the entire world as a dance unfolding according to certain cosmic laws. From this view, everything is indeed perfect.

Like the thank-you mantra, it's possible to use the affirmation "Everything's perfect" as a reminder to yourself throughout the day. Recently I got my eyes checked. As the doctor examined my eyes, he made various grunts of concern. I was getting nervous. I felt the frailty of growing older, a lack of control, and the grief that comes from losing some of the vigor and strength of youth. By reminding myself that everything's perfect, I was able to relax with the feeling of being out of control, rather than resist it. When the doctor announced that all I needed was glasses, it was pretty easy to switch to the thank-you technique!

Cosmic Potholes

Knowing that, on one level of reality, everything is perfect is not a valid excuse for ignoring suffering. The trick is to feel the peace of realizing that everything is perfect, while at the same time working to help better the conditions in the world.

The words *everything's perfect* can be a helpful mantra to use during times of stress, suffering, or just as a peaceful reminder at any time. When I use it, it helps me realize there is a whole other world that exists outside the dramas I create in my own head and life. I don't say it to deny that there is plenty of distress around, but rather to remind myself that beauty and stillness always exist as well. Of course, you'll never know of its power unless you try it for yourself. Simply repeat the words to yourself and see if they help you let go of worry. Even if it doesn't work, it's still perfect.

Amazing Grace

The spiritual teacher Ram Dass once shared a lesson about how everything is perfect. He was complaining to his guru, Neem Karoli Baba, about how much suffering there was in the world. His guru just kept saying, "Don't you see that everything is just perfect?" Ram Dass wouldn't accept this, but his teacher kept saying it. Finally, Ram Dass opened up to the level of reality where he could see the perfectly unfolding drama of cosmic laws. It felt truly peaceful. Once Ram Dass was enjoying this perspective and peace, his guru told him, "Now go out and feed people; go out and serve people."

In order to experience the sacred in daily life, it's nice to know that you don't have to change anything in the material world. What a relief. You do have to change the point of view with which you look at the world. Viewed from the right level of awareness, everything is meaningful, purposeful, and even "perfect." It is our job to try to find that level of being within ourselves. Ironically, the more one sees the world from such a place, the better one is able to be of true service to a hurting world.

The Least You Need to Know

➤ Despite today's busy lifestyle, one can still experience the sacred in daily life.

➤ Feeling grateful for each thing in your life is a great way to open the heart and let Spirit slip in.

➤ By watching for acts of beauty in yourself and others, you can become inspired.

➤ Seeking beauty in art, nature, and music can help you feel aligned with the Divine.

➤ Knowing that, on one level, everything is perfect can help you tune into the stillness and peace within.

Chapter 20

From Fear to Magic

In This Chapter

➤ The drabness of being all "WET"

➤ Turning small fears into growth opportunities

➤ Reaching for goals and living your dreams

➤ The role of spontaneity and meaningful questions in your awakening

---

When I was four years old, my brother was having his ninth birthday. With a little help from my mom, I was able to understand that my brother was more than twice as old as I was. Once I had this realization, I turned to my mom and said, "Boy, is he *old!*" When I was four, a day seemed like forever, while a year was a totally absurd length of time. Even an hour seemed like a long time, since I knew that in an hour I could learn many new things and have several new adventures.

Such is the life of a child. Of course, as we grow older, time seems to accelerate. Some people say it's because we measure time relative to how long we've been around. I believe time seems to go by more quickly as we get older because we're less present and available to the myriad adventures each day offers us.

The difference between a 3-year-old and a 5-year-old is immense, whereas the difference between a 30-year-old and a 32-year-old isn't. Why is that? When we're children, we learn rapidly, we take chances, we're always reaching out for new adventures. Sometime around the age of 20 or 30, our inner growth spurt tends to peter out. We settle down.

There's nothing wrong with settling down, unless that means you live your life in a way that smothers the spiritual spark within. As spiritual beings, our job is to make sure we keep learning, keep following our dreams, and keep taking the risks needed to become a fully alive person. The ideas and methods in this chapter can be of help in keeping the childlike spark in us alive and well.

The Way of the Easiest Thing

Why do so few adults seem as alive and open to learning as the average child? There are a lot of answers to that question, but let me give you one you may not have heard before.

I believe it's because of a little-known force in the universe I call "way of the easiest thing," or *WET* for short. The WET force eventually soaks our brain with a very rational and safe way of doing just about everything. Like other forces in the universe, such as gravity, there's no escape from the WET force. By knowing more about this force and how it operates through people, it's possible to circumvent it in certain ways. Just as the principles of gravity actually enable airplanes to fly, so can the WET force actually enable us to reach a higher state of consciousness.

To understand how the WET force works, it's helpful to consider how it is operating through you right now. Currently, you're reading this book. Why? Probably because, all things considered, it seemed like the thing you most wanted to do right now. When it no longer seems like the thing you want to do, you'll do something else. Perhaps you'll go to the refrigerator and look for something to eat. What will you choose? Undoubtedly, the thing that pleases you most, because that's the easiest thing to choose. Where will you eat this food? Probably at the closest table. Why? Because that would be the easiest thing to do. When you're done with it, what will you do? Probably the easiest thing that occurs to you at that moment.

From Allah to Zen

WET, or way of the easiest thing, is a force in the universe that encourages people to do what's easiest for them and what pleases them. It is also an approach to life that, if not veered from occasionally, leads to a lack of growth, boredom, and an avoidance of activities that could rekindle a person's spiritual longings.

The WET force permeates our every decision with the question, "What's the easiest thing to do now?" That's why life can lack adventure and feel so mechanical after a while.

Even people who seem to be daredevils are subject to WET. For example, I often speak in front of hundreds of people. To many folks, that seems like a brave thing to do. The truth is that speaking to hundreds of people is easy for me, even easier than spending a night alone reading a book. Since each person has different things that are easy for him to do, this prevalent force is camouflaged. But it's there, guiding our actions in a way that dampens our aliveness and curiosity.

Risking Your Way into Life

When a person realizes how safe and mechanical his life has become, he can do one of two things. He can either try to forget about it, or he can try to fight ending up all WET. While the WET force is constantly dousing our spiritual spark, it does not take much to reignite the flame inside. You don't have to go skydiving or hang gliding to feel like you're facing fears that inhibit your natural aliveness. All you have to do is take small, growth-oriented chances in areas where you normally play it safe.

Facing Your Fears

Normally, people focus on one or two areas of life, while the other areas of their life lag far behind. For example, some men take lots of risks at work, but not in their relationships; they never learn how to face their fears. People fear their fear, instead of using it as a signpost for growth.

Fear is the harbinger of the unknown. If you feel a little fear while trying something new, it means you're growing. You're expanding your boundaries. Congratulations! By regularly facing your fears in various areas of your life, you can accelerate your growth as a human being.

Cosmic Potholes

When choosing what risks to take, choose small ones at first. If a big risk, like skydiving, doesn't go well, you're in big trouble, whereas if asking someone out doesn't go well, you'll survive the experience. As you take more risks, you'll learn what is an appropriate growth step for you.

Getting Stronger

There are many different areas of life that we can grow in. Since your level of happiness is largely determined by what's *not* working well in your life, it's a good idea to try to grow in the areas you're weakest in. For instance, if your relationships are great, but you hate your job, it's smarter to try to grow in your job, since that is your main obstacle to being more fulfilled. Unfortunately, people don't usually do that. Instead, they tend to focus on what's easiest for them—in this case, their relationships. It's like strengthening your strong arm, while leaving your weak arm to grow even weaker.

Once a person sees the wisdom of taking chances in areas he's weak at, the question becomes how to do it. A good first step is to consider making a list of the various categories of your life. Here are some I've thought of:

➤ Friends and intimate relationships

➤ Career and finances

➤ Family connections

➤ Body and health issues

➤ New areas of learning

➤ Spirituality

➤ Recreation and hobbies

➤ Personal goals

Feel free to add to the preceding list. Once you have your list, ask yourself, "In which of these areas do I feel the least experienced, confident, or fulfilled?" Then vow to take growth-oriented chances in this area.

Like everyone else, I fall into routines of just doing what I'm already good at, and avoiding other areas of life. Fortunately, I have a lot of friends who are willing to challenge me when they see me playing things too safely. Recently, a friend challenged me to learn to cook—something I've historically been totally inept at. It was exhilarating (and a bit scary) to make my first gourmet dinner.

Heavenly Helpers

Once you recognize an area of life in which you feel a need to grow, find a mentor who can inspire and help you. Even books can sometimes act as mentors, but all growth takes practice—not just reading. Consistent, small steps toward your goals is the best way to grow.

Going against the WET force can not only expand your abilities, but it can lead to a "high." Although facing fear is always difficult, with practice you get better at trusting the process and understanding the many benefits of continuously challenging yourself.

Living Your Dreams

The goal of a spiritual seeker should not be to avoid the material world. Denial and avoidance are not the way to enlightenment. Rather, each of us needs to fully live out our hopes and dreams until we're no longer pulled so strongly by them. A mature spiritual seeker is someone who has tried most of the things the world has to offer, and is now ready for the next step. If you try to skip doing what's meaningful to you in the material world, you'll likely find that it pulls on you like bubble gum stuck to your shoe.

Since people generally do what's easiest for them, most people end up being out of balance in their life. Spiritual seekers often avoid their material desires, while businesspeople often deny their spiritual longings. But spirituality isn't just going off alone to meditate; it's being a fully aware and engaged person in life. Just as a plane needs two wings to stay balanced and fly, a spiritual person needs to be experienced and capable in both the material world and the inner world.

What dreams do you have buried in your heart? A good way to know is to ask yourself, "If I had a billion dollars, and knew I could not fail, what would I do?" Would you try to end starvation, travel around the world, or get married and have children? If a dream is important enough to you, part of your job is to figure out how to manifest it.

At one time I had a dream to talk about spirituality on the *Oprah Winfrey Show*. This desire pulled at me for a long time. Then, after writing my book *The Little Book of Big Questions,* my dream came true. Oprah devoted the entire show to the spiritual questions in the book. Once the show was done, and the book became a best-seller, I saw that my life didn't really change. Rather than try to become richer and more influential, I realized that money and fame weren't really that useful to me. Having accomplished my dream, I was able to let go of my nagging desire for riches—and devote myself again to diving deeper within.

Had I not pursued my dream, I think it would still be nagging at me today.

Amazing Grace

In the Jewish mystical tradition known as the Cabala, people are discouraged from beginning their studies until they are at least 40 years old. It is believed that a person needs to have a lot of life experience before he can truly be a seeker of the "other world." Teachers of the Cabala believe that only when a person has lived some of his desires and experienced a lot of life can he fully turn toward spiritual seeking.

Scheduling Your Spontaneity

Children are naturally spontaneous. They can find magic and miracles even in a sandbox. Then they go to school. After a few years of "learning," they become transformed into a new species—adults. Adults are rarely spontaneous. They have a hard time finding magic even where miracles are actually taking place. It's a sad state of affairs. If you haven't lost your hunger for the play, fun, and magic you probably knew as a kid, then there's always a hope you can get it back. After all, you were born with it. You just need to unlearn the lessons you learned along the way.

Jesus said that "Anyone who will not receive the kingdom of God like a little child will never enter it." Indeed, we all need to be more childlike if we're going to uncover the heaven within. Since most adults are pretty bad at being spontaneous, it can help to begin with baby steps. The first step is to make spontaneity a priority. The ability to reach one's goals is an important characteristic of being an adult. However, if your goals are reached at the expense of your capacity to be silly, have fun, and laugh, then perhaps you have the wrong goals.

While scheduling your spontaneity sounds like an oxymoron, it can be a good place to begin. Give yourself an hour here and there to just be silly and childlike. Take a long walk with the goal of creating a magical moment with a stranger. Buy some fun toys that you can share with your kids. Simply having a clear-cut intention to let your childlike essence have its way is a good first step.

Recently, to help me bring spontaneity into my telephone conversations, I decided to answer the phone in a new way. Every once in a while when I pick up the phone I say, "Hi, I'm answering the phone in order to have a magical experience with you. If you're not into that, I suggest you hang up now." It's fun to see how people respond, and it usually leads to a unique conversation.

Cosmic Potholes

Striving for goals should not be done in a way that interferes with your natural spontaneity. Nor should being spontaneous and going with the flow interfere with living your dreams. Each person needs to find a balance between striving for goals and enjoying life moment to moment.

In one memorable conversation, the person calling me was trying to sell me a new long-distance service. Such salespeople normally read from a script, but my caller had no place on his script for responding to what I had said. Finally, he blurted out, "I'm just trying to sell you long-distance service." I responded, "Well I'm trying to sell you on the value of listening to your soul." There was a pause. After a moment he responded, "I think you have the better product!" We both laughed, and we began a wonderful conversation. I asked him if he liked his job, and he said he hated it, that he really wanted to be an artist. I suggested he work part-time and give his art more of a chance.

Last week I got another call from him. This time he told me he's now working part-time and he just sold his first painting. Magic!

The Inspiration of Conversation

The average person says about 20,000 words a day. Most of those words are said simply to get things done, to complain about stuff, or to engage in trivial chitchat. If you listen in on people's conversations, you'll notice a lack of inspiring discussions taking place. This is unfortunate. The words we speak can be a powerful tool for learning, inspiring, and exploring—if you know how to use this "technology" properly.

Ask Big Questions

There are many possible uses for talking that can enliven and enhance one's spirit. First you can discuss inspiring subjects. In my book *The Little Book of Big Questions*, I created more than 200 questions people can ask each other to begin interesting conversations. A few of my favorite questions include the following:

➤ What's one of the most miraculous things you've ever experienced?

➤ What's one of the most important things you've learned in your life?

➤ What would you do with only six months left to live?

➤ What does spiritual growth mean to you? What is the "goal" you're after?

➤ What do you consider to be the most spiritual experience you've ever had?

➤ Why is it that 95 percent of Americans report they believe in God, and yet our culture is so materialistic?

➤ How do you think the rise of technology has affected our culture's spiritual pursuits?

By asking these and other thought-provoking questions to your friends, family, and co-workers, you can add a sense of depth and meaning to your daily life. When people discuss meaningful topics, it raises their spiritual vibration and awareness. It feels good, and creates a sense of intimacy.

Exploring the Depths

So why do these conversations happen so infrequently? Because people are often afraid to explore conversations that have depth. It's easy to talk in a superficial manner, and avoid being vulnerable about what we really believe. Yet after a while, such conversations feel empty. As you ask people big questions, you'll find some people react poorly, while others will love to go exploring with you.

When asking people deep questions, it can be helpful to say a little bit about why you're asking. Before someone reveals his innermost thoughts to you, he wants to make sure you're being sincere, and that you're a safe person to talk to. I often say something like the following: "I'm trying to learn new things about life and spirituality, and you seem to be a person who has thought a lot about these

Amazing Grace

I have been a long-time fan of the rock band the Moody Blues. A year ago I got to meet their keyboard player, Michael Pinder. Since he often wrote very spiritual lyrics for the group, I asked him what he saw as his spiritual path. He said, "I see my path as trying to find the quality, depth, and magic in as many of life's moments as I can." A profound answer from a man who has inspired millions.

Heavenly Helpers

When asking thought-provoking questions, see if you can follow your curiosity and allow other questions to come up with each answer given. When you're answering a question, try to be as vulnerable, honest, and thorough in your answer as you can. Use questions as a method to explore new ideas and learn new information.

213

From Allah to Zen

An **agnostic** is someone who disclaims any knowledge of God, but does not deny the possibility of God's existence.

things. Is it okay if I ask you a couple of questions to see what you think and what you've experienced?"

Most people are honored to answer meaningful questions when they're presented to them in the right way. One of my favorite questions is to ask people, "What's one of the most miraculous things you've ever experienced?" I've often been surprised by the answers I've received. Even atheists have told me miracle stories that have inspired and uplifted me.

When I asked my dad (who is *agnostic*) this question, he rattled off several miraculous experiences he knew of. Although he has not pursued spirituality the way I have, this question allowed us to share a wonderful moment of intimacy and exploration. Try it.

Within every person is a desire for more meaning in life. Normally, we're moving too fast to explore the depths of our minds and souls. There is resistance, usually in the form of fear, to exploring our depths. Whether you try to live your dreams, take small risks, or ask meaningful questions, you are going against the force that says to always do the easiest thing.

But fear and resistance aren't bad. In fact, they're a sign that you're doing something right. By facing small amounts of resistance consistently, you'll grow spiritual muscles. You'll learn the art of transforming fear into magic.

The Least You Need to Know

➤ To keep growing, you need to overcome the tendency to do the easiest thing.

➤ By facing small fears in different areas of life, you can keep expanding who you are as a person.

➤ Striving toward meaningful goals is an important facet of becoming a balanced spiritual seeker.

➤ Being spontaneous and childlike will help you enjoy life more and help you be open to the wonder all around you.

➤ Asking questions and engaging in uplifting conversations can help you feel connected to Spirit in daily life.

Part 6
Spiritual Accelerators

It's easy to get lost in mechanical ruts in modern life. Fortunately, there are numerous ways to dislodge yourself from routines that no longer serve you. You can find a spiritual group that motivates you, a teacher who inspires you, or a workshop or retreat to soothe your soul.

To accelerate your spiritual progress, it's often important to find something or someone that can help you stay true to your highest aspirations.

Besides finding like-minded people to help you on your path, there are other ways to hasten your growth. You can travel to sacred spots or create them in your own home and heart. Sometimes life gives us sickness, pain, or inklings of our own mortality. If properly "used," these events can give us a sense of urgency and renewed interest in our spiritual pursuits.

Chapter 21

Retreats and Workshops

In This Chapter

➤ What spiritual retreats and workshops are and why they're helpful

➤ Choosing a retreat that's right for you

➤ Retreat resources

➤ Choosing a workshop that's right for you

➤ Workshop resources

Though it is said that life is the ultimate spiritual teacher, sometimes it helps to have a little extra tutoring. This is why an increasing number of spiritual seekers make it a point to spend time at some of the thousands of spiritual retreats and workshops offered worldwide.

This chapter will tell you what you need to know about spiritual retreats and workshops—what they are, why you would want to attend one, and how to go about choosing and finding them.

The What and Why of Retreats and Workshops

Retreats and workshops are similar in that each offers a special environment that one enters into in order to obtain certain experiences or understandings. However, they actually fulfill two very different functions.

A *retreat,* as the name implies, enables us to withdraw from the noise and commotion (internal and external) of daily living. It allows us to contemplate the quiet inner truths—about who we are and our purpose for being here—that tend to get drowned out by the noisy demands of our everyday lives.

From Allah to Zen

A **retreat** is a quiet, private place—a refuge from the ordinary demands of life in order to pray, study, or meditate. It's interesting that the word retreat also has the connotation of withdrawing from an enemy.

The retreat approach is essentially a passive, humble one: By slowing down the pace of our lives, we quiet our internal chatter enough to hear the voice of the Divine. By creating the right conditions, a retreat can help us solve a problem, feel inspiration, obtain a clearer perspective, rekindle hope, or provide a sense of connectedness with something larger than ourselves.

Workshops, on the other hand, teach specific lessons or impart an understanding of particular ideas. The environment is usually more concentrated and focused than that of a retreat. The fact is, modern industrial society does a lousy job of teaching us how to live harmonious lives, and for most of us, some form of remedial schooling is necessary. Ideally, workshops can teach us things we might otherwise learn only after a string of failed relationships, a bout with addiction, a great tragedy, or years of therapy.

Spiritual Retreats

The notion that disengaging from ordinary life can accelerate one's spiritual journey is not a New Age concept. The spiritual benefits of disengaging from the clamor of everyday life have been known for millennia. Devotees of virtually every major spiritual tradition and religious order have recognized the importance of spending time in a quiet, peaceful setting free from the distractions and problems of life in the workaday world. The proverbial yogi meditating on the mountaintop is one well-known example of such a seeker, but it is by no means the only one. For thousands of years, ashrams, monasteries, and temples have served as lifelong retreats for seekers of God.

Retreats have assumed a new importance in recent times, however. The rising hunger for spiritual sustenance over the past decade has coincided with the faster pace of modern life. We now face a dizzying proliferation of demands for our attention, and an inexorable rise in the number of hours required to work and raise a family. The well-documented exodus of educated professionals from high-paying jobs to slower-paced lives in the hinterlands exemplifies the dissatisfaction of middle-class Westerners. While most people still live busy lives, we have begun to realize that if we don't spend time in "idle" once in a while, we risk burning out our internal engine.

Okay, sounds good, you say, kind of like what most people would call a vacation. But retreats—the better ones, at any rate—aren't just vacations. Nowadays many people end up needing a vacation from their vacations. Rushing around from city to city, or from amusement park to museum, is not a retreat. A true retreat is a purposeful withdrawal from society in order to go deeper inside oneself. Of course, grace can descend at any time and in any situation, but it is probably less likely to appear when you're playing blackjack in a hot and smoky casino. Inner quiet is an indispensable part of the process, and a retreat is one way to find it.

Still not convinced? Think of it as clearing out room inside your mind and heart for God, to make him feel welcome to visit. As an example, suppose you wanted to go chat with one of your neighbors. At the house on the left, you hear the stereo blasting and see the owner mowing his unkempt lawn with one hand and wolfing down a sandwich with the other. Meanwhile, your neighbor on the right is sitting quietly on the front porch of her well-tended house with a peaceful, relaxed smile on her face. Which neighbor would you choose to visit?

A retreat can help you silence the cacophony of complaints, worries, and fantasies inside your head and make it more likely that God's voice and your own wisdom can be heard.

Heavenly Helpers

Some people prefer frequent retreats of short duration, versus infrequent retreats of longer duration. I've found that even a half day "retreat" in nature or locked away in a room without a phone can help me break free of the pace and momentum of daily life. Try both short and long retreats and see what effect each has on *your* life.

Amazing Grace

One way to ensure that you will enjoy peace and quiet on a retreat is to go on a silent retreat. One of my first retreats was a 10-day meditation retreat in Japan where speaking was not allowed. Each day the silence was broken only by the pealing of the bell that served as our morning alarm clock. I grew to love the sound of that bell, and at the same time I acquired a profound reverence for silence and a personal understanding of its importance to spiritual growth.

So Many Choices ...

There are an amazing number of organized retreat facilities available all over the world, each offering its own unique environment. When trying to decide which one is right for you, you are well advised to consider the following factors.

Length

In my experience, there's a pretty simple rule at work here: The more time you spend at a retreat, the greater the benefit. If a weekend is all you can manage, by all means go do it. But if you can find the time, a week or two is even better. Why? If it's your first retreat, or even if you're a veteran, you may find you spend the first day catching up on your sleep and getting used to your surroundings, and the second day feeling agitated and uncomfortable at suddenly having nothing to do all day. The third day is often when you really begin to unwind and the magic starts to happen.

Of course, a good weekend retreat can still be a powerful experience. And some people might feel they just can't afford to spend time away from work (though such a person is probably most in need of a longer retreat!). In general, shorter retreats should be light on activities (either physical or mental) and consist largely of solitude and quiet. Otherwise, the benefits of a retreat are easily lost, and a workshop—or simply a quiet weekend at home—might be a better choice. This leads us to the next factor to consider.

Pace

Some retreats are designed to let guests truly get away from it all, and accordingly minimize contact with other people. Others combine the isolation of a retreat with courses, workshops, discussion groups, counseling or guidance sessions, or recreational activity. Some retreats are relatively structured, while others are almost totally unstructured. Before choosing a retreat, you should figure out your preferred balance between socializing and solitude, and how much freedom you have to withdraw when you feel the need to be alone.

Cost

There is a wide range in the cost of retreats, depending on whether it is run by a church or a private group, the location, the amenities offered, and the types of activities available. Some church-sponsored retreats do not charge for use of the retreat facilities, but they ask for a donation.

Focus

Many retreats emphasize a particular theme or focus. For example, there is a large number of religious retreats, where some time is spent on contemplation and study of the principles of a particular religion, denomination, or spiritual tradition. Other types of retreats include the following:

➤ Yoga retreats

➤ Silence retreats

➤ Relationship retreats

➤ Spa or health retreats

➤ Nature retreats

➤ Fasting retreats

➤ Meditation retreats

➤ Family retreats

Each of these types of retreats provides a specific environment tailored to the goals and interests of the participant. Each has its own benefits, and there is no hard-and-fast way to choose. Naturally, you will need to assess your own capacities and objectives. For some people, a yoga retreat might be physically inadvisable, while for others fasting might be too extreme a step. A religious component is attractive to some, but a turnoff to others. Only you can decide what's right for you, and it's a decision made by the heart as much as by the head.

Comfort/Discomfort Level

Having read all this, you should keep in mind that the type of retreat that appeals to you most isn't necessarily the best one for you.

Our nature is to stick to what's comfortable—to stay in a well-worn groove. This ingrained tendency to avoid situations where we feel uncomfortable or out of control is one of our greatest hindrances to spiritual growth. If you want your retreat to be more than just a momentary decompression from a stress-filled life, an experience that is truly out of the ordinary, you may want to select a retreat that challenges you in some way, that brings some resistance to your life. Think about going somewhere that brings up *more* initial discomfort, rather than less.

This advice is especially applicable to those who are attracted to the abstract notion of attending a retreat, but who are in fact uneasy with prolonged

Heavenly Helpers

Certain Christian retreats can be "preached retreats," where guests are expected to listen to talks or sermons given at the retreat, or "directed retreats," which offer personalized spiritual counsel. If you feel you need outside inspiration to get you going, these types of retreats may be the most helpful to you.

solitude. Such people prefer to avoid quiet surroundings that force them to listen to the chatter in their heads. As a result, they are drawn to retreats that offer a high degree of interaction and activity. They cope well with this type of "retreat," even enjoy it. They sometimes obtain useful insights, which confirms to them the wisdom of their choice. But they have not been on a retreat in the true sense of the term. They have simply substituted one form of talking, thinking, and activity for another.

This is why you need to make sure that your retreat gives you adequate opportunities to be quiet and alone. A good retreat not only gives you a chance to think about things you want to think about, but slows you down enough to bring to the surface those important questions you may be avoiding by filling your life with activity.

Cosmic Potholes

Be sure to book retreat reservations early. If you wait till the day you need to "get away," you may find that there's nothing available. Some of the more popular retreats are booked solid during certain times of the year, especially summer.

Finding a Retreat

All right, I'm in, you say—now what? Do I just look up "Retreats" in the phone book?

Well, you could, actually. My local Santa Barbara phone directory carries listings under the heading of "Retreat Facilities and Houses," right between "Retreading and Recapping—Tires" and "Reunion Planning Consultants." (Amazing what you can find in there, isn't it?) So if you feel you have to get away immediately, that might be a good place to begin.

Fortunately, though, there are other resources available for finding the right retreat. Certain spiritually oriented magazines, such as *New Age Journal* or *Yoga Journal*, contain ads for retreats.

For the computer-equipped, the Internet is another place to look. My search using the keywords "spiritual retreats" produced a list of around 100 retreats worldwide, which is only a small fraction of what's out there. There are also a number of books that provide a description of the retreat experience and a list of suggested retreats. A few of these books are:

➤ *A Place for God: A Guide to Spiritual Retreats and Retreat Centers,* by Timothy K. Jones; Doubleday, 2000.

➤ *101 Vacations to Change Your Life: A Guide to Wellness Centers, Spiritual Retreats, and Spas,* by Karin Baji-Holms, Vincent Terrace; Carol Publishing Group, 1999.

➤ *Silence, Simplicity and Solitude: A Complete Guide to Spiritual Retreat,* by David A. Cooper; Skylight Paths, Publishing, 1999.

➤ *Parent-Child Retreats: Spiritual Experiences for Parents and Their Children Ages 7–10,* by Mary Ann Figlino, Kathy Coffey, Blanche Sims; Morehouse Group, 1998.

➤ *Quiet Places: A Woman's Guide to Personal Retreat,* by Jane Rubietta; Bethany House, 1997.

➤ *Parent-Child Retreats: Spiritual Experiences for Children Ages 3–6 and Their Parents,* by Maggie Pike, Lynne Knickerbocker, Eleanor Sheehan; Living the Good News, 1997.

➤ *Wilderness Time: A Guide for Spiritual Retreat,* by Emilie Griffin; Harper San Francisco, 1997.

Another source of information can be your friends. If you have friends who go on retreats, they might know of something nearby that is a great value. If you don't have friends who take periodic retreats, maybe you need more spiritually oriented friends. A great place to meet such people is at spiritually oriented workshops. Read on!

Spiritual Workshops

If the idea of a retreat feels a little intimidating, or if you're in the mood for a more active spiritual undertaking, you might consider a workshop rather than a retreat.

Workshops covering a vast range of topics and approaches to spirituality are held all over the world, 365 days a year. While a comprehensive discussion of all of the different types of workshops is beyond the scope of this book, knowing a few basic principles will help you find the right workshop for you, and will prevent you from becoming lost in a sea of similar-sounding brochure descriptions.

Choosing a Workshop

The first thing is to know what you're looking for. As you'll discover, a "spiritual workshop" can involve anything from chanting at sunrise in the Andes to lying naked in a tub of warm water reliving birth trauma. Generally speaking, there are a few basic types of workshops:

➤ Workshops that emphasize one or more physical or mental activities, such as yoga, chanting, prayer, meditation, visualization, writing, art, massage, energy work, and so on.

➤ Seminar-type workshops that focus primarily on intellectual discussion and understanding.

➤ Workshops that emphasize getting in touch with one's feelings, getting closer to others, or reaching an *emotional catharsis.*

➤ "Peak performance" workshops or courses that employ hypnotism, guided imagery, role-playing, and other exercises to effect behavioral change as well as spiritual breakthroughs.

From Allah to Zen

Emotional catharsis refers to when your emotions get stirred up and reach a peak of intensity, followed by a healing release of tension, tears, laughter, or anger. Through cathartic exercises, a person can move through blocked feelings more quickly than he normally would in ordinary life.

Heavenly Helpers

Since some workshops cost a fair amount of money, it can be helpful to talk to people who've already taken them. Ask them, "What did you get from it?" and, "Have you noticed any ongoing changes in your life?" Workshops that offer ongoing support after the workshop is over tend to be more helpful in the long term.

As with finding a retreat, you will need to think not just about which approach sounds most enjoyable, but which would be best for your spiritual progress. Remember that growth requires sacrifice—a willingness to go against the grain and do what's difficult. For example, if you are the logical, unemotional type, you may well have negative judgments (feelings of discomfort) about feeling-oriented workshops, and prefer the intellectual-type workshop, which most closely resembles the academic environment you've already mastered. This means you should almost certainly choose the touchy-feely type of workshop, as it is far more likely to lead you to a real breakthrough.

Don't Become Addicted

One danger of workshops that I have noticed over the years is that they can become a substitute for a true spiritual practice. Workshops can be highly entertaining and uplifting, and at the end there are often powerful feelings of euphoria and inspiration, which inevitably fade. As a result, some people become what I call "spiritual groupies," compulsively attending workshop after workshop to maintain the high. They are often sincere seekers, and believe they are doing the best they can to live a spiritual life, but they seldom progress very far. They are essentially dilettantes, who have chosen to rely on workshop leaders to teach and uplift them. They are unwilling to commit themselves to a disciplined spiritual path that requires consistent, daily effort.

So remember, a workshop should serve as a map explaining how to get to a hidden paradise, but your job is to get to paradise—not to become a skilled map-reader.

Finding a Workshop

Workshops, while plentiful, can be a little trickier to find than retreats, because they generally don't have fixed addresses.

Advertisements in New Age, Christian, and natural health–oriented magazines can be a particularly good source for information on upcoming workshops. Many retreat centers provide regular workshops, so an Internet search for these centers could prove worthwhile. In addition, yoga studios, vegetarian restaurants, church bulletin boards, health food shops, organic food stores, herbal products outlets, and similar establishments often have bulletin boards where people post notices and flyers for spiritual activities and events.

Go for It!

Once you've located an interesting-sounding workshop, decided to attend, paid your money, and actually arrived, you now face one of your biggest challenges: the temptation to hold back and judge rather than participate. Workshops often encourage us to do things we don't normally do at home—that's part of the reason they're effective. You might be asked to hug or hold hands in a circle with someone you don't know, gaze into someone's eyes, tell your partner you love him, or reveal painful memories or secret dreams.

Amazing Grace

I've been to a lot of workshops that have asked me to do some strange things, from walking barefoot on burning hot coals to standing naked in front of a room (yikes!). While most of them have had only temporary impact, in a couple of them, I learned something that altered the course of my life. You never know when you'll learn a tidbit of knowledge that changes everything for you. In one workshop, the leader suggested I make no effort whatsoever when I meditate. For some reason, that changed my experience of meditation forever.

While you may find these things difficult or uncomfortable, they are not life-threatening. What's more, your resistance is your friend, because it reveals—if you're paying attention—the obstacles inside you that prevent you from being truly alive. Overcoming the fear of intimacy and the need for control at a workshop might be your first step to reclaiming your spirit and redefining your relationship to others and to God.

Retreats and workshops have been an important part of my spiritual development. Not only have I quickly learned things that may have taken me years to learn, but I have also met people who have become lifelong friends and spiritual buddies. In cultures where there is a slower pace of life, workshops and retreats are probably not that useful or necessary. Unfortunately, most of us don't live in such a culture. Until we do, it's nice to know that there are many varieties of spiritual help available for the asking.

The Least You Need to Know

➤ Retreats and workshops can be valuable and important parts of your spiritual practice.

➤ Make sure that a retreat offers plenty of time for solitude and quiet reflection.

➤ Be careful not to use the excitement and energy of workshops as a substitute for your own day-to-day spiritual efforts.

➤ Once you decide to enroll in a workshop, participate enthusiastically, even if it's difficult at first—overcoming your discomfort is a big part of the reason you're there.

Chapter 22

Back to School: Students, Teachers, and Groups

In This Chapter

➤ Being a student

➤ Learning with a teacher

➤ Finding a teacher

➤ Accelerating the learning process in a group

You've been around for a while, and you've decided that there must be more to life than work, errands, worry, cheap thrills, and exhaustion. So you picked up *The Complete Idiot's Guide to Awakening Your Spirituality* hoping to learn something about how to enrich your life. In the moment you picked it up, it's doubtful you thought of yourself as a student. Yet by purchasing and reading this book, you are manifesting qualities of hope, curiosity, and openness to learning—the key qualities of a good student.

This chapter shows you how to deepen your ability to be a student of life—how to seek out opportunities to learn on your spiritual path. We'll explore the value of teachers, and how to find the type of teacher that you can most benefit from at this stage of your search. We'll also talk about groups and how a group can accelerate your spiritual awakening. Good luck on your homework!

Amazing Grace

When I was 20, after a couple of years of feeling spiritually stuck, I made the difficult decision to spend a year in a Zen Buddhist monastery. Right before moving into the monastery, I went to a talk given by a spiritual teacher in the town that I live in. I was very impressed by what he said, and how he came across. I decided to begin going to his talks and meetings. That was 18 years ago. I found it an interesting coincidence that I met my teacher only after I decided to commit to a monastery. It reminded me of the old adage, "When the student is ready, the teacher will appear."

Why Be a Student?

At the beginning of our lives, we all start out in a "student" position. Everything is new, and we are naturally curious and eager to learn. We don't question our vulnerability and dependence on others; we hunger for the lessons that are stepping stones toward our independence. And as we become more independent, we receive the congratulations of those who have helped us along the way. Eventually, we even start to pat ourselves on the back. Unfortunately, that's where the trouble starts.

From Allah to Zen

"Dependentitis" is the unrealistic fear that dependence on other people for help is always bad. This fear is taught to us as we grow up, and when we're faced with situations where we actually need help from others, it can prevent us from getting the help we need.

At a very young age, one of our first lessons is that to be independent is good. Take the example of a child learning to walk. The parents guide the child, holding her fingertips, until one day she takes a step on her own. Her parents cheer and celebrate this accomplishment by smiling, cooing, repeating the story, and telling the child how proud they are. She gets the message that walking independently is a good thing, and wants to walk on her own as much as possible.

As she gets this message with each lesson—eating, getting dressed, talking—an additional message becomes apparent: Dependence is *not* good. And so starts the disease of *"dependentitis."*

By the time we're adults, we don't want to acknowledge our vulnerability and dependence on others. We live in a me-oriented society, geared toward independence and separation. "More" of "mine" is better, and *my* car, *my* computer, *my* house, *my* job, *my* relationship, and *my* independence are what we spend our time striving for.

When it's time to start down your spiritual path, you find yourself buying a book. You hope the book will give you a few pointers, and you probably think, "Then I'll take it from there." Until you're enlightened, you must be willing to be dependent on those who are wiser than you—if you want to make sure you're consistently headed in the right direction.

The Challenge of Dependence

It's hard to be dependent when life is going well for you and you're successfully independent. Independence feels good and dependence makes you feel vulnerable. Fortunately, just by buying this book you acknowledged that you don't know everything. That means you're way ahead of many other spiritual seekers! In the game of spiritual growth, it's better to be in the don't-know position as much as possible. The way to do that is to always hang out with people (other students or teachers) who are even wiser than you.

Interestingly enough, there are certain situations in which we willingly seek help. When we have a serious illness, we go to a doctor. When the car breaks down, we take it to the mechanic. When we have a problem with an appliance, we call the repair technician. Yet when we feel the deficiencies in our own life, we think we can fix them ourselves. Perhaps the most helpful mantra we could chant at such times is, "I need help, and I can't do it alone, so I'm going to seek help from others now."

After working hard all our lives to become independent, to come full circle and admit that we are dependent upon someone else for our spiritual growth seems less than enlightened. And yet deep down inside we hear a little voice saying, "I'm not changing. Despite my new job, my new relationship, my new house, my new car, and my new book, I still feel the same."

The thought of someone knowing something more than we do about how to live our lives differently is unpalatable. The vulnerable, dependent act of asking someone to lead us on a spiritual journey is unthinkable. We'd rather read a book than try to do something different. And at the same time, we have a longing inside. In our heart, we know that the relationship, the job, the car, the house, and the book will take us only so far.

Heavenly Helpers

Before you can truly learn, you have to be able to admit that you are a student. Admitting that you need help, and are dependent on another for that help, might feel humbling if you're addicted to your independence. Being humble is good. Dependence on others is good. Vulnerability is good. This is more your natural state, which is closer to God.

Being a Student of Life

The good news is that being a *student* of life is easy, since the availability of lessons is unending. Every moment of our lives gives us an opportunity to learn something—if we're looking for the opportunity.

If we're lucky, we begin to see the deficiencies in our independence. We feel dissatisfied with our lives, and start to question some of the lessons we've learned up to now. If we're really lucky, our questioning starts before we've gone through so much crisis that we can't cope.

Unfortunately, we often don't feel our dissatisfaction until we go through a major crisis. With the death of a loved one, an accident, or a natural disaster, we get a glimpse of the possibility that our lives are not in our control as much as we had hoped. When a loved one dies and we find ourselves asking why, we realize that our ability to be in control is definitely limited, if not a facade. We start to question some of our fundamental beliefs, and wonder what the deeper meaning of life is.

It's also at these times that we're more receptive to people who have a deeper perspective on life. We start to realize that, if we pay close enough attention to others, we can learn from them.

Who and Where Are Teachers?

In a sense, teachers are everywhere we look. Once you get good at being a student (and it is a skill that one acquires), you will find this out. A child can teach us how to be honest and direct. An elderly person can teach us about kindness and gratitude. A waiter can teach us about patience. A counter clerk can remind us the value of being friendly. Almost always, however, we have to learn how to look at ourselves before we notice our teachers in the world.

"But that's why I'm reading this book," you might be thinking. "To learn what I need to know to become a more spiritual person." Well, the information you've gotten here should give you a lot of food for thought and a few suggestions that you'll be willing to try. Books are valuable sources of information, inspiration, and perspective, to which one can turn throughout the spiritual journey.

Consider the friend who takes a trip to Paris. When she comes back and tells you about her journey, you don't reply that you've read the book. You know that a book about Paris could never replace the experience of going to Paris. Likewise, in a spiritual search, reading about how to approach God is just a small step in the right direction. Once you're hungry enough for a deeper spiritual life, you realize that the path to God is going to require active exploration in your everyday life.

Cosmic Potholes

One can gain much of value from reading books. In addition to being valuable sources of information, books offer inspiration and perspective. The danger of using a book as a guide on your spiritual journey is that you can *imagine* you are doing well, even if you're not. A book can't tell you where you need help.

Looking for a Teacher

So how does one find that one special *teacher?* How did the apostles find Jesus? How did Carlos Castaneda find Don Juan?

As I mentioned previously, there is an old saying that goes "When the student is ready, the teacher will appear." Often one is introduced to his teacher by someone who knows the teacher. At other times, one finds a teacher through research, or luck or fate brings them together. Each student's path is unique, just as the events leading up to your reading this book differ from those of another reader's life.

With today's computer-based high-speed technology, students can turn to the Internet to find information about spiritual teachers. In addition to sites about spirituality and spiritual teachers, one can attend church and participate in a congregation online. On the Web you can join virtual Bible-study groups, read and write reviews about spiritual books, and enter into chat sessions with other seekers.

From Allah to Zen

Teachers are of two types: intentional and unintentional (those who are not necessarily aware that a student is learning from them). Both types can help others to learn about themselves and the world. Animals and other creatures may also serve as teachers to students who are willing to regard them in that manner.

As with books, the Web can be a good source of inspiration and information. Until you actually pursue help from a teacher in person, however, your prospects for enlightenment are about as good as someone trying to enjoy a meal by watching food commercials on TV.

Recognizing a Teacher

Occasionally, we happen across someone in our everyday life whom we recognize as a teacher. I first experienced this when I was 12 years old. I saw my uncle hypnotize my normally shy, 14-year-old sister Lori into thinking she was Mick Jagger. As she belted out a pretty good rendition of "Satisfaction," a whole new world of satisfaction opened up for me.

At that time, I had been depressed, withdrawn, and suicidal. I had no friends and barely spoke. Until that day, life had seemed predictable and devoid of meaning. I saw through the illusions that many adults had, which made me even more depressed. Growing up in an unhappy, somewhat wealthy family, I knew that having money was not going to be the answer to my woes. When my uncle showed me the latent powers of the mind, I was like a drowning man who'd been thrown a life preserver. At the ripe old age of 12, I began devouring books on psychology, hypnosis, and spirituality. I became a student of consciousness, and my uncle became my first teacher.

Later, when I was 15, I read about chanting a mantra in the lyrics of John Lennon's song "Mind Games." He wrote about chanting a mantra as a way to create love and peace on Earth. If John Lennon said it would work, I was willing to give it a try.

Cosmic Potholes

A teacher at one point in your life may not be the right teacher at a different stage of your life. Also, just because *you* can learn from a particular teacher doesn't mean your friends or even fellow seekers will be able to learn from the same teacher.

I did some research and came across the Transcendental Meditation (TM) movement. I had no idea what to expect from it. If my uncle could turn my sister into Mick Jagger with a few ordinary words, who knew what an Indian guru could turn me into with a magical technique? I got my mantra and began meditating. I loved it. While my teenage friends were getting stoned, I was getting high on meditation.

After about five years of practicing TM, I noticed that things weren't progressing as fast as I had hoped. I began looking for a monastery that might help me move forward more quickly on my path. At about the same time, I came across a poster of a spiritual teacher who said he was going to talk on a way to "become free of the mechanical nature of ordinary life." I attended the lecture and was immediately spellbound by what he said. For 18 years, I have stayed in contact with my teacher, Justin Gold. It's been an amazing experience.

Chances are that you will go through a few spiritual teachers before you find the one who holds the key to your path. Skepticism is good. You may have to get to know a teacher before knowing whether or not what he teaches is of value to you. The first meeting you have with a teacher will probably not give you a complete picture of the teacher or what he or she is presenting.

Questions you might ask yourself when considering a potential teacher include:

➤ Is this teaching theoretical or practical?

➤ Am I drawn to this teaching/teacher despite any skepticism I may have about the teacher/teaching?

➤ Does this teacher present deep, thought-provoking questions I have never considered?

➤ Is this a "feel-good" course, or is this teacher willing to challenge me—even in ways I may not like?

➤ Does this teacher possess a mysterious quality I am attracted to?

➤ How much money, if any, is involved in learning from this teacher?

➤ What is my gut feeling after at least three meetings?

Having a teacher is both exhilarating and scary. In Western society we're not used to thinking that someone else could know a lot more about life, love, and God than we do. It is humbling to really be a student.

Heavenly Helpers

While a pilgrimage to Lourdes or India may be beneficial to one seeker, traveling great distances to find spirituality may not be necessary for another. If you are planning an exotic trip, consider an inventory of unexplored possibilities closer to home. Which of your local churches and temples have you visited? Go with an open heart and reap the rewards!

How Teachers Can Help

My teacher has taught me the importance of a scientific system of learning to see yourself as you are. A concept like this can only be alluded to in a book. Some teachings can only be adequately transmitted directly from teacher to student. Even if it could be conveyed in written form, it would lose the spirit of the teaching, and therefore be of little use. Reading something is an invitation to the mind to think it understands the words. A live teacher who can see your actions will know whether or not you understand a concept. Imagine if Caine in the TV show *Kung Fu* tried to simply take a correspondence course!

Most teachings don't address the fact that we all tend to imagine we are better (or sometimes worse) people than we actually are. Why would anybody want to learn that his oh-so-pure intentions are in reality leading him to hell? Yet this is what we have to learn—to see ourselves as we actually are.

233

Another advantage of many spiritual teachers is that they often have many students who are already following their teachings. Finding like-minded seekers is a great help in following any path. They can help keep you inspired and "in the game" when your own motivation falters. In addition, other seekers can help accelerate your awareness by providing you with more ways to receive honest feedback about yourself.

Spiritual Groups

Often, the way to find a *spiritual group* is to first find a spiritual teacher, and then become part of his or her group. There are many spiritual groups whose teacher lives in another country, is long dead, or is rarely available. In such cases, the dynamics of the specific group are probably equally as important as the particular teachings of the teacher.

So where do you find a good spiritual group? As with finding a teacher, you can ask friends, look on the Internet, or check out your local newspapers. In any city, there is usually at least one "alternative" paper that lists spiritual groups and activities. You can also look through various spiritual magazines that have advertisements for workshops, courses, and retreats offered by various groups and teachers. Two of my favorites are *New Age Journal* and *Yoga Journal*. The best way to know if a group or a teacher is a good "fit" is to simply go to the group and see what it's like.

Just as when looking for a certain type of car, you notice them everywhere you go, if you have enough interest in finding a group, they start to show up for you.

Chances are that any known spiritual teacher you come across will have other students. When students help each other, the results can be incredible. Watching a fellow student on his path is inspiring to one's own path. Learning from each other's risks and mistakes can greatly accelerate the individual learning process. If one is astute enough, one can learn from another's lesson and not have to make the same mistakes to learn the same lesson. In this way, the learning can be exponential.

There will always be lessons that you will have to learn without the benefit of someone else's mistake. We are all human, and you need not journey far before you come across or create a situation that you can learn from.

But pooling spiritual resources in a group is like being part of a mountain-climbing team. There's always someone in front checking out the situation to help you know where to take your next step. And you play your part by helping those below you on the rope. And so together you climb.

From Allah to Zen

A **spiritual group** consists of students and teachers who share the common goal of wanting to know God, love, or peace within. They acknowledge their interdependence and work together in their quest for higher possibilities.

After I met my teacher, I spent at least 10 hours a week with him for the next seven years. With about 15 other of his students, we all lived together, traveled together, and worked on becoming true students of life and consciousness. With a system of techniques he gradually taught us, we learned to study how we really were, rather than how we liked to think of ourselves.

With the help of my teacher and the other students, I began to see I was more selfish, more robotlike, and less peaceful than I had ever imagined myself to be. Yet, as a well-known verse says in the Bible, "The truth will set you free." Through the process of becoming more aware of how I really was, I began to change.

After some time on my own, I'm once again studying with my teacher. People often ask me, "Why do you need a teacher when you've been doing spiritual work for so long?" While working on myself, I've learned that the human ego is almost infinitely deceptive. Because the ways of true spiritual growth are often subtle, I've found that having a teacher has helped me avoid many major potholes on the path of spiritual awakening. I can learn at an accelerated pace by receiving help from my teacher and fellow group members to remember my spiritual goals. We have an agreement to call attention to the times when we stray from our goals, as well as to the times when we make progress toward our goals.

Cosmic Potholes

One of our biggest obstacles to learning from others is our arrogance in thinking that we already know. This comes from our age-old "dependentitis" disease. As you're reading this right now, your arrogance might be telling you that you are not arrogant. To learn, you must overcome the ways arrogance can keep you protected from learning from others.

Recently, my teacher has given me the task of beginning to teach others. In my position as teacher, I've been equally humbled. While my goal is to be a pure servant who can help guide my students forward, I often see that I fall short of what I'm being called to do. I may give feedback to a student from a place of impatience or superiority, which shows me how far I am from being a pure and humble servant of a higher power. But I've learned that it takes enduring these small failures before I'll see any true success. I've learned that whenever I take on more than I can handle, grace and growth inevitably result.

The Least You Need to Know

➤ Recognizing your dependence on others is the first step to becoming a true student of life.

➤ Without a teacher, it's probable that you'll imagine your progress toward enlightenment to be more than it is.

➤ Finding a wise spiritual teacher can take time and effort. Choose carefully, and know what you're looking for.

➤ As part of a group of like-minded seekers, your learning will increase exponentially.

Chapter 23

Enjoying Sacred Space

> ### In This Chapter
>
> ➤ Creating sacred space to connect with Spirit
>
> ➤ Assembling altars and meditation spaces
>
> ➤ Recognizing sacred space outdoors
>
> ➤ Energy lines and power centers
>
> ➤ The pilgrimage—a vacation for your soul

Since prehistoric times, humans have created sacred spaces, responding to a deep longing to connect with Spirit. This longing has inspired the construction of everything from small personal altars to rural chapels, from sacred stone circles to soaring cathedrals. All are holy to those who feel the need to reach out to God. All are able to help remind and stimulate our desire to more deeply know the sacred.

Altars

The earliest known *altar* is a limestone structure excavated in the Middle Eastern country of Palestine, at the ancient Canaanite town of Megido. It dates from about 2000 B.C.E.

In the Christian traditions, altars are focal sites for rituals such as communion, praying, and singing together. Roman Catholic altars contain relics of the saints for whom the churches are named. Offerings of flowers, incense, and food are common at Buddhist and Hindu shrines. In Japan, Shinto devotees offer symbols such as prayer papers and small works of art meaningful to the deity being petitioned.

Your Own Sacred Space

Assembling an altar in your home can be a soul-affirming way to honor your connection to Spirit. Place a slab of wood or stone on the floor or a tabletop. A quiet area where you can sit before it in peace and comfort is ideal.

Your altar can include items that have personal meaning to you, perhaps a piece of artwork that speaks to your spirit, a religious image, or objects collected from nature. Many people include the elements of earth, fire, and water. Native American traditions hold that Spirit communicates with us through all creation; each pebble, acorn, shell, or feather expresses the sacred wholeness, and its power moves in a resonant current between object and human spirit. Soothing sounds from wind chimes or a fountain can enhance the stillness within you, as can soft music. Lighting a scented candle or incense is another way to honor the time you set aside for spiritual contemplation.

From Allah to Zen

An **altar** is a structure that provides a focal point for religious practices such as petitionary prayer, meditation, penance, dedications, offerings, and purification.

Heavenly Helpers

You can let nature itself enhance your meditation. I find it peaceful to sit before my own small altar at the beginning or end of the day when the natural light is low and changing.

You may want to renew your altar display from time to time. You could change it with the seasons, or to acknowledge significant events in your life, or simply to attend to your evolving sense of Spirit.

Sometimes it's difficult to include an altar in your workplace. But a special object or two, perhaps a single perfect flower, can bring your spirit into a room and provide an occasional respite from business demands.

When I labored in a hectic office environment, I posted a photograph of a favorite place in a redwood forest that I particularly loved. In addition, somewhere I had picked up a lifelike figure of a little frog that sat companionably on my computer. When I looked at that silly little frog, I could hear in my heart the singing of his live counterparts in the creek near my home.

A friend of mine is fortunate enough to have a unique meditation room in her home. The room is a cozy, quiet grotto lined with warmly colored native rock gathered on the property where her house was built. Numerous niches in the stones hold candles, which provide the room's only light. The room is simply furnished, with a soft rug and large cushions.

My friend shares the room generously, and it is a wonderful place to honor Spirit. However, it is not necessary to have a luxurious room set aside for meditation. Another friend meditates in her small walk-in closet with the door shut, earplugs firmly in place, after the children have gone to sleep. The Spirit honored is the same in both instances.

Community Altars

A special energy comes about when people assemble to meditate together. Sacred spaces created by social groups reflect the worldviews of their creators. The Pueblo Indians' *kivas* acknowledge the Earth as the source of sustenance for the Pueblos' agricultural society. Likewise, the sweat lodges of the Chumash Indians, longtime natives of the California coast, were places for ceremonies of spiritual cleansing and renewal.

Japanese Shinto shrines blend with the natural environment to subtly enhance each element of the whole and express reverence for the harmony of nature. These holy places are believed to be the actual dwelling places of the gods. In the town where I live, worship places as diverse as the Vedanta Temple and the Christian Science church provide space for meditation. The Episcopal church provides a labyrinth to walk.

From Allah to Zen

A Pueblo **kiva** is a circular underground chamber that is entered through a hatchway in the roof. Kivas are used for council, ritual, and meditation.

Tuning in to Sacred Space Outdoors

Earth contains myriad places of superb natural beauty that resonate with our spirits and require little or nothing to bring spiritual focus to bear on them. Spending time in the company of a tree or a large boulder is a wonderful way to access your own inner peacefulness. The sight of my favorite sycamore tree lightens my heart when I pass her on my way home. She stands between a creek and a narrow road. She has great character, limbs curving wildly about like those of a ballerina. When looking at nature, let your imagination play freely.

Places where land and water meet hold an elemental appeal for most of us. The sight and sound of water lapping at a shoreline or roaring over a waterfall can free our spirits.

Experiencing nature at night can also greatly heighten our senses. A desert walk in the bright moonlight is an otherworldly experience that can create an intense awareness of the inner Spirit. The darkness, the open terrain, and the vast sweep of the desert sky can help your soul soar.

I have a slightly eccentric friend who loves to bundle up and sit in the nighttime woods in winter—when the great horned owls are courting. Listening to their low, melodic hoots, she loses bodily awareness and becomes completely absorbed in the music and the darkness. I used to make fun of her "odd" behavior. Yet after seeing how much joy she gathered from the experience, I realized it was me—watching TV inside—who was the odd one.

It can be fun to arrange an outdoor altar or meditation space in your garden. A flat place created by a slab of stone or wood, or an arrangement of several surfaces, can support favorite evocative items. A fountain is more manageable outdoors, as are wind chimes and bells. Plants, insects, and birds can be newly appreciated. Usually, the space can be larger than is possible inside a house.

An offering of water and birdseed near a statue of St. Francis will attract birds. They will hide momentarily when you arrive, but sit very patiently for 10 minutes or so, and you will be rewarded with the sound of small wings fluttering nearby. Bright eyes will look you over—be still—and then the boldest bird will make a dash for the birdseed. The birds will become accustomed to you and will learn to watch for your arrival with the refreshments. There is something sweet about winning a modicum of trust from a wild creature, a bit of connection with the wild spirit of earth.

If you include a statue in your meditation space, remember the need to evoke peacefulness. An offering of flowers nestled in the lap of a Buddha or a bunny is a sweet and fragrant tribute. A tiger or bird of prey? Not so relaxing!

Amazing Grace

In her poetic book *A Sense of Wonder*, naturalist Rachel Carson wrote of taking her nephew Roger to the seaside on a stormy autumn night: "Together we laughed for pure joy—he a baby meeting for the first time the wild tumult of Oceanus, I with the salt of half a lifetime of sea love in me. But I think we felt the same spine-tingling response to the vast, roaring ocean and the wild night around us."

Spiritual Monuments

Ancient design principles are being used today in the creation of outdoor spaces for meditation and spiritual practices. Labyrinths symbolize our own path of spiritual seeking, leading to a central point of revelation and inner peace. Megalithic-looking monuments are created with very large stones, and can take the form of stone figures, lines, circles, pyramids, or cairns (a heap of stones).

Medicine wheels are stone circles containing lines that radiate outward from a marked center. In the Native American tradition, they are often aligned with astronomical events such as solstices. Stonehenge, an elaborate stone circle, is an example of a megalithic monument. The form of a circle symbolizes wholeness and cyclic processes, and naturally imbues a space with spiritual significance.

While traveling in Sedona, Arizona, I came across many medicine wheels. My first thought was "What a bunch of New Age crap." However, I was open-minded enough to enter into the configuration of stones and dirt, and quietly sit on the ground. To my surprise, it seemed to dramatically alter my consciousness. I was so "high" that I couldn't even feel my body, much less move it. After what seemed like a very long time (hours?), I struggled to leave the wheel. According to my watch (which has been known to lie just to play tricks on me), only 14 minutes had passed.

I now have a new respect for such ancient artifacts as medicine wheels and other spiritual structures.

Cosmic Potholes

Ancient monuments and power spots (see the following section) should never be altered! To protect yourself and the place, do not remove anything except trash. There are those who believe that stone fragments and other "souvenirs" can carry negative energy that can attach to you. Crystals or other objects should not be hidden or buried. To preserve the sanctity of the place and show respect for the original builders, do not disturb the site in any way.

Ley Lines and Power Spots

Ancient beliefs hold that the Earth is covered with ley lines created by cosmic forces originating outside the Earth. Ley lines create a web of meridians and intersections that guide Earth's energy flow.

The Chinese art of feng shui and the European understanding of ley lines both deal with these elemental forces. According to ancient beliefs, ley lines penetrate and leave the Earth vertically, at nodes. The penetrating nodes are called power centers, and are known for their spiritual energy. Knowledge of ley lines was used prehistorically to place temples, megalithic monuments, and other important structures.

Alfred Watkins

The study of ley lines was revived in 1921 when a miller named Alfred Watkins was out walking in Hertfordshire, England. He noticed that the

Amazing Grace

Black Elk, a Native American elder, once said, "The first peace, which is the most important, is that which comes within the souls of people when they realize their relationship, their oneness, with the universe and all its powers, and when they realize at the center of the universe dwells the Great Spirit, and that this center is really everywhere, it is within each one of us."

countryside seemed to be covered with a network of straight lines linking prehistoric sites. By consulting a map, Mr. Watkins found that the sites were systematically aligned.

The most powerful spots tended to be located at high points; so also did castles. (And in modern times, so do microwave antennas.) Clusters of Scotch pine grew along ley lines, and roads and tracks appeared to follow them. The "Straight Track Club," which Watkins started, continued until 1948. Watkins first observed the obvious prehistoric points of standing stones and tumuli (mounds). Then he found that medieval churches and castles were often located on the alignments.

Dowsing and Mapping

In the seventh century, Pope Gregory had directed the conversion of the country's pagan temples into churches. Thus, a number of Roman Catholic churches were inadvertently located in places formerly chosen by mystical methods! Like underground water, the underground energy of ley lines can be located by *dowsing*.

Using map dowsing, Eileen Roche and Gordon Millington of the Surrey Earth Mysteries Group found the E-line. The E-line is thought to be the widest and most powerful ley line known. It runs through England, Nepal, New Zealand, Australia, and South America.

Seattle, Washington, is the first city in America to have had its ley lines mapped. The Seattle Ley Line Project's creators and supporters believe that when power centers are enhanced by praying, meditating, and otherwise honoring them, they can have a positive, perceptible influence on people and give energy back to the Earth.

From Allah to Zen

Dowsing is a technique for using the body's energy currents to perceive the energy of underground water and ley lines. Although controversial, practitioners say it can be done on site, or on a map by experienced dowsers.

Energy Vortexes

The special Earth energy and the scenic beauty around Sedona, Arizona, has always attracted shamans, visionaries, artists, and spiritual sages. The place is so attractive to spiritually oriented people that a large New Age community has developed there. It has even been called a spiritual Disneyland!

In Sedona, the power spots are known as energy vortexes. A vortex is a swirling center of subtle energy emanating from the surface of the earth and carrying a magnetic charge. It leaves a slight measurable residual magnetism where it is strongest.

The energy of the vortexes is said, by the spiritual seekers who study them, to resonate with the energy centers present in the human body. Some of the vortexes carry a positive magnetic charge, and some a negative charge. These charges are held to enhance masculine or feminine personality characteristics. Other vortexes carry both positive and negative charges, and can have a balancing effect on the personality. Juniper trees are native to Sedona, and they respond visibly to the vortex energy by growing in a spiral pattern that is sometimes even strong enough to bend the branches.

There are four main energy vortexes in Sedona. *The Airport Vortex* bears a positive charge, and twisted Junipers grow where the energy is strongest. *The Cathedral Rock Vortex,* at the Red Rock Crossing, is said to strengthen the feminine aspect with its negative charge. Its strongest energy is where the creek is closest to Cathedral Rock. *The Boynton Canyon Vortex* emanates from a 30-foot knoll above the canyon. Very twisted Junipers grow along the trail around the knoll. Its combination of positive and negative energy is believed to strengthen the masculine/feminine balance. *The Bell Rock Vortex* is near the village of Oak Creek. It is covered with twisted Juniper trees, and is especially powerful with its combination of positive, negative, and balanced forces.

Having spent time at all of these vortexes, I can attest to their power. My personal favorite was the Boynton Canyon Vortex, which is spread out over a wide area. While hiking in this canyon, I felt very high. It was an amazing experience to feel that the earth was "massaging" me into an altered state of consciousness.

Heavenly Helpers

Sedona has an abundance of vortex enthusiasts and guides. Excellent information about vortex tours, hiking trails, and other activities is available from the Sedona Chamber of Commerce, at many of the local shops, and on the Internet.

Pilgrimages: Travel with a Special Purpose

For centuries, people have been drawn to worship in places where spiritual energy is concentrated. Multitudes of pilgrims travel to sacred places all over the world, to connect with Spirit and to be healed in body and mind. Just the act of starting a pilgrimage can help to transform one's sparks of spiritual hope into a raging fire.

The Pilgrimage in History

Pilgrimages have played a part in the religions of ancient Persia, Egypt, India, China, and Japan. The Greeks and Romans consulted the oracles of Delphi, and the early Hebrews traveled to Shiloh and Dan (Israel) and Bethel (Jordan). Every Muslim who is physically fit and can afford it is required to make the traditional pilgrimage to

Mecca. The sacred cities of Kairouan in Tunisia, Ourzzane in Morocco, Karbalá in Iraq, and Mashhad in Iran are also important Muslim pilgrimage destinations.

In India, so rich in Spirit, Varanasi is the holiest of all cities to Hindus. Buddhists travel to Bodhagaya, India, where the Buddha attained enlightenment. Christians, Muslims, and Jews all visit Israel, where tourists are the only people who can travel freely in the divided city of Jerusalem. Shrines to the Virgin Mary are found all over the world. Miraculous healings have occurred at the tomb of Saint Olaf, in Norway. In Italy, Assisi, home of Saint Francis, is open to pilgrims though the area is still recovering from the disastrous recent earthquakes.

In the Middle Ages, the pilgrimage industry was almost as well developed as package tourism is today. Shelter, food, drink, souvenirs, entertainment of all kinds, as well as protection, were provided along early pilgrimage routes.

From Allah to Zen

A **pilgrimage** is a journey to a holy place made with spiritual intent.

Today we have the Internet. A host of Web sites provide the traveler with information about travel to holy sites, from individual walking tours to glamorously packaged group tours. Recently, I took an amazingly detailed virtual tour of the Holy Land in Jerusalem while working at my computer. It wasn't as good as the real thing, but it wasn't bad considering I never left my sofa.

It is rather jarring to see the juxtaposition of the ancient pilgrimage tradition with the Internet, the newest of the new. But it is good to know that the sights and sounds of faraway places can be accessed by those unable to travel.

A Few of My Favorite Pilgrimage Destinations

Here are a few of my favorite pilgrimage destinations.

El Santuario de Chimayo

El Santuario de Chimayo, in the Sangre de Cristo Mountains of New Mexico, is sometimes called the "Lourdes of America." This shrine is dedicated to El Señor (Our Lord) de Esquipulas.

Around 1810, a Chimayo Indian priest was performing penance and saw a light shining from a hillside. He dug into the hill and found a crucifix. The crucifix was taken to the church in Santa Cruz, but miraculously it reappeared in its original burial place. Twice more the crucifix was taken to the church, and twice more it returned to its hole. So it was agreed that El Señor wanted to stay in Chimayo. Miraculous healings occurred in the little chapel built there, and it was soon replaced by the much larger Chimayo Shrine. The shrine's powers are centered behind the main altar, in El Posito, the sand pit where the crucifix was found.

Assisi

The town of Assisi in Umbria, Italy, is the home of Saint Francis and his friend, Saint Clare. Saint Francis was a charismatic visionary whose spirit energy continues to inspire pilgrims. As a young man, Francis renounced his wealthy family and spent the rest of his life in joyous poverty.

Amazing Grace

In 1219, Saint Francis went to Israel to end the war between the Muslims and the Christians. He told the sultan about the Gospel, and offered to walk into a fire with a Muslim to show whose faith was stronger. No Muslim volunteered, so Francis offered to walk through the fire alone. The sultan was deeply impressed. He agreed to the armistice proposed by Francis. Then the Christian leaders turned down the proposal! But because of Francis's effort, the Franciscans were given permanent custody of the Christian shrines then in Muslim hands.

Santiago de Compostela

One of the world's oldest Christian pilgrimages leads to Santiago de Compostela, the tomb of Saint James, in Spain. The cathedral believed to contain the relics of Saint James was the destination of Chaucer's Wife of Bath. It was visited by John of Gaunt, Saint Francis of Assisi, Louis IV of France, and King James III of Scotland. Trails to Santiago de Compostela begin in France, Portugal, Ireland, Switzerland, and Germany, and merge in Spain at Puente la Reina, near Pamplona.

Heavenly Helpers

Santiago de Compostela is a good choice for less affluent pilgrims who have good, strong legs. Along the way, villagers traditionally offer food and drink to travelers, and very inexpensive lodging is easily found at monasteries and hotels.

The route to Santiago de Compostela is 500 miles from the Spanish border. *Peregrinas* (pilgrims) still walk about 20 miles per day. To obtain a certificate of completion of the pilgrimage, peregrinas must prove that they have traveled at least 60 miles on foot or horseback, or 120 miles by bicycle. Long ago, when France and other countries offered felons a choice of prison or pilgrimage, the paths abounded with opportunists selling forged certificates of completion of the pilgrimage.

Jerusalem

The old city of Jerusalem is a favorite pilgrimage site for millions of people. I spent a couple of weeks there and was overwhelmed with all there was to see. For more than 3,000 years, people have fought over this small portion of land. After visiting the Dome of the Rock (now a Muslim temple), I realized why so many battles have taken place over this 100-yard piece of land. The area is thought to be a power spot of unparalleled intensity. During a visit to the Dome of the Rock, I was so inundated by its spiritual vibration that I could barely move!

India

For those with an Eastern connection to spirituality, a pilgrimage to India can be an amazing experience. More so than almost any culture, India is a complicated mix of religion, ritual, third world poverty, and total chaos. The lack of control and efficiency that one experiences while traveling in India can become part of the pilgrimage experience. I remember traveling on an Indian train with a child I didn't know and two chickens on my lap, thinking that I was getting a crash course in the art of surrender. Visiting the many ashrams, gurus, and holy temples can keep any spiritual adept occupied for many weeks.

Whether creating an altar, looking for a power spot, or beginning a pilgrimage, one's intent and level of sincerity are key to enjoying sacred space. Since they all can be used to reawaken one's spiritual passion, it's helpful to keep in mind the different levels of effort required and factor them into the time you have available. In my own case, I take a "pilgrimage" to a beautiful nearby park about once a week, to my altar once each day, and to a power spot or special city about once a year. As you get into the habit of creating sacred space for yourself, you'll find that your soul will feel well nourished.

The Least You Need to Know

➤ You can create a sacred space of your own, to answer your need to connect with Spirit.

➤ Nature provides ready-made sacred places; all we need to do is relax and tune in to them.

➤ Ancient monuments and structures located all over the world can help us see our connection to eternity.

➤ Modern spiritual seekers are relearning ancient traditions about cosmic forces that may unite us all.

➤ Holy places of traditional pilgrimage still inspire us, and are easier to visit than ever before.

Chapter 24

Going Beyond the Body

In This Chapter

➤ Death as our greatest teacher

➤ How to study death before we die

➤ The healing powers of illness

➤ Softening around the pain

There is much to learn from sickness, pain, and death. They are possibly our greatest teachers. We do everything we can to avoid them but, in the end, many of us will have learned our most profound lessons from them.

We may attempt to grow spiritually when we feel like it, or when our friends and fellow seekers instigate it. We do it as it pleases us. We meditate or go to the lecture of a famous guru—if we can fit it into our schedules. Then along comes the spiritual storm: an accident, a malignancy, an incurable virus. Suddenly we appreciate life for how short it is, and how lucky we are to have the chance to live it. We see the green of the leaves and the blue of the sky in a new way.

Death: The Cosmic Shake-Up of Old Routines

The process of dying is a spiritual storm that affects not only the one who is dying, but his or her family and friends as well. Death is final and unrelenting. It cannot be bought or coddled. But as it sweeps through our lives, it has the potential of leaving a positive spiritual mark that stays with us.

I knew a man who was stricken with intestinal cancer. He was 70 years old and led several spiritual groups. He meditated daily and was deeply respected by his students. Although he meditated daily, beneath his calm veneer, he was often restless. However, in the nine months before his death, he transformed. He became more peaceful and wise. He walked by the ocean almost every day that he was able. He moved increasingly slowly. Yet he smiled more. He openly admired the water, the people, the dogs, the trees. One day, about a month before he died, he turned to me and said, "I wouldn't give up this cancer experience if I had it to do over. I have learned so much from this." This is a man who experienced death as a final stage of growth.

Heavenly Helpers

Pretend you have only one month to live. Whom would you say good-bye to? Whom would you thank? Whom would you forgive or ask forgiveness of? What would you like to do? Do you have your papers in order? Dying is inevitable and does not schedule itself according to your timetable. The best time to do these things is now.

The Miracle of Life

To remember the inevitability of death is to be more aware of the miracle of life. Death reminds us of what is important. The famous shaman Carlos Castanada writes about death and the spiritual warrior in his book *The Journey to Ixtlàn.*

> A warrior must focus his attention on the link between himself and his death. Without remorse or sadness or worrying, he must focus his attention on the fact that he does not have time and let his acts flow accordingly. He must let each of his acts have their rightful power. Otherwise, they will be, for as long as he lives, the acts of a fool.

Castanada continually reminds us that death hovers over our shoulder, available as the final advisor in every decision.

Any act may be your last on Earth. Today, after you read this chapter, you may be hit by a car. Someone will be. Are you ready?

Death as a Part of Life

There are cultures in which death is considered an active part of life. Tibetan Buddhists, for example, see life as a training ground for death. (Life is, by the way, a short blip in the continuum of the soul.) The famous Buddhist book *The Tibetan Book of the Dead* contains explicit directions on how to successfully negotiate what happens directly after physical death. It also explains that there are realms you'll pass through in which your goal is to remain peaceful so that you can attain a higher outcome, which is to stop the cycle of reincarnation from body to body and move to the next level of the soul's evolution.

The Tibetans, like some other cultures, believe that we die as we live. The spiritual attainment and service that we did during this life on earth *do* matter. They create the state that we die from. That state is the keynote of what comes next.

It's interesting to compare this view of death to the way that we in the West contend with it. In the West, death is often something that happens in the sterilized atmosphere of a hospital. Bodies are quickly carried away in a bag afterward. If someone isn't instantly cremated and handed back to us in an urn, he's injected with chemicals, glamorized with makeup, and dressed in his best Sunday suit. Old folks often end up in nursing homes waiting to die. Discussions of death are minimal and are seen as depressing. The West is a death-denying society that deifies youth and physical beauty.

Some cultures, like the Native American peoples, look to their elders for advice and wisdom hard won by their years on Earth. The older population lives in the home as an integral part of the family unit. In contrast, we do everything we can to pretend that death is never going to happen. What is sadder than a formerly glamorous actress getting her third face-lift? Is it any wonder that we can't graduate to a peace with the inevitable last phase of our lives?

"When I look back on the time my father was ill," wrote a friend, "I see that I missed the opportunity to really *be* with him." She continued:

> I was so busy trying to save him with pills and machines and different doctors. I didn't want to seem to him like I was giving up the fight, so we rarely talked about how the whole thing was for him. At the end he was so weak, and I finally had to let go. I told him then. I hope he knew. And since he died, now three years ago, I have never been the same. The day-to-day things that used to seem important seem silly to me now. We are all going to go the way he did. I decided to work less, spend more time with my kids, and in nature. I began a regular meditation practice and to study a spiritual path. I think my father worked too much and I don't think he got to enjoy things enough. I miss him so much and his absence is a daily reminder that we have only a short time here.

My friend got a wake-up call from her father's death. She saw the shortcomings of the way we deal with death in this culture. More important, she took some steps to change her own life. Certain behaviors and habits had predetermined her day-to-day life. The life-changing event of losing her father gave her a new way to view her days here, which we must remember are finite, for all of us.

Studying Death While Alive

Elisabeth Kübler-Ross was a medical doctor credited with being the first to study the stages of dying. She labeled five stages:

➤ Denial

➤ Anger

➤ Bargaining

➤ Depression

➤ Acceptance

Not all dying patients make it to the stage of acceptance. In fact, the mind, which is constantly changing, may loop from stage to stage. However, the stages do give us a framework for seeing the possibilities of spiritual growth for the dying person. Of course, the family and friends of a dying person also go through these stages, for they, too, are involved in the letting-go process.

These five stages can even apply in the ordinary circumstances of daily life. Recently, I was waiting in a theater for a movie to begin. It was half an hour late. A theater employee came out and announced that we could get our money back because the projector was broken. My first reaction was "Oh no, this can't really be. They must be able to fix it" (denial). Then I became irate with the theater management for not having an extra projector on hand or being too dumb to fix it (anger). Then I thought I would give them a half-hour to figure it out (bargaining). Next I felt the disappointment of not seeing the movie I had been looking forward to seeing (depression). And last, I thought about what I could do at home and other ways I could make use of the evening after I got my refund (acceptance). You may notice the same progression in yourself when things don't go as you expected.

From Allah to Zen

Hospice is an international group dedicated to the care of the terminally ill. Rather than try to "fix" patients, hospice workers are trained to make them comfortable and to be there for them in a heartfelt way. Hospice care is provided in the home of the patient, a nursing home, or at special hospice houses, not in hospitals.

The Hospice Example

As well as the stages Kübler-Ross designated for the dying process, she is also responsible for improving the quality of *hospice* care and bringing increased awareness to the dying process.

Because we are such a death-denying society, we have lost the ability to communicate in a deep way with the dying patient. When Kübler-Ross studied the situation of the terminally ill, she found that they craved honesty and the chance to express themselves. Hospital-room talk was often superficial and nervous. She found that visitors usually talked to each other about unimportant matters—as the dying person lay there, quiet.

In hospice, the workers are taught to be *with* the patient. The qualities of a good hospice worker include an ability to listen, to be caring, to be open, and to be willing not to try to change things. Surrounded by people with these attributes, the dying person has the possibility to make peace with his death and, it is hoped, to experience spiritual growth.

The dying person is not the only one who benefits. By learning to be vulnerable and open with people in this way, hospice workers improve the quality of their own day-to-day lives. Maybe we should all aspire to be hospice workers and take on those attributes with the living, as well as with the dying.

"Little Deaths"

So what is it with this fear of death that makes it so hard even to talk about? If I think, "I won't exist," I become afraid. If I think about how much I won't get to see, or whom I will miss, I become afraid. If I stop my thoughts, and am present in the moment, however, I am not afraid. So am I my thoughts or am I something more?

We all experience many "little deaths" in our lives. For example, recently a special friend visited me from across the country. She stayed a few weeks and then flew home. I don't know when I'll see her again. As we said good-bye, I felt sad. The part of me that had grown close to her was about to "die," since I wouldn't be seeing her for a long time. I thought, "Oh, I'm going to really miss her."

The thought created a sense of loss. It wasn't good or bad; I just noticed it as a miniature version of dying. I also noticed that I could either get lost in my thoughts, or I could stay in the present moment. Shortly thereafter, another good friend of mine called, and we began a great conversation. As I was able to let go of my friend who had flown home, I could appreciate the other friend who was on the phone with me. In life and in death, as one door closes, another opens.

Many spiritual traditions have used the analogy that we are like drops of water in a vast ocean. To remain "the drop" is a lot of work, requiring a tremendous effort of thought. To relax into the ocean-ness fosters an experience of being connected to God. Maybe this idea is why most spiritual paths emphasize the importance of meditation. Meditation helps us slow down our thoughts and communicate with the ocean we are part of. In this way, meditation can be a great way to practice the art of dying.

Losing Control

The pain of sickness, accidents, or dying is a way to experience spiritual growth.

Daniel Santos is a healer who has studied extensively with Chinese and Native American shamans. He writes that our individual spirit longs to contact the ocean of energy all around us. It presents people or episodes to guide us:

> If we fail to respond, then the spirit uses its medium-range missiles. These are more like emotional upsets, problems at work; basically situations that require a little more attention. If the gentle reminders and medium-range missiles fail to get our attention, then the heavy artillery is called in. Sickness, disease, accidents. These will really grab our attention and disorient us from our limited approaches to life.

While I don't know if God works this way, attributing some meaning and purpose to difficult times can often be helpful.

A nutritionist friend of mine was flattened, recently, by a string of health problems. The illnesses ranged from respiratory to digestive problems, none of which she had experienced before. This string of problems happened consecutively over a period of months. At first she pulled out her arsenal of supplements, herbs, and homeopathics. She saw her acupuncturist and chiropractor. She added naps, tried various exercises, visualizations, and juice fasting. All the things that had helped her before and had helped her clients didn't work this time. "I remember standing in front of my supplements," she said, "and I realized I knew nothing. I had been so cocky, so falsely confident, like anything I could do could actually control anything else."

Eventually my friend got well. She said she gave up and began reading books and being okay with staring out the window. She finally accepted help from her friends, instead of always being the one to help. In the past few years she hadn't had time to read books or really take time off.

Her illnesses taught her a certain humility that she could not have learned within the lifestyle she had been living. They ended up being her spiritual friend, scraping away, like a Brillo pad, a layer of her self-importance. Without the backpack of arrogance she used to carry around, she is one step closer to the Creator.

Cosmic Potholes

Have you ever heard this joke? "How can you make God laugh? Tell him your plans." Listen to your tone of self-importance or self-assurance when it comes to health issues. Remember that none of us are self-employed. We all answer to a vaster energy than we sometimes care to admit. When we forget that, we set ourselves up for a fall.

This example brings up the question of whether doctors really help us when they fix our pain. Some teachers see pain as positive, illness as a crossroads. A person at these crossroads can make new choices in his life or go back to the ones that made him sick. To make new choices takes courage. Speaking of one female patient, healer Daniel Santos told me "She has nothing to guide her except for a slender connection with the spirit inside. All I can do as a healer is lend her the strength to continue on, to help her to turn around and face the void."

This crossroads, to someone who wishes to choose a spiritual route, is critical. It's easy to go back to the people and situations that contributed to our imbalance because that is what we know. Someone with an alcohol or drug problem, for example, will be tempted to go back to the nightlife or friends who encourage that behavior. To change, a person must die to who he was—to be reborn as who he wants to be. In this way, spiritual growth is really the art of dying (to your old self) while you're still in a human body.

Amazing Grace

I once knew a spiritual teacher named Ken Keyes. He was known for writing a wonderful book called *The Handbook to Higher Consciousness*. Most people didn't know he was quadriplegic. I once saw an assistant spill food on him just before he was going to do a TV interview. While everyone got upset around him, Ken just laughed. Finally, he said "I really feel sorry for you folks with hands. You always have the illusion of control, while I long ago let go of that illusion." It helped me see how a person could joyously let go of control, and even appreciate it for its spiritual value.

Our society is not geared for the spiritual life. To choose a life following the call of Spirit sometimes requires drastic changes, and drastic changes usually come with great pain.

Your pain can be a tragedy, a motivator, or a blessing—depending upon how you respond to it.

We Are Not Our Pain

Most of us have great dedication to eradicating our pain. We have so many painkillers that we can barely fit them all into one cabinet. We have M.D.s, chiropractors, acupuncturists, and body workers, all to eliminate our pain. And the more we identify with our pain, the more we feel the victim of it. Likewise, the more we identify with our body as who we are, the more pain we feel.

Rather than trying to eliminate the pain, it can be helpful to accept it and learn to *soften* around it. In his book *Who Dies?*, Stephen Levine says, "We have seen that much of what is called pain is actually resistance, a mental tightening reflected and experienced in the body."

Levine has worked intensively with people who are dying, and who are sometimes in great pain. Those who have been able to experience themselves as more than their physical body have been the most successful at living with pain.

Heavenly Helpers

"Softening around the pain" means, according to Levine, experiencing the pain fully and openly. By describing the sensations, one can see how much resistance has played a part in maintaining it. As one sees the fear and relaxes, the fist of tension around the pain can begin to relax and dissolve. With the letting go of resistance, the moment-to-moment experience of pain is softened.

Levine has found that, through the exploration of pain, grace can come. The greater the pain, the deeper people seem to explore their lives. Not only do they find fear and resistance to the difficulty in life at the core of their pain, but they see analogies to other aspects of their lives. "Many who have worked with these exercises have said that it wasn't just the pain in their body that they hadn't understood," says Levine, "it was also the fear, the boredom, the restlessness, the self-doubt, the anger which they had always pulled back from, which they had never allowed themselves to enter into."

By entering into these feelings, via the doorway of pain and sensation, people uncover deeper states of mind. After a while, this journey leads to the freedom of experiencing these states as clouds that come and go, instead of as personal property to be held on to. By learning, admittedly the hard way, that we are vulnerable and that control is suffering, we can let go and experience a more connected and expanded state of being.

The Least You Need to Know

➤ Death can be the most profound spiritual teacher.

➤ To remember our death, in the midst of life, is to have a wise advisor.

➤ We can study the letting go process of dying, in little ways, via the frequent opportunities to let go that life brings our way.

➤ Illness can be the voice of a new beginning, if we listen to it.

➤ By courageously exploring our pain, we can go through a doorway to expanded consciousness.

Part 7

Spiritual Inspiration

We are born as fiery, fully expressive infants. Yet, the years take a toll on our soul. By the time most of us are adults, it's easy to succumb to the cynicism, greed, and apathy that surrounds us. In this part, I discuss ways to rise above such tendencies and keep one's hopes and dreams alive.

Fortunately, there is more inspiration accessible than ever before. Books, movies, music, and the advice of experts are all within easy reach. In addition, ways to use sexual energy, supplements, and ancient techniques for feeling closer to Spirit are also readily available. In this part, I discuss some of the easiest and best ways to become spiritually inspired. Once inspired, the job we have is to journey, one step at a time, toward being a humble servant of the source that keeps us alive.

Chapter 25

Inspiring Movies and Books

> ### In This Chapter
>
> ➤ The impact movies and books can have on your life
>
> ➤ Thirty movies with a spiritual message
>
> ➤ Thirty books to feed your soul

When I was eight or nine years old, I picked up a book lying on the table at my dentist's office. It was a story about a little boy who was in the hospital with cancer and was near the end of his life. The book had pictures that showed the boy's parents and his doctor standing next to his bed.

The boy had just been told that he was going to die. He responded by saying that he was afraid he was too small for God to notice him and take him to heaven. His mother told him that if he raised his hand in the air, God would see him and take him up to heaven. The little boy said that he was too weak to raise his hand, so the doctor propped the boy's forearm up with pillows. At the end of the story there was a picture of the little boy with rays of light shining down on his head.

Although I read this story many years ago, it has stayed with me. I've often thought that, through my daily spiritual practices and efforts, I am trying to lift my arms up to heaven, just like that little boy, hoping that the forces of grace will notice me.

Certain scenes from books and movies have had enormous impact on me and my spiritual search. Books and movies can expose you to ideas, inspiration, and lessons you might not normally receive. They can strike a chord within your heart that allows you to feel a depth in life that can inspire you for a long time.

This chapter lists 30 movies with short descriptions. Rather than describe the plot of each, I suggest the spiritual themes to look for. I also list 30 inspiring books. What we get out of a movie or book is largely based on the quality of our attention. As you watch or read the selections that follow, try to do so based on the questions and theme I include for each. Have fun!

Inspiring Movies

I've noticed that when I go to a video store, I am often in the mood for a certain type of movie. Some nights it's a comedy, other times it's a drama. While some of the movies that follow don't fit neatly into any category, I've done my best to divide them up into three categories. In this way, you will be better able to choose a movie that fits your mood and desire.

Movies to Tickle Your Funny Bone

Being There with Peter Sellers. 130 minutes.

A funny and refreshingly simple movie guaranteed to slow you down. A great movie to see with others so you can share your thoughts afterward. In American culture, we do, then we do some more in a never-ending effort to control the outcome of our lives. What about dropping all the "doings" to get there and start "being there." Watch this movie and really try to become absorbed in the character of Chance the gardener. Next, try approaching your life as if you were Chance for a few hours and see how your life feels different—or, if you are one of the lucky ones, how it feels the same.

Cosmic Potholes

In watching these movies you will have both positive *and* negative reactions to the content. As an experiment, don't let small things you may not like about the movie get in the way of its message. It's easy to discount a movie for minor mistakes—and miss the treasure it offers. Don't let this happen to you.

Big with Tom Hanks. 102 minutes.

One of the characteristics of enlightened people is that they are playful. You know—light! Lighten up and watch a boy in a man's body experience life. Your assignment is to stretch yourself and be more playful than you normally would be—at least three times after watching this movie. Do this in moments where it's safe and there are no consequences to anyone. An example would be asking someone to dance where you might normally hold back.

Bronco Billy with Clint Eastwood. 119 minutes.

Have you ever thought "I think I'll quit my job and join the circus," or something similar? Well here's what happens if you do. This movie shows that if a person takes on bigger responsibilities, he is given the help he needs to fulfill them. I love that thought! Why don't we try to follow our dream? After seeing *Bronco Billy*, sit down in a quiet place where you won't be disturbed for 30 minutes and write down *your* dream. Good luck!

Dave with Kevin Kline. 100 minutes.

"If it's Tuesday, everybody works!" This is a line from Dave, the main character in this wonderful film. *Dave* is a great portrayal of a person who knows how to serve other people. Dave doesn't serve food, but compassion, humor, and perspective. Watch this with friends if possible, and afterward talk about all the ways Dave served the people in his life. Then have each person you watched the movie with tell how he feels he serves the people in his life. It should lead to an insightful discussion!

The Final Countdown with Kirk Douglas. 104 minutes.

Watch this movie for the incredible technology that Western society has developed. What would our society look like with an "inner" technology of the same magnitude? Is it possible that this inner technology exists and is available to those people ready to receive it? If so, how would you go about finding someone who is privy to this technology? If not, what obstacles keep you from finding a person who has discovered this incredible inner technology?

Forrest Gump with Tom Hanks. 142 minutes.

I think the line went something like this: "I may be stupid, but at least I know what love is." When I heard this line I asked myself, "Do I know what love is?" Is love simply taking care of something or somebody? Think of what God takes care of. Look and see what Forrest takes care of and then look to see what *you've* taken care of. Make a list of those things you have loved and then make a list of the things about you that prevent you from loving or taking care of others.

Groundhog Day with Bill Murray. 103 minutes.

The last day of Bill Murray's waking up to the sound of Sonny and Cher is a day I would like to be able to live every day of my life. Receiving the ability to live life that way is quite a process, as you will discover. Have a great viewing and remember the adage, "Every day is a new beginning."

Oh, God! with John Denver. 104 minutes.

I loved the humility in this movie! One of the biggest faults of a person who has a glimmer that there is more to life than fame, financial clout, and fast living is that he develops a different form of separation. He feels better than those who don't have a sense of deeper possibilities in human existence. As you watch this film, as an experiment, take what God says as if he is talking to you. Do you feel confronted or receptive?

Cosmic Potholes

When people eat, talk, or take breaks during a movie, it lessens its impact. I've included the running length of all the movies here so you can set aside time to watch with no interruptions (bathroom breaks okay). You can do it!

Heavenly Helpers

To get the most possible out of each movie you see, imagine that it was written specifically to teach you an important lesson. Your purpose is to figure out what your lesson is.

From Allah to Zen

Clues are signposts directing your way to Spirit. For instance, if you do something and it leads to a feeling of contribution or peace, that is a clue that it is likely good for your soul.

Shirley Valentine with Pauline Collins. 160 minutes.

We would all agree that there are ruts (patterns that keep repeating themselves) in our lives. Shirley Valentine can be our teacher on how to get out of our ruts. As you watch this movie, look to see what emotions lead Shirley to change in her life. What personal strengths do you possess that will free you from your ruts? If you don't feel you have the personal strength to pull yourself from your rut, what people do you know who do have that kind of strength? If you don't know such people, where would you look to find them?

7 Faces of Dr. Lao with Tony Randall. 100 minutes.

What would it take to bring magic into all the different activities in your life—your love life, your work life, your spiritual life, your play life? See how one man lives his life with a touch of magic and how that life enriches the lives of all who know him. After watching this movie, sit down, relax, and write down all of the activities in your life where magic exists, and also where it doesn't.

They Might Be Giants with George C. Scott. 88 minutes.

What are the *clues* that a person needs to follow to lead him down the path of heart? How do we know where to look for them? What do we do with a clue once we find one? This movie is about a man who is an expert at finding clues. Watch what he and his assistant do as they explore and experiment. Notice where Holmes advances indirectly toward his goal. After seeing this movie, think of each of the situations in which Holmes proceeded indirectly and ask yourself "What was the payoff for his doing that?"

Spiritual "Drama" Movies

Lost Horizon with Ronald Colman. 132 minutes.

Before watching this film, promise yourself not to get hung up on the dated sets and acting styles. Instead look more at the adventurous spirits of the people in the film. Look at how these people do things in moderation. After the movie, think about the activities you engage in and ask yourself "Do I do things in moderation?" Examples of activities to evaluate might be eating, sleeping, working, getting angry or upset, being happy or content, saying what you think, and so on.

The Man Who Would Be King with Sean Connery. 129 minutes.

What would it be like to follow your greatest dream? Here is a story of two men who take the chance of attaining their highest aspiration. Look for what personal attributes it takes for a person to follow his dream. Also look for what personal weaknesses hindered his progression toward his goals.

Meetings with Remarkable Men with Dragan Maksimovic. 102 minutes.

This film shows how a Russian mystic, G. I. Gurdjieff, grew into a major spiritual leader of the twentieth century. Gurdjieff had a hunger from a young age to reach the highest of human spiritual attainment. The movie is set in Turkey and Afghanistan and depicts situations that you have probably not seen before on the screen. After viewing, sit down and think of the people who have contributed to your spiritual life and then send each of them your loving thoughts.

Heavenly Helpers

To increase the impact a movie has on your life, try thinking about it during the days after you initially watch it. You can even try to imitate being one of the characters that inspired you in the movie. By play-acting a character, you can get a sense of how new behaviors might benefit your life.

The Razor's Edge (1946) with Tyrone Power. 146 minutes.
The Razor's Edge (1984) with Bill Murray. 128 minutes.

These two films provide one of the best depictions available of a person's search for his purpose in life. One miracle of these two films is that they show a Westerner contacting a guru and eventually becoming his student. Watch with friends and discuss the obstacles you have, if any, to searching out a spiritual teacher and becoming her or his student. Then discuss what a person would actually need to do to find his guru.

The Seventh Sign with Demi Moore. 94 minutes.

In this movie, Demi Moore's character is asked to make a rather big sacrifice. On the spiritual path, we are all asked to make little sacrifices. For example, let's say someone does something and you become hurt, and you react with anger. A "sacrifice" would be to make yourself vulnerable and say "I feel hurt!" A sacrifice is anything different from the way you would normally handle your negative reactions. The day after you watch this movie, take a small step back from a normal reaction you would have; make a little sacrifice of your pride. Write down how you feel about it.

2001: A Space Odyssey with Keir Dullea. 139 minutes.

Here is a movie that is a life experience! Let your problems melt away as you open up to the big picture of human evolution and transformation. Ponder what you think might be the next evolutionary leap of humanity, and what it might look like. Will we be a different race 100 years from now? How about 1,000 years? As in the movie, it may happen more quickly than we expect!

The Valley Obscured by Clouds with Bulle Ogier. 114 minutes.

If you've seen the movie *EdTV* in which a cameraman follows a man around filming his daily life, then you'll have the flavor of this movie about a group of friends searching for paradise. Watch with adult friends before allowing young folks to see this movie, since the camera doesn't stop at the bedroom door. After viewing the film, discuss the reasons friends are so important on the spiritual path. Who are *your* spiritual allies?

The Year of Living Dangerously with Mel Gibson. 115 minutes.

Living on the edge, grasping for every morsel the feast of life can offer. Not taking no for an answer—pushing, pushing, pushing until you get some piece of the whole for which you search. Mel Gibson shines in one of his earlier movies as an inspired newspaper reporter sent on location into a troubled foreign government. Mel meets a fellow reporter, Billy Kwan, who turns out to be a "teacher" for him. Hint: Pay close attention to Billy's words. After the movie, discuss what she said and relate it to your own life.

Movies of Hope and Joy

Brother Sun Sister Moon with Graham Faulkner. 121 minutes.

This movie is a depiction of the life of Saint Francis of Assisi. It begins with Francis as a teenager going off to fight in the Christian Crusades. It follows his life through to his acceptance by the pope to begin his own order of monks, which are known today as the Franciscan Order. This film is beautifully done, with superb acting and directing that really gives one the idea of a simpler life. As Saint Francis states to the pope, "The birds live free—why can't we?" You'll enjoy this true tale of inspiration.

City of Joy with Patrick Swayze. 134 minutes.

Self-pity is a negative emotion that relies on self-importance, or the thought "I deserve," to survive. The more self-importance one suffers from, the bigger the possibility of self-pity in one's life. This movie shows a land of people where self-importance is rare. After viewing this film, think about the following question: "Where in my life do I feel I deserve a lot, and how does that cause me unnecessary suffering?"

Dersu Uzala with Maxim Munzuk. 140 minutes.

Nature is one thing that doesn't require anything from you. You don't have to plug it in, buy tickets to go see it, feed it, wash it, rent or buy it; you don't even have to believe in it. We can relax in nature because it's beyond our control. Since you can't beat it, there's a tendency to just *be* with it—and that's relaxing. Sit back and absorb the nature in this film. Afterward, think about how you felt the last time you spent time in nature. Perhaps this movie will inspire you to spend time in nature in the near future.

The Inn of the Sixth Happiness with Ingrid Bergman. 158 minutes.

This is a wonderful and exciting depiction of a woman whose service to humanity really happened. She put herself on the line because she cared deeply for the people she served. Notice what inspires you about the main character. Notice how she is able to transform all the people she meets, despite her many obstacles. Ask yourself "What are the obstacles I have to living my dreams? How might I overcome them?"

Julia with Vanessa Redgrave. 118 minutes.

Try to feel the spirit of Julia as she lives her life. Could you feel that deeply about your spiritual life? Notice how Julia is willing to give up her personal plans to serve others in their time of need. Could you do that? If not, what stops you?

A Man for All Seasons with Paul Scofield. 120 minutes.

This movie gives me a picture of a hero I would want to emulate. There is a certain "wholeness of character" about Thomas Moore that I use as a model of how I want to be someday. After watching this film, sit down and think of a person or persons who fit your idea of a complete human being. Who are your heroes?

The Milagro Beanfield War with Rubén Blades. 117 minutes.

How do the actions of one person affect many? In this movie you see how one man's gesture changes the history of a whole village. After viewing this film, write down the effects key decisions you've made have had on the lives of others. For this exercise write down only the positive decisions and their positive effects. Then, for 24 hours after you write your list, look at how the small decisions you make every day affect others. Remember—keep it light!

The Nun's Story with Audrey Hepburn. 152 minutes.

This is a true story about a woman's process of discovering her true self. After viewing this movie with friends, discuss some of the major events of her life and what she learned from each. In addition, discuss the scene in which Sister Luke describes a spiritual life beyond the boundaries of the Catholic faith.

Heavenly Helpers

Watching a spiritual movie with someone who is open to spirituality is helpful because afterward you can discuss the nuances of the film.

Resurrection with Ellen Burstyn. 103 minutes.

This is a powerful movie that depicts many spiritual lessons. Ellen Burstyn's character receives the power to heal, and people have many different reactions to her power. Have you ever been around someone with special powers? What was your reaction? How do you think you'd handle such power? Notice how she passes on the gift she's been graced with. Discuss with friends whether or not you feel you pass on the gifts you've been given.

Reading Your Way to Spirit

Going to read a book? There are many ways to do it. You can skim, you can go slowly, you can read for entertainment, or you can read to savor each and every word and lesson.

Here are some suggestions to help you get more from your reading:

➤ Read fewer pages at a sitting. The speed at which you read the lines matters. Read slowly and assimilate the words.

➤ Where and when you read matters. Read only when you have no place else to go. You should read at a time when you're able to fully open to the wisdom a book has to offer.

➤ Highlight or underline words that strike a chord in you. Later, reread what you highlighted.

➤ Don't read the suggested books that follow for mere entertainment. There are plenty of books that are suitable for entertainment. If you're not in the right state of mind to read something profound, choose lighter fare.

If you use these suggestions, I'm confident that what you read can affect you deeply. Books can be a precious help on the spiritual path. If you give them the attention and respect they deserve, they will provide you with much inspiration.

Amazing Grace

About four years ago I was given a 1,200-page book to read by a spiritual teacher. I came back two weeks later with a feeling of accomplishment and told him that I was ready for my next book. He did not congratulate me as I expected. In fact, he said that it took him six months to read the same book and that I read it too fast to appreciate the subtleties. He had me read it again, but at a much slower rate. The second time I read it, it was as if I were reading a completely different book.

The following books contain essential ideas to feed your spirit. Review the four suggestions above before reading each book. Take your time with each—this isn't a contest to see how fast you can read. You'll get more from reading a single book slowly and deeply than you will by reading all the books quickly.

➤ *The Razor's Edge,* by Somerset Maugham

➤ *The Chronicles of Narnia,* by C. S. Lewis

➤ *The Essential Rumi,* translated by Coleman Barks

➤ *The Magus,* by John Fowles

➤ *Steppenwolf,* by Herman Hesse

➤ *Demian,* by Herman Hesse

➤ *Siddartha,* by Herman Hesse

➤ *Narcissus and Goldmund,* by Herman Hesse

➤ *The Experience of God,* by Jonathan Robinson

➤ *Dreams,* by Olive Schreiner

➤ *The Way of the Peaceful Warrior,* by Dan Millman

➤ *In Search of the Miraculous,* by P. D. Ouspensky

➤ *Meetings with Remarkable Men,* by G. I. Gurdjieff

➤ *The Screwtape Letters,* by C. S. Lewis

➤ *Story Like the Wind,* by Laurens Van Der Post

➤ *Far Away Place,* by Laurens Van Der Post

➤ *The Last Unicorn,* by Peter Beagle

➤ *Mount Analogue,* by Rene Daumal

➤ *The Aquarian Gospel of Jesus the Christ,* by Levi H. Dowling

➤ *Journey to the East,* by Herman Hesse

➤ *Childhood's End,* by Arthur Clarke

➤ *Be Here Now,* by Ram Dass

➤ *In Watermelon Sugar,* by Richard Brautigan

➤ *Another Heart in His Hand,* by J. Jaye Gold

➤ *Lost Horizon,* by James Hilton

➤ *A Nun's Story,* by Katherine Hulme

➤ *Undiscovered Country,* by Katherine Hulme

➤ *The Starseed Transmissions,* by Ken Carey

➤ *Witness,* by John Bennett

➤ *A Separate Reality,* by Carlos Castaneda

Cosmic Potholes

Try not to read a book in the midst of a lot of activity. Ringing phones, screaming kids, or beepers can take you away from really getting into a book.

By learning to open up and fully receive from inspirational books and movies, you can increase the amount of wisdom you're exposed to in a simple and easy way. Technology has its drawbacks, but it also has its benefits. Make sure you take advantage of the ease with which inspiring books and movies are now available.

The Least You Need to Know

➤ Books and movies can influence and inspire us for many years.

➤ It's a good idea to watch movies with friends so you can discuss them afterward.

➤ Try to bring the essence of inspiring books and movies into your daily life.

➤ It's better to read spiritual books slowly, savoring their contents as much as possible.

Chapter 26

The Creative Spirit

In This Chapter

➤ Creativity as a way to explore your spirituality

➤ Using your creative talents to open yourself to the magic of life

➤ Using creativity to promote healing

➤ Exploring your shadow to enhance your creativity

"… Art must realize that its task is to carry the spiritual-divine life into the earthly; to fashion the latter in such a way that its forms, colors, words, tones, act as a revelation of the world beyond."

—Rudolf Steiner

The words flowed across the paper like a raging river racing to the ocean. It was as if the forces of creation manifested through my hands. With my fingers flying across the keys, I elucidated ideas so beautiful that at times I felt swept away in inspiration. I watched in awe as the creative spirit blessed me with divine words. The inner resources seemed infinite as I ventured forward, welcoming the challenge with all the presence I could bring forth.

My aim was to express the relationship between creativity and spirituality. At times, my mind drew a blank, stopped by the fear of the calling. Yet I soon broke through the self-imposed wall, and the words that follow represent what Spirit created through me.

When it comes to exploring the relationship between *creativity* and spirituality, words can seem inadequate, yet also rich with potential. A writer could soar into the sublime with his or her descriptive writings, or crash into the bargain basement section of hurried expression. In this chapter, I will discuss the insights I've gained from my own creative explorations as a writer and musician, and from my work using creativity with others as a counselor, teacher, and workshop leader.

The Magic of Creativity

When we create, we express our highest nature. Whether we create a song, a painting, or a moment of intimacy with our mate, we often feel as though we have been blessed by the experience. In the process, we leave the ordinary world of habit and mechanical behavior, and go boldly into the unknown.

This journey into the formless can be quite invigorating. The unknown is like a wellspring waiting to burst forth. When we experience its power, we can sense its link to a source much greater than our normal sense of self. When in the flow of creation, we feel as though grace surrounds us and nurtures our expression.

From Allan to Zen

Creativity can be simply defined as the act of making something using one's imagination. Creativity can be explored through gardening, parenting, painting, photography, writing, songwriting, pottery, sewing, filmmaking, furniture painting, remodeling, jewelry making, lovemaking, storytelling, work projects, and presentations. Through creativity, we manifest part of our being into artistic form.

Have you ever created something and then felt bad? Probably not. The experience of expressing oneself through writing, painting, songs, presentations, and other enlivening adventures is almost always uplifting. It's as if each creation sprinkles the designer with the stardust of wonder and the sunshine of joy. The Creator created us so that we could become cocreators. In the process, we accelerate an internal process that brings us closer to the light.

The Artistic Calling

Not long ago I made a major creative leap. In the mid-1990s I had a strong calling to write a musical. This urge seemed like guidance from a force greater than myself. I thought, "I can't do this. Besides, it'll never sell." Yet several months after my fearful retreat, I found myself in a music class learning to write music.

I practiced for many hours, and took lessons. Several years later I felt comfortable enough to write some songs down on paper. In summer 1999, it became clear to me that to get my life back on track, it was imperative that I write this musical.

Today I have an entire play written with 25 songs. Just the other day, when I played the songs to myself, I got goose bumps. I stopped to savor the joy of realizing what had been created through me. The whole process felt incredibly alive and divinely guided. I don't expect to sell the musical; the writing of it was its own reward.

The Product vs. the Process

In this culture, we tend to value the final product rather than the process that created it. Looking back over the process of creating a musical, I realize that the journey of creation is what has truly blessed my life.

Art is an opportunity to boldly explore life. Creation is the natural province of the divine. Looking at works of art helps us to realize that creative genius belongs to no individual, but rather to each of us through the divine source from which everything comes.

When I paint a picture, there is a flow and energy that works through me. Sometimes the results are clearly divine, and other times clearly pedestrian. When creating something, our job is to get our ego out of the way and let Spirit do its thing. Of course, sometimes that's easier said than done.

Creativity offers each of us endless possibilities of expression. The way we interact with others can be rich with creative expression. We can give and care for those around us with a flourish of creative ideas. Imagine being a loving partner and parent, using your creative urges to do the best job you can. Wouldn't that be fun? How many creative ways can you find to express your love? After all, isn't expressing love the most divine of activities?

Heavenly Helpers

Places to stimulate your creativity include nature, museums, classes, workshops, and the inexhaustible resource of your mind, emotions, and intuition. Tools recommended to have on hand: a journal for writing, art paper and paints or pastels, colored pencils, musical instruments, scissors, glue, poster board, good music, and anything else that can stimulate your creativity.

Heavenly Helpers

An aid in getting your ego out of the way when trying to create something is to begin the creative process by trying to do something badly. Paint, sing, or write as bad as you can. Have fun with it. This can help to loosen you up and allow your true talents to shine forth without such fear of doing a poor job.

Opening to Creation

What creative urges have you had lately? When was the last time you allowed yourself to follow those urges? What stops you from pursuing them?

Amazing Grace

Recently I spoke to a kindergarten class. I asked them, "How many of you know how to sing?" All hands went up. I asked, "How many of you know how to paint?" Once again, all hands went up. Later that day, I spoke to a high school class. I asked them the same two questions. Interestingly, only two or three hands were raised. I surmised that creativity is a process we can "unlearn" by going to school and listening to our inner critic. Of course, since we are born creative, we can always learn to overcome our blocks to being creative.

I have learned that the biggest roadblock to creativity is myself. I have seen myself and others sabotage the creative process by holding onto ridiculous expectations and judgments. I call these blocks to creative expression my "inner critic."

The Inner Critic

The inner critic tells each of us that what we've created is not good enough. The inner critic speaks to us in many voices—voices that mimic one's parents, former teachers, and well-meaning friends.

We can all learn to overcome the thoughts that stop us from creating. As you do, you open up more fully to the joy of manifesting whatever your imagination conjures. When I write, I often feel like a fully charged battery. Sometimes I feel like the Energizer Bunny, sitting at my keyboard, unable to go to bed.

Here are several ideas to help quiet your inner critic:

➤ Acknowledge the inner critic when it speaks to you. Acknowledging it will help you to release it.

➤ See all your creative work as positive. Some of it will move you and some of it won't, but it's all positive.

➤ Watch out for the part of you that wants to look good at all times and expects perfection.

➤ Learn to love what you create. All of it is you and you are worth loving.

Liberating Ourselves

Chasing the inner critic out of the driver's seat is liberating. When you let yourself create for the pure pleasure of creating, you will find yourself exploring wonderful artistic territories.

The great Creator has given us a palette of colors and a yearning for expression, two tools we can play with. It's our job to stay open to exploring as fully as we can all the possibilities on the palette before us. Keeping artistically alive means pushing the critic aside; being present; opening ourselves to guidance; being willing to explore; and freeing ourselves from debilitating expectations and perfectionism.

Cosmic Potholes

Sometimes there are people in our life who seem to enjoy telling us what they think we're doing wrong. They even like to criticize our creative adventures. These people often are frustrated with their own lack of creativity. Don't let them get in the way of your fun. When sharing your creative work with others, choose supportive people.

Creating Our Lives

It helps to look at our lives as a creation. When we see that we can create our experiences of life through our choices, we feel empowered. We come to understand that there is a guidance within us that goes far beyond our personality. When we listen to this guidance, it leads us down a path of fulfillment. When we ignore this guidance, we create suffering for ourselves.

This source of inner guidance seeks aliveness. It encourages us to take risks, to be open to change, to go boldly into life. As the noted mythologist and philosopher Joseph Campbell stated, "We must follow our bliss." Life lived this way truly is a creation.

As children, we knew creating was where it was at. We didn't need to set time aside to create. We created our lives moment by moment. Most of our days were spent having fun and exploring life.

Creating was natural then. As adults, creating often gets placed on the back shelf. It becomes a to-do project. Instead of creativity being who we are, it becomes a part of us we put aside. We tell ourselves we must get serious about life in order to make a living, raise a family, and realize all the other goals we were taught were so important. We can lose our zest for life and passion when we move toward the rational and away from the creative.

Inviting Creativity into Your Life

What is calling you to read this chapter? How could you use what you're reading to open yourself to a different type of spiritual experience?

Here are some ideas to experiment with, to invite the spirit of creativity back into your life:

➤ Write a poem about the beauty around you.

➤ Place a blank canvas in front of you, sit quietly until moved to action, and then paint a picture. Allow what comes out to be an expression of something deep within you.

➤ Write a story about a spiritual experience you have had.

➤ Draw an abstract picture of God as an energy force.

➤ Dance as if you were expressing your gratitude for living.

➤ Invent other ways to have fun and be yourself creatively.

How would your life change if you saw it as a nonstop creative project? Each day you have an opportunity to express yourself in new and fun ways. What would you do differently if you sought to be fully yourself in the moment? Would you more frequently speak your truth, express your feelings, follow your curiosity, play, dance, sing?

Heavenly Helpers

There are a number of wonderful books you might want to explore to inspire your creativity. Authors I recommend include Julia Cameron, Betty Edwards, Natalie Goldberg, Mickey Hart, Don Campbell, Natalie Rogers, and Sark.

Creativity brings us more fully into the moment. When we are truly involved in creating, all our attention is focused on the task at hand. Usually our minds are busily off in other directions, planning for later or reviewing the past. When engaged in the creative process, we're totally involved in what we're doing. One could say we are just being.

The partnership between myself and my tools of expression is an alliance that can create magic. When playing my guitar, I invite the words of a song to invent themselves. As my brush spreads color, images begin to form and I get to witness the miracle of something being created. The potential for the partnership between me and the creative spirit is present in each moment of life. To know that, to sense that, makes the creative process more than just an occasional project, but instead a way of linking up with Spirit in daily life.

Seeing the creativity of others can be an inspiration. When we watch a great performance on the screen, in concert, or even on the basketball court, we might think "How blessed they are to create so beautifully!" When we read a well-crafted novel, or gaze at an inspiring piece of art, we long for the realization of our own God-given talent. We admire the courage of the individual, and are in awe of the spell cast on those who are put under the magic of their mastery. The creativity of others can be a reminder to each of us of the ultimate Creator of everything.

Overcoming Resistance

There is often initial resistance to entering this higher state of being. To pursue your creative impulses, you must be willing to push past your initial resistance in order to enter the promised land of higher expression.

Writing, like all creative processes, is rich and rewarding when you feel "in the flow." You can begin to feel the energy of inspiration and the unity of all things. However, when you don't feel in the flow, it can be quite a chore. In my own writing, I have come to realize that sometimes I'm "hot" and sometimes I'm not.

When people ask me how I manage to write two books a year, I give them my secret for being creative: Each day I sit in front of my keyboard for at least five minutes. I push past my initial resistance to sitting down at the keyboard. If I'm not in the flow, after five minutes I give up. If I'm in the flow, I keep writing until I'm too tired to write any more. Having a lot of "at bats" in front of the keyboard has helped me to hit home runs more often.

Heavenly Helpers

A great way to stimulate your creativity is journal writing. Writing daily is a wonderful practice that stimulates ideas and provides inspiration. Begin by turning off the inner critic; ignore the impulse to censor and forget about punctuation. Write freely and discover the vast landscape inside of you. Setting a goal of writing for a number of pages or minutes each day is helpful.

Art and Healing

In my role as a therapist, I've seen many clients create images that provided them with insight into a healing that needed to take place.

A student in a counselor training program I taught was asked to come up with an image that represented where she was in her life. She painted a scene with a big black block right in the middle of everything. When we explored this scene later, she discovered the source of her constant anxiety. The black block represented a past of traumatic experiences. With this discovery, she was able to see herself in a different way. This block of anxiety had been in her way for many years, yet she had not seen it until she drew it on paper. As we explored this block, a richer life began to unfold for her.

Extraordinary Forces

Creative work can tap into extraordinary forces. Through singing an uplifting song we can be transported into realms conducive to healing. Painting an image for recovery can set us on a journey to insight and wholeness. Writing about unexpressed emotions can liberate us from constriction and depression. Dancing can release us and open us up to being more alive and expressive. Each of these modes of creative expression can help us overcome obstacles that prevent us from deeper union with Spirit.

Can you imagine a song that could uplift your spirits when you're down? How about a dance that could chase the demons of self-doubt away? How about a story that could give you courage when you're afraid? What about an image of healing for an inner discontent? Through the process of trial and error, you can discover things that can get you out of creative funks, and into creative fun.

Amazing Grace

On the wall in my room is a painting by a five-year-old girl I once knew. It depicts a child going down a slide, with the big yellow sun shining and her mother and dog at the bottom of the slide. Everyone in the painting has big smiles, including the sun. When I first saw the painting, it brought tears to my eyes. It exudes innocence, optimism, and joy. Whenever I feel creatively blocked, I look at that picture and try to tune into the mind and heart of the girl who created it. It usually works.

Sometimes we discover the healing power of art during times of endings, change, or transition. Images created and expressed through words, drawings, and movement can bring us nearer to understanding and acceptance. In difficult times, the source can be called upon to guide us, through creative expression, toward healing and letting go.

Many of the greatest creations of history have manifested when people were being called to deal with their greatest challenges. The dark night of the soul has pushed many artists to paint and write their way through personal crises. In studying the lives of creative geniuses, one sees that struggle and suffering often precede a great artistic birth.

The Shadow Side

The most powerful pieces of art have often come from the shadow side, the normally unexpressed parts of ourselves. These parts can be our rage, our fears, our repressed memories, or any other aspect of ourselves we might be ashamed of. In our expression of our shadow side, it's as though we are reclaiming parts of ourselves we have pushed away. If we are to be whole, these parts must be integrated into our awareness. Through our artistic creations, this process can happen at an accelerated rate.

Participation as an observer, listener, or reader is also important in healing and spiritual fulfillment. Think of how many times we have been moved by a particular painting, the melody or words of a song, or writing that is full of life. Such creations leave us basking in the light of insight and grace. We can be left with lasting impressions so profound that even the artist could never grasp the impact. Each creative expression, no matter how small or imperfect, has the potential to touch a soul.

Each of us has been significantly influenced by the creations of others. The blessings of human creation fill our lives. When we truly feel the grace of the creations around us, we have to conclude there is a great creative force. This Creator has filled our lives with the tools necessary to become creators ourselves.

In the process of manifesting what's inside us, we move closer to the heart of creation. We move closer to the depths of human suffering and joy. We move closer to our creative, playful, spiritual essence.

The Least You Need to Know

➤ Through creativity, we can discover powerful images for healing.

➤ When we write, paint, sing, dance, or engage in any other creative endeavor, we open ourselves to a greater sense of Spirit.

➤ The least we can receive from artful expression is increased energy, fun, and the satisfaction of going for more in life.

➤ Keeping a playful, accepting attitude when creating silences our inner critic and frees us up to experience more joy in our life.

Chapter 27

Sex, Drugs, and Rock 'n' Roll

In This Chapter

➤ Using material pleasures to transcend the ego

➤ The ideas and methods of sacred sexuality or Tantra

➤ The historical use and abuse of drugs to achieve higher states of awareness

➤ Using singing, drumming, and dancing to experience ecstasy

Any teenager can tell you that sex, drugs, and rock 'n' roll are pretty cool. Each can elicit powerful experiences, which is partly why they're so popular. What most people don't know is that each of them can also be the doorway to intense spiritual experiences—if used properly.

Any powerful technique, technology, or experience has the potential to enhance one's spirituality, or detract from it. For example, in Chapter 17, "The Alchemy of Money," I talked about how having money can be used to magnify a person's inner aspirations, or distract him from looking within. It all depends on what a person's intention is, and how he uses it. When it comes to sex, drugs, and music, it's possible to use these modalities to commune with the sacred, or commune with the sinister.

In Chapter 3, "Diving into Now," I talked about how outer presence, or losing yourself in an activity, is one form of spiritual experience. In a way, sex, drugs, and music are the average person's way of having a temporarily higher or spiritual experience. Only if cultivated can such powerful experiences be of any lasting value. By discussing how these avenues can be used to elicit profound states of awareness, I hope you'll explore them in a way that leads to much joy and inspiration.

Amazing Grace

I once attended a spiritual growth workshop with a famous teacher. More than 400 people were in attendance. This teacher asked everyone to say one sentence about what started him on the spiritual path. While there were many answers, the most common was that they had taken some drug (usually psychedelics), and as a result become convinced there was more to spirituality than they had thought. The next most common answer was that they had been through a profound experience, usually triggered by sex, music, or being near death. They hoped spirituality might help them have such experiences more often.

Tantra: The Spirituality of Ecstasy

In India, from the eighth to twelfth centuries, a movement arose called Tantric Buddhism that was championed by the common people. At the time, the monasteries were rather elitist organizations, and people wanted a religious system that was more accessible and inclusive. They wanted to be able to perform their own spiritual practices—without having to be celibate or live in a monastery.

From Allah to Zen

The word **Tantra** derives from the Sanskrit root word *tan*, which loosely translated means "to extend, expand, weave, or manifest." Tantra is a spiritual approach that emphasizes the use of the senses and sexual energy to aid in one's spiritual evolution.

The Tantrics believed that spirituality could be developed within the context of daily life. They viewed having a family, making love, and doing business as grist for the mill of personal awakening. They even thought that desire, passion, and ecstasy should be embraced as part of the inner journey, rather than avoided.

In general, *Tantra* is an approach to life that accepts experience fully, making no division between what is "spiritual" and what is "profane." Tantrics try to make no moral judgments. Rather, they view each situation as an opportunity to learn something and become more aware. They believe that avoiding sense pleasures, such as sex, leads to repression and a lessening of connection to the life force. Tantrics feel that true mastery of one's body comes from being able to control such powerful energies, and not become a slave to them.

In Tantric practices, one goes beyond ordinary pleasure. The goal is to find the source of all pleasure, one's innermost being, which is considered to be pure bliss. It is a discipline that uses the senses to go beyond the senses. Unfortunately, when dealing with states of ecstasy, it's very easy to become addicted or attached to such experiences. To overcome this tendency, Tantrics are encouraged to meditate on "emptiness," and to go beyond the grasping ego to a pure, unattached present-time awareness. Of course, this is not easy to do without a lot of practice and training.

In many religions, the ecstasy induced by sex, drugs, music, and dance was considered a distraction to the discipline needed for more "acceptable" approaches to God. Tantric Buddhism helped put forth the idea that we have a natural, ecstatic essence worth exploring. According to Tantrics, even one's shadow side is worth exploring. By meditating on and allowing the expression of negative emotions, Tantrics believe that such feelings can be better integrated into one's awareness, rather than denied and repressed.

Cosmic Potholes

When using the senses to go beyond the senses, the tendency is to forget the discipline part of the practice and just enjoy the ecstasy. This usually leads to a nice experience, but no real internal mastery. To truly go beyond one's attachment to pleasure, much instruction, meditation, and practice is normally required.

Sacred Sexuality

In 1988, while in a meditative state, I became inspired to learn about Tantric sexuality. After reading many books and taking several workshops, I wrote a video, titled *Intimacy and Sexual Ecstasy*. Once this video became a best-seller, I started to lead Tantra workshops. In these workshops, I learned the difference between what Tantra really was, and what Westerners were willing to actually do as a practice.

Originally, Tantric sex was a spiritual discipline in which one's partner was used as a vehicle to become closer to God. It consisted of elaborate rituals, the repetition of certain mantras, and various meditative methods that culminated in an energetic ecstasy. Since most Westerners are not inclined to perform the elaborate rituals of ancient Tantric practices, over the years a more modern approach to sacred sexuality has developed. Nowadays, Tantra is usually taught as a combination of breathing and meditation methods, energy control, and various pleasure- and relationship-enhancing practices. While Tantra originated in India, many of the best methods associated with modern-day Tantra actually came from ancient China—as part of the Taoist system of spirituality.

Heavenly Helpers

Tantra can be learned from books, workshops, or videos. The Web site www.tantra.com offers many resources. Many of the most powerful Tantra methods are best practiced on one's own, without a partner—at least at first. Once you have some skill with these techniques, then you can use them more effectively while making love with your partner.

To give you a sense of how one might use sexual energy to elicit more intimacy or even a transcendental experience, I'll give you a couple of simple Tantric techniques.

Circular Breathing

The first method you can do with a partner while fully clothed, although it can also be done while making love. It's called circular breathing. In this technique, the couple lies down in a cuddling position, with the man's front to the woman's back. This is often referred to as "spooning," and it's a common way for many couples to sleep. While in this position, the man should have one hand over his partner's heart, the other near the top of her head—wherever is comfortable.

A first step to circular breathing is to simply synchronize the breath of both partners. When the woman inhales, the man should inhale at the same time. When the woman exhales, the man should exhale. Breathing together in this manner creates a feeling of connection, harmony, and intimacy.

Once a couple has done this for a while, they can begin circular breathing. This involves inhaling and exhaling at opposite times. In essence, the man imagines breathing energy up from his groin, and sending it from his heart to his partner. When the man exhales, the woman imagines breathing in this energy from her heart area and exhaling it down her body and out her groin area. In this manner, a couple circulates the life-force energy between them. As the woman exhales, the man inhales, and the circle is complete.

Amazing Grace

While watching the *Tonight Show with Jay Leno* one night, I was surprised to hear Leno refer to my book *Communication Miracles for Couples*. He mentioned that I suggested couples practice "spooning" in order to avoid arguing and promote more harmony, and that he found the technique really works. Then, as a punch line, he added, "It worked so well that maybe we can get Bill Clinton and Paula Jones to do it together."

When a couple does this method as a break from lovemaking, a lot of energy is circulated, and it's possible to feel like one united breathing organism. It can be quite a high.

While most couples greatly enjoy circular breathing, it is quite different than the elaborate rituals of ancient Tantra. If you don't care to read a lot about those rituals, feel free to create your own. In Tantra, the goal of many of the rituals was to see one's partner as the embodiment of the pure masculine or feminine force. By washing each other's feet, looking into each other's eyes for long periods of time, and generally serving each other, partners set the stage for "devotional lovemaking."

Once the stage was set, they would begin making love, but not quickly proceed to orgasm. In fact, in traditional Tantra and Taoist sexology, the male is supposed to never have an orgasm. Instead, both partners are trained to circulate the sexual energy and move it up their spine in an effort to experience union with God. The combination of acts of worship, energy control, meditation, and the circulation of sexual energy often led to transcendental states of bliss.

Although this is not a text about Tantra, I'll give you one method you can try to better understand the power of what's possible.

Slow-Motion Love

After connecting with your partner through whatever rituals you prefer, try making love in slow motion. Go just fast enough to maintain the man's erection, and a wonderful sense of tension. Whenever the man is near orgasm, stop all movement and look into each other's eyes for a while. If you want, you can practice synchronized or circular breathing during this short break from intercourse. Before losing his erection, the man should begin thrusting again.

Keep doing this stop-and-go cycle until the energy is so intense you can barely stand it. Allow yourself to open to greater amounts of energy than you have before, and if possible, let go into the ocean of bliss and love that's always within you. Good luck!

From Acid to Zinc

For thousands of years, cultures around the world have used various plants to induce altered states of consciousness for spiritual purposes. There is much evidence that the famed Eleusinian Mysteries of Ancient Greece actually used an LSD-type of mixture to initiate people into the wonders of creation.

Throughout history, priests, shamans, and witch doctors have also been known to induce trances via "secret potions" for themselves or whole groups of people. For example, the dried head of the peyote cactus, whose active ingredient is mescaline, was used by the Aztecs as early as 300 B.C.E., and is currently still used by some Native Americans for religious ceremonies. The Aztecs also ingested a mushroom they called "the flesh of the Gods," whose active ingredient induced an LSD-like experience.

From Allah to Zen

An **entheogen** is a plant or chemical taken to elicit spiritual or mystical experiences. Literally, it means "becoming God or Spirit within." Common entheogens include psilocybin (found in certain mushrooms), mescaline (found in certain cacti), and LSD, sometimes referred to as "acid" (a synthesized chemical derived from ergot fungus).

In anthropology, plants or chemicals taken for religious purposes are called *entheogens*. Nowadays, with the debilitating problem of drug abuse, the line between the religious and recreational use of drugs has grown very thin. Since the sacramental use of drugs has been around for thousands of years, there must be a reason.

Indeed, studies done in the 1960s by Harvard researchers Leary, Alpert, and Pahnke showed that psychedelic drugs could induce experiences that were seemingly identical to mystical states of consciousness. Even long-term follow-up studies indicated that the double blind–controlled subjects maintained a positively changed worldview as a result of their experiences.

When LSD became illegal in 1964, research with various entheogens became difficult. Young people began getting powerful psychedelics from drug dealers, and using them in questionable ways and settings. The drug problem exploded.

Despite the illegality of most psychedelics, they still play a major role in introducing many people to new and expanded states of consciousness. In the 1980s, the drug MMDA—better known as XTC—hit the streets. At the time, I was a graduate student doing research with this drug (it was legal at the time). My own and other people's research indicated we could often accomplish a year's worth of therapy in a few hours with this unique substance. Unfortunately, it was quickly abused by thousands of kids, and therefore the government soon had to classify it as an illegal drug.

With so much hype, hysteria, and difficulty surrounding drugs in our culture, it's hard to use them in a responsible manner. It's ironic that many of the most useful consciousness-expanding drugs are illegal, whereas the most deadly drug on earth, nicotine, is available almost everywhere!

If you plan to ingest any nonfood substance, from a psychedelic to a vitamin, as a means of expanding your experience, you should follow a few simple guidelines:

➤ Before ingesting any substance, research what its potential for addiction is. Highly addictive drugs, such as heroin and nicotine are, in my opinion, too dangerous to try.

➤ Before trying a drug, even one prescribed by your doctor, know what its likely side effects and addictive potential are.

➤ Never use any mind-altering drug (especially alcohol) while driving or operating heavy machinery.

➤ When using any substance, create an appropriate setting to have an uplifting experience. For example, you may choose a nice nature spot, have a friend as a guide, or any other setting that appeals to you.

➤ Avoid using any mind-altering substances, even coffee, just to make yourself feel better. If you use any substance just to make yourself feel better, it'll make it nearly impossible to use it for higher exploration.

➤ Know that many street drugs are illegal, dangerous, and do not have "quality control"— meaning you can never be sure what you're getting.

While in college I studied the ways drugs are used around the world. I concluded that there is no such thing as a good or bad drug—it all depends upon how you use it. For example, tobacco was (and still is) incorporated into a beautiful ritual of friendship by many Native American tribes, whereas now it's most widely used as a harmful addictive substance that takes an average of 10 years off a user's life. Therefore, before ingesting any nonfood substance, ask yourself, "Am I taking this for the right reasons?"

The Muse in Music

Ever since humans could beat two rocks together, music has been a way to alter consciousness and help people feel connected to Spirit and each other. Starting with instruments made from items such as trees, bamboo, and animal skins, ancient people would sit around a campfire and play music. Soon music took on religious significance as people played it at births, funerals, and important sacred nature rites.

If you've ever sung or played music with a group of people, you know the magic that is possible. Music has a way of seducing us into a different part of our being. From simple drumming to the singing of hymns, it's easy to lose your normal

Heavenly Helpers

Many legal and easily available substances can get you quite "high" if taken infrequently, and if you keep your body in good shape. For example, caffeine, alcohol, kava kava, valerian root, and many other herbs in health food stores can lead to profound or new experiences if they are taken with a higher intention, and not overly used.

Amazing Grace

When I was in a remote village in Fiji, I found that the villagers huddled around a fire each night, drank a substance called Kava (a bit like alcohol), and sang for many hours into the night. Besides being fun, it created a wonderful sense of community. Occasionally, they sang chants that seemed to induce states of ecstasy in all who sang along. It sure beat a night watching sitcoms!

Heavenly Helpers

In every city there are drumming circles and choirs whose focus is to get everyone fully into the music that's created. To find such a group in your area, ask at a local music or drum store. For singing, a good gospel choir can be especially helpful in discovering the joys of singing to and with Spirit.

sense of self in a combination of rhythm and melody. You probably find that hearing certain music inspires you, while other music makes you feel reflective, "soft," or even sad. The most intense musical experiences often come from playing or singing rather than from simply listening.

While it can help to know how to play an instrument to enjoy the power of music, it isn't necessary. After all, everyone can enjoy the benefits of singing. Most people are reluctant to sing because they're afraid they won't sing on key. In spiritual singing the goal isn't to sound like Whitney Houston, but to let go of your inhibitions and dive into ecstasy!

To reach this goal, all you need is a sincere desire, an ability to go beyond your fears, and a willingness to let loose. If you've ever tasted the sheer joy of singing in a choir or in the shower, you know what's possible. With practice, you can learn to use singing as a method to attain states of bliss, joy, and even surrender to a power bigger than you.

Drumming is especially conducive to producing altered and ecstatic states of consciousness. The great thing about drumming is that you don't have to have any experience to really get into it. Although I've had no instruction in how to drum, and have no natural talent for it, I find I can completely lose myself within the ecstatic rhythms of a drumming circle (a group of people drumming together). Buying a set of bongos or just a simple single drum is all you need—along with a like-minded group—to explore this primeval art. It can be a powerful and deeply moving experience.

The Romance of Dance

Dance, along with music, has been around as long as humans have. Before a plethora of "formal" dances were invented, ancient people would simply shake their body to the rhythms of drums. Once again, the goal was not to look good or be cool, but to lose oneself into the ecstasy of movement.

While specific dances, from waltzes to tangos, have broadened the art of dancing, the goal of using dance to go beyond one's normal sense of self has become less popular. Nevertheless, this ancient art can be as near as the next time you turn on some music, and let your body guide you into the world beyond your thoughts.

"Ecstatic dancing" is dancing with the aim to fully immerse yourself in the dance. While no formal instruction is needed to do this form of dance, some guidelines can be helpful:

➤ Play music that has energy to it and inspires you.

➤ It helps to dance without a partner so you don't have to think about anything other than fully letting go into the music and your own movement.

➤ Some people find it easier to let loose in a group of like-minded dancers, while other people prefer to dance on their own. Choose what works for you.

➤ Focus on the music, rather than your feelings of inadequacy or embarrassment. The aim is to go beyond your self-consciousness.

➤ Close your eyes so you can better get in touch with your body.

➤ Like everything else, you tend to get better with practice.

While free-form dancing is a great way to go beyond your thoughts, there are actually methods of dancing that were invented for the purpose of inducing a thoughtless state. The best known of these is the whirling that comes from the Sufi school, known as whirling dervishes (see Chapter 12, "Body-Centered Practices"). These dancers twirl rapidly for long periods of time, without getting dizzy, in an attempt to surrender to the whirling.

Another form of dance to help people transcend their normal sense of self has been made popular by dance teacher and author Gabrielle Roth. In her book *Sweat Your Prayers: Movement as Spiritual Practice*, and her video *The Wave*, she describes a method for freeing one's body by entering into five universal rhythms. By dancing to these rhythms in a specific sequence, Roth explains that anyone can learn to move beyond self-consciousness and into a connection with his or her soul.

Whether a person uses sex, drugs, music, or dance to transcend his ego, the process is really very similar. The idea is to get so fully into an experience that outer presence spontaneously blossoms. The result is a joy and ecstasy that swells up from within and has no boundaries. From this thoughtless state, the world appears as a blissful dance of energy and beauty. May you explore and enjoy such exquisite experiences.

Cosmic Potholes

Although it may look easy to do, the art of whirling usually requires some instruction to do properly. Without it, you may find yourself getting nauseous or crashing into walls as you fall over in a dizzy funk. A local Islamic or Sufi group may be able to tell you where you can find instruction.

The Least You Need to Know

➤ Sex, drugs, music, and dance can all be gateways to higher states of awareness—if used with the right intention and method.

➤ Tantric Buddhism is an ancient spiritual system predicated on the idea that you can use the senses to go beyond the senses.

➤ Sacred sexuality or Tantra is a system of rituals and methods to convert sexual energy into higher states of consciousness and connection with the Creator.

➤ Herbs and drugs can, if carefully used, help many people to experience modes of perception that are inspiring and that go beyond their normal sense of self.

➤ Music, singing, drumming, and dance can all be used to go beyond self-consciousness and into an experience of outer presence—where the ego is temporarily dissolved.

Chapter 28

The
Experience
of
God

Final Words
of Wisdom

In This Chapter

➤ Why it's important to know the fundamentals of spirituality

➤ The value of learning from spiritual notables

➤ Advice on how to develop a closer relationship with God

➤ How differing advice can eventually create a fuller picture of what it is we're after

For my book *The Experience of God,* I asked 40 well-known spiritual writers and leaders for their best ideas and methods for connecting more deeply with the Divine. One of the questions I asked each of these spiritual notables was, "If you had just one piece of advice to give to a person who wanted a deeper relationship with God, what would you tell them?"

The contributors enjoyed this question. After all, most of us like giving advice. Unfortunately, few of us enjoy hearing it—especially when it comes to spirituality. People often get defensive about anything that sounds even remotely like advice. Yet this question allowed the interviewees to express what they felt other people really needed to know.

In any long-term endeavor, there are good times and bad times. When a business begins to go sour, managers often sound the battle cry, "Let's get back to basics." In business, the basics are such items as cash flow, customer satisfaction, and effective marketing. In the realm of Spirit, the basics are not as clearly delineated.

Heavenly Helpers

Watch for your reaction to the words of these spiritual notables. If any of them say something that resonates with you, you may find it helpful to read one of their books.

The purpose of this question is to help us reconnect with the most important aspects of the spiritual path. Remember the connect-the-dots drawings you did as a child? What looked like a random assortment of dots on a page would, once all the dots were connected in the right order, turn into a clear picture. In the same way, the many "dots" of advice offered here may seem random at first, but when taken together they paint a beautiful picture of the way we can grow spiritually.

Whenever possible, it's good to learn from people who have already traveled the roads we wish to take. The timeless truths offered here could save you or someone you love many years of trial and effort. I have taken excerpts from 20 of the notable seekers I interviewed so you can get a flavor of the answers offered. After a brief bio about each person, each offers his or her response to the question, "If you had just one piece of advice to give to a person who wanted a deeper relationship with God, what would you tell them?"

Lynn Andrews

Lynn Andrews has devoted her life to the study of age-old rituals and shamanism. She is the author of Medicine Woman, Jaguar Woman, *and* Woman of the Wyrrd, *among others.*

From Allah to Zen

An **ally** is a spiritual being of energy (like an angel), often invoked or called upon in shamanistic systems to help a person battle inner or outer forces.

To form a deeper relationship with God, you have to ask for something to come in. My teacher, Agnes Whistling Elk, has told me many times that you have to become receptive to your prey. This means you have to make a place within yourself for your prey to live. When I say "your prey," I mean anything that you might be looking for. If, for instance, you're looking for a guardian angel or an *ally*, you have to make a place within yourself that is receptive to that energy.

Some people I talk to tell me they simply don't feel the presence of the Great Spirit in their lives. But as I talk to them longer, I realize that they have so much doubt, anger, and confusion that there's no place for God to live inside of them. They haven't become receptive to their prey. It's necessary to create a place within ourselves where God can live.

Pat Boone

Pat Boone is a popular singer, actor, author, and TV and radio host. He has authored more than a dozen books, including the best-seller Twixt Twelve and Twenty.

In forming a relationship with God, what we have to do is to really get ourselves "in neutral" and seek His will rather than our own. If you can get yourself out of the way and genuinely seek to find the will of God, He can shape your thinking and lead you to the right kind of decisions. We don't always know exactly what God's will is, but if we can just decide that we want it, whatever it is, it's easier to ascertain his will and come much closer to it.

Though we can learn something from the example of others, our own prayer lives should never be purely imitative, or static, or ritualistic. They should be growing and innovative and changing and fun! Come up with your own style! Invent! Create—that's one of your God-given characteristics. So spend some time in prayer, both asking for general forgiveness and cleansing and being specific about individual acts that you want to be washed away and corrected.

Joan Borysenko

Joan Borysenko is a pioneer in mind/body medicine, and the author of several best-sellers including Minding the Body, Mending the Mind, *and* A Woman's Book of Life.

I would remind readers of the words of the Greek Orthodox priest, Kido Coleander, who was once asked what monks did all day long in the monastery. He replied, "We fall and get up again, fall and get up again." I think the most important thing in forming a deeper relationship with God is to be gentle and loving with ourselves and to recognize that we are made up of both light and shadow. Accepting all of who we are is probably the most difficult, and yet the most beneficial, spiritual practice.

What I would specifically tell a person would depend on the person, and where that person was in his or her life and faith. In terms of my own gradual awakening to God's presence, I needed first to heal the wounds of childhood that left me feeling unworthy of my own love or anyone else's, never mind God's! Second, I needed an understanding that God was complete and perfect love, a forgiving God. After all, who wants a relationship with a bogeyman or a cosmic Peeping Tom? Third, I needed to know that God was both immanent and transcendent within and beyond—that the Divine truly dwells behind every pair of eyes, including my own; that I would see and know God in moments when I was truly open to giving or receiving love.

Finally, once the stage was set, the most important thing for me was asking for help in knowing God. By this, I mean praying things like, "I want to know You, I want to love You, I want to be of service. I'm sick and tired of feeling scared, alone, and judgmental. Please reveal yourself to me." You see, I'm a great believer in free will. As much as the Mystery may want to enfold us in its love and wisdom, we have to want it too. Ask and you will receive—still good advice 2,000 years later.

Levar Burton

Levar Burton is an actor best known for his role as Kunta Kinte in Roots *and Lt. La Forge in* Star Trek: The Next Generation.

My advice for forming a deeper relationship with God would be to create a quiet space within and ask the question, "How can I have a deeper relationship with you?" Then listen for an answer. The other way would be to bring playfulness and enjoyment into your spirituality. When it comes from a joyful place, it's more natural and you'll feel more like pursuing it.

Mantak Chia

Mantak Chia has worked to create a workable energy system for Westerners. He is the author of many books including Awaken Healing Energy with the Tao *and* Taoist Secrets of Love.

The first thing people need to do in forming a deeper relationship with God is open the energy channels inside themselves. The body is the temple of God. If you want to make a connection with the Tao, with God, you have to open the energy blockages within yourself. That helps make your body a conductor for God's energy. This can be done through proper meditation. The second thing you need to do is eat natural, nutritious food. A third thing you need to do to connect with God is learn to have good thinking and good virtue. And last, you need to retain sexual energy. If you lose all your energy through sex, you won't have enough energy to connect with the Tao. If you consider monks, nuns, holy men, you will realize they all refrain from sex. This helps them retain more energy so they can connect with God.

Deepak Chopra, M.D.

Deepak Chopra, M.D., is the author of several best-sellers including Ageless Body, Timeless Mind, The Seven Spiritual Laws of Success, *and* The Path of Love.

Amazing Grace

Levar Burton originally had his sights set on becoming a Catholic priest. After becoming disillusioned with religious dogma, he looked for other means to use his talents and desires to make a better world. So, he turned to acting as a way to reach the hearts and minds of his audience. Against all odds, while a student at USC, he got the role of Kunta Kinte in Alex Haley's TV miniseries *Roots*.

Cosmic Potholes

Trying to refrain from sex before you are ready, or without the proper sexual control techniques, can be extremely difficult or even harmful. If you are interested in transforming your sexual energy into spiritual energy, consider first reading one of Mantak Chia's books.

You need to find an outlet for your love, a place where you can give it freely. The more openly you experience love, on whatever terms, the closer you will come to finding its essence. Love that doesn't flow is no love at all; it is just yearning and longing. The renowned mythologist Joseph Campbell pointed the way for expressing love when he said, "Follow your bliss." Bliss is the tingling rush of love in action, the flow of Being as it reaches out to meet itself and curl back with delight in contact. Love wants to find itself, and when the circuit is complete, bliss flows. Nothing is more important than reconnecting with your bliss. Nothing is as rich. Nothing is more real.

Alan Cohen

Alan Cohen is a speaker and an author of many popular inspirational books, including The Dragon Doesn't Live Here Anymore *and* Handle with Prayer.

I would tell people who want a deeper relationship with God to follow their heart and trust that deepest longings and intuitions are coming from Spirit. God is trying to work through us, and we just need to open a channel and let it happen. It helps to make the connection between what your intuition tells you and the results that follow.

Life is always giving us feedback about whether we're following our true paths. If we're following our true, joyful voice, we are in a state of great creativity. People will receive what we have to offer, and the universe will support us for it. We need to start making associations between what we're feeling and the kind of results we're getting.

Ram Dass

Ram Dass researched the use of psychedelics with Timothy Leary at Harvard University in the early 1960s before meeting his guru in India. He has written many books including Be Here Now, Journey of Awakening, How Can I Help? *and* Still Here.

God is always present in our lives, and it's only the veils of our own minds that keep us from appreciating that presence. One strategy you might use for obtaining a deeper relationship with God is to think of God as an imaginary playmate, and to imbue that playmate with all the qualities you would like God to have: infinitely wise, funny, loving, compassionate, etc. Then just hang out with your imaginary playmate the same way a child does. Talk with your playmate, and just be with it as if it's always there with you. Having a friend with all these wonderful qualities will make you want to move closer to it by changing your own qualities. Finally, you change enough so that you realize that your friend was real and you were imaginary—because, after all, there is only God.

When I asked my teacher, Neem Karoli Baba, "How can I get enlightened?" he said, "Serve people." He went on to say what Christ said: "Whatever you do to the poorest people, you're doing to me." Mother Teresa describes it by saying, "I only serve my beloved Christ in all His distressing disguises." So that's a practice, but as you merge more into the Oneness, there's no longer anybody to serve but yourself—because there's only one of us. When your foot gets hurt, your hand will naturally do what it can to relieve its pain. In the same way, as you lose your sense of separateness, the spontaneous generosity of the heart comes forth.

Bruce Davis

Bruce Davis is a leader of spiritual retreats and the author of several books including Monastery Without Walls, The Magical Child Within You, *and* My Little Flowers.

Getting closer to God is a matter of setting priorities. We have to give our spiritual self time and space. We have to take the time to meditate and pray. For most people, their souls are their last priority. God is at the bottom of their list. This is because people don't commonly know the fruits of the spiritual life. They look for those fruits in transient, temporary pleasures. So the first step is to realize that the fruits of the spiritual life are truly satisfying.

Heavenly Helpers

As a way to open up to devotion to God, you can try feeling your devotion to your kids (or your pets) as a "primer." Once you get in touch with devotion to those you love, you can then relate that love you feel to God—the source of all love.

I think for most people, spirituality is a pretty intellectual thing—but that's not really what it is. I believe that devotion is the core of the experience of spirituality. It's a very expansive love. But most people, even "spiritual" people in our culture, don't know this experience of devotion. The closest thing to this experience would be the devotion we feel toward our children, or toward our partners. If you multiply that by 100, then you have a sense of what devotion toward God is like. And devotion is what really opens up the heart. Unless the heart is totally involved, we do not really find God.

Wayne Dyer

Wayne Dyer is a leader in the personal development field and has written 15 best-selling books including Your Erroneous Zones, Your Sacred Self, *and* The Wisdom of the Ages.

I think of the words of Melville when he said that God's one and only voice is silence. If people want to get closer to God, they really have to learn to quiet down their inner dialogue. They say that people have 60,000 thoughts a day, every single day. And most of the thoughts we have are the exact same thoughts that occurred yesterday. Rather than our being a servant of the mind, the mind needs to be made a servant to the higher part of yourself. It was Pascal who said, "All man's troubles stem from his inability to sit quietly in a room alone."

By emptying the mind through meditation, you begin to realize you're not what you think about—that there is a part of you that can *watch* what you think about. You see, that's the entry point for beginning to realize that there is some part of you who can observe yourself. That "witnessing" part of yourself is the doorway to another realm.

Wayne Farrell

Wayne Farrell is the author of several best-sellers including Why Men Are the Way They Are, The Liberated Man, *and* The Myth of Male Power.

I would tell those who want a deeper relationship with God to go inside themselves and tune in to their feelings. Pay attention to your dreams, to what's worrying you, to the tension points inside your body and what triggers them. What your inner self is bothered and motivated by is your inner God speaking. God is all the accumulated wisdom you've gathered in your lifetime. Your body can give you something like a computer printout of this wisdom when you pay attention and listen to it.

Louise Hay

Louise Hay is a metaphysical teacher and the best-selling author of numerous books including You Can Heal Your Life *and* Empowering Women.

I suggest that those who want a deeper relationship with God release all judgment, practice forgiveness whenever they can, and learn to truly and deeply love themselves, for as their self-love deepens they will find the tremendous Power and Essence of Life that many call God. This Life Essence lies within each and every one of us.

The Dalai Lama

The Dalai Lama is the exiled political and spiritual leader of Tibet who now lives in Dharamsala, India. He has authored many best-selling books, and in 1989 His Holiness received the Nobel Peace Prize.

The essence of all religions is love, compassion, and tolerance. Kindness is my true religion. No matter whether you are learned or not, whether you believe in the next life or not, whether you believe in God or Buddha or some other religion or not, in day-to-day life you must be a kind person. When you are motivated by kindness, it doesn't matter whether you are a practitioner, a lawyer, a politician, an administrator, a worker, or an engineer: Whatever your profession or field, deep down you are a kind person.

Love, compassion, and tolerance are necessities, not luxuries. Without them, humanity cannot survive. If you have a particular faith or religion, that is good. But you can survive without it if you have love, compassion, and tolerance. The clear proof of a person's love of God is if that person genuinely shows love to fellow human beings.

Kenny Loggins

Kenny Loggins is a Grammy Award–winning singer/songwriter, an activist in various charities, and the author with his wife, Julia, of The Unimaginable Life.

The journey to the Spirit is the path inward, and we are all upon it. Some choose straighter paths than others, but we are all headed to the same place. To hear the Spirit more clearly, learn to hear the voice of intuition. To hear the intuition more clearly, learn to feel your life.

Nothing cuts us off from God, but the ego/mind can make us feel pretty bad. It can give us a false sense of isolation and unloveability. At times like these, all Light is just a vague memory. Stay in the pain, in your heart, and ask for help.

Dan Millman

Dan Millman is a past world champion gymnast and the author of several books including Way of the Peaceful Warrior, No Ordinary Moments, *and* The Life You Were Born to Live.

I'd advise anyone who wants a deeper relationship with God to do the work of consciousness—to clear those internal obstructions in the body, mind, and emotions that bind attention to the self. Once the body finds relative balance (or at least, freedom from pain); once the mind lets go of its addiction to thought; once we accept our emotions and rise above fear, sorrow, anger, up into the heart, we notice what has always been with us, around us, living us, breathing us, loving us, sustaining us. Ultimately, words can only point toward it.

Bernie Siegel, M.D.

Bernie Siegel, M.D., is involved in humanizing medical education and is the author of several best-sellers including Love, Medicine and Miracles *and* Peace, Love and Healing.

One of the things that happens when you get into heaven is you're asked, "Would you like to be introduced to God?" If you say yes, then the next question is, "How would you like to be introduced?" If you say, "I've been president of such and such a company, or I raised five children," they say, "No, that's not you. We need to know who you are." The ultimate answer is, "I am a portion of God, so God already knows me—I don't really need an introduction." God and I are one, and as one minister I know said, "God is in production, and I'm in distribution, so we're all in the same system."

People simply need to be aware of what is already there. They don't need to develop a relationship with God, they just need to be aware of it. I think it's just our intellect that gets in the way of such a relationship. The Bible tells us that God speaks to us in dreams and visions. I think it helps to be in touch with God's language, which is not intellectual but symbolic. Being in touch with dreams and visions will help you understand and communicate with God. So pay attention to your dreams, your visions, your drawings, your intuitive side.

Amazing Grace

Dr. Siegel was one of the first people willing to give me an interview, and was always willing to write nice things about my books before I became a best-selling author. Despite his incredibly busy schedule, he practices what he preaches by reaching out to people with his humor and helpfulness.

Marsha Sinetar

Marsha Sinetar is a prolific author of many books including Do What You Love, the Money Will Follow *and* Ordinary People as Monks and Mystics.

Just turn toward God. That's all. Adjust your attention upward. Steer your heart's movement toward that which is divine. That is enough. Remember Scripture's injunction. "Be still and know that I am God." These lines suggest that if we simply do this task—a doing which is our attentive, silent, worshipful response—connection is assured.

Charles Tart

Charles Tart is a former professor of psychology at U.C. Davis and the author of many books including the classics Altered States of Consciousness, Transpersonal Psychologies, *and* Waking Up.

The piece of advice that I find extremely helpful is one attributed to a group called the "Sarmouni Brotherhood." It says, "There is no God but Reality. To seek Him elsewhere is the action of the Fall." To me, this means you need to seek for *truth* first. Whenever you put your ideas about how things are ahead of actually trying to see what's really there, you're inevitably going to create trouble. No matter how you'd like things to be ideally, you have to keep coming back and checking in with what actually is.

Actually, I'm not an authority on enlightenment. I'm an authority on "endarkenment." I think that, rather than looking for truth, it's easier to start at the other end and look for error. That is, try to see the error that you generate. By observing myself directly, I find that I live in a constant, ongoing sea of activity, beliefs, attachments, aversions, hopes, and fears—and a lot of the time I'm not paying attention to the simple sensory input I get from the real world around me.

Cosmic Potholes

I frequently speak at churches around the country. The biggest problem I see is the tendency for people to pretend to be how they think they should be, rather than be who they are. The inevitable result is "phony holiness," which feels fake and is far from the vitality of living in God's presence.

From Allah to Zen

A Course in Miracles is a self-study program of spiritual psychotherapy that consists of three books. The purpose of the Course is to train the mind to relinquish the thoughts of fear and to begin to think the loving thoughts of God. It teaches that the way to experience the peace of God is through total forgiveness of yourself and all others.

Whatever truth ultimately is, I know it's got to be more than just this constant sea of fantasies that I generate. So I start by trying to be alert for error. I ask myself, "What kind of story am I telling myself instead of looking at what's in front of my eyes? What kind of fear am I holding onto instead of listening to what I can actually hear with my ears? What kind of belief do I have about how things should be instead of feeling my actual emotional feelings?"

It's not a matter of constantly thinking and analyzing, talking to yourself in your head about what you might have done wrong. That just feeds the superego, causes no real change, and can go on forever! The emphasis is simply on making a deliberate effort to be more attentive to my moment-by-moment sensory inputs and bodily feelings. By seeking reality in this fashion, I find that errors come to light, but not just as grist for endless rumination.

Mother Teresa

The late Mother Teresa founded the Missionaries of Charity whose mission is to help the "poorest of the poor." She is the author of No Greater Love *and* A Simple Life, *and in 1979 she received the Nobel Peace Prize.*

My message to the people of today is simple. We must love one another as God loves each one of us. To be able to love, we need a clean heart. Prayer is what gives us a clean heart. The fruit of prayer is a deepening of faith, and the fruit of faith is love. The fruit of love is service, which is compassion in action.

Marianne Williamson

Marianne Williamson is a popular lecturer on A Course in Miracles *and the author of many best-sellers including* A Return to Love, A Woman's Worth, *and* The Healing of America.

Any time I'm upset and feeling disconnected from God, the highest support I can receive from someone is their asking me, "Marianne, did you meditate today? Did you read something inspiring today? Are you attacking someone in your thoughts?" Most people don't really need advice. They just need support and discipline in doing what they already know works.

There has been a shift in the past few years from the path of the Seeker to the path of the Pilgrim. Being a seeker means you're looking for a path. Most of us generally know what our path is by now. This is a pilgrimage, not just a search. There are other pilgrims all around us, some walk faster and some slower. Sometimes the road is easy, and sometimes the curves are treacherous—but we know where we're going, and we know it's possible to get there.

Jonathan Robinson

As the author of this book, I have given you a lot of advice already. If I had to give you just one piece of advice to leave you with, it would be this: If you want to consistently grow spiritually, find a teacher or a group of people who will help you. There's little that we can do on our own. With a group of like-minded seekers, there is no limit to what is possible. Unfortunately, many spiritual groups are rather dull and mechanical in how they approach spiritual growth. You may have to try out many groups or teachers before you find one that feels right to you. Have faith that every sincere effort you make toward God will be heard and rewarded. I wish you well on your sacred journey.

The Least You Need to Know

➤ There are certain fundamentals that are always important while on the spiritual path.

➤ To have a deeper relationship with God, a first step is to make that more of a priority in your life.

➤ Many spiritual notables agree that love, kindness, and service are critical to whatever spiritual path you follow.

➤ Listening to your body, feelings, and intuition can help you develop a deeper relationship with God.

➤ Many techniques for knowing God can be helpful, such as prayer, meditation, service, seeking truth, and cultivating inner energy.

From Allah to Zen: Glossary

active meditation   Any meditation involving slow or vigorous movement of the body. Its methods can include dancing, shaking, twirling, certain martial arts, or movement-oriented yoga postures.

agnostic   One who disclaims any knowledge of God, but does not deny the possibility of God's existence.

alchemy   A term that refers to the medieval art of turning base metals, such as lead, into gold. However, in a spiritual context it refers to the art of turning mundane pursuits, such as money and sex, into a means of spiritual growth or awakening.

altar   A structure that provides a focal point for religious practices such as petitionary prayer, meditation, penance, dedications, offerings, and purification.

ally   A spiritual being of energy (like an angel), often invoked or called upon in Shamanistic systems to help a person battle inner and outer forces.

Bhakti-yoga   The science of devotion to God, emphasizing the importance of surrender, love, service, and an intense personal relationship with whatever form of God one is worshiping. Bhakti adherents often use chanting, prayer, various rituals, and pilgrimages as part of their spiritual practice.

bodhisattva   A saint in the Buddhist tradition. They seek enlightenment purely for the benefit of mankind. Bodhisattvas devote their life to the service of others, and even vow to forego their own personal enlightenment in order to make sure they can continue to help all beings.

Buddha   Means "the awakened" or "the enlightened one." It commonly refers to Siddhartha Gotama, who became enlightened around 500 B.C.E., but it can also refer to anyone who becomes enlightened.

clues   Signposts directing your way to Spirit. For instance, if you do something and it leads to a feeling of contribution or peace, that is a clue that it is likely good for your soul.

The Course in Miracles   A self-study program of spiritual psychotherapy which consists of three books. The purpose of the course is to train the mind to relinquish the thoughts of fear and to begin to think the loving thoughts of God. It teaches that the way to experience the peace of God is through total forgiveness of yourself and all others.

darsan   Translated from Sanskrit as "seeing and being seen by God," or an act of respectful worship.

devotee   A student or disciple of a philosophy or guru.

Dowsing   A technique for using the body's energy currents to perceive the energy of underground water and ley lines. It can be done on site, or on a map by experienced dowsers.

ego   Our normal sense of who we are. It creates a feeling of separateness from other people that is slowly dissolved by traveling the spiritual path. As infants, we need to develop a strong separate sense of self or ego to survive. Yet, when an ego becomes too strong, it interferes with a connection with people and God.

entheogen   A plant or chemical taken to occasion spiritual or mystical experiences. Literally, it means "becoming God or Spirit within." Common entheogens include psilocybin (found in certain mushrooms), mescaline (found in certain cactus), and LSD, sometimes referred to as "acid" (a synthesized chemical derived from ergot fungus).

experimental attitude   The determination to try something out for a short period of time in order to learn new things or have new experiences.

feng shui   Literally means "the way of wind and water" or "the natural forces of the universe." It was developed by the ancient Chinese as a way to live in harmony with the environment. Nowadays, it is popularly known as a way to arrange items in one's house to bring in positive energy and dispel negative or blocked energy.

food   A word that can be used to describe the substance that physical bodies feed on, as well as the substance our soul feeds on. For example, it could be said that our soul feeds on the foods of compassion, quiet time, and reflection on nature.

God   The absolute, omnipresent, Living Being in all things; the source of all existence.

Hatha   Has been translated to mean health. We must have health to have union. We must have a healthy body to prepare for spiritual illumination. The *ha* means "sun." The *tha* means "moon." Hatha is the union of the sun and the moon. This union of the positive and negative creates a new force, a force that is needed to grow spiritually.

Hinayana   A branch of Buddhism sometimes referred to as "Little Raft." This does not mean it is a lesser path. It is a narrower path, open only to those who want to be monks or nuns, and it sticks conservatively to Buddha's original teachings. It is also known as Theravada, or, the Way of the Elders.

Hospice   An international group dedicated to the care of the terminally ill. Rather than try to "fix" the patient, hospice workers are trained to make them comfortable and to be there for them in a heartfelt way. Hospice care is done in the home of the patient, a nursing home, or at special hospice houses, not in hospitals.

hot-and-cold game   A method of discerning whether you are getting closer or farther from your goal. By listening to internal and external feedback, you can better determine whether you are on the right course.

inner presence or **mindfulness**   The ability to watch your thoughts, feelings, and behaviors in a way that helps you to feel separated from them. In this state, your thoughts and feelings are objectified, and you start to identify yourself with the part of you that is watching.

intuition   The capacity of knowing without the use of rational thought processes. It is a direct knowing usually attained by quieting one's mind and connecting with an intelligence greater than one's own.

Islam   Means "the peace that comes when one is surrendered to God."

karma   Refers to the cosmic law of cause and effect. In the traditions in which it is used, it is believed that everything you do has an effect on the universe that will echo back to you in some way. In Karma yoga, through selfless action and service, one tries to become free of the binding effects of past karma.

kiva   A circular underground chamber which is entered through a hatchway in the roof. The Pueblos use kivas for council, ritual, and meditation.

kosher   Means ritually fit for use according to Jewish law. You will usually see it in reference to Jewish food. Kosher slaughtering is designed to be as fast and painless as possible. If there is anything that happens during the process that indicates the animal has suffered, the flesh may not be eaten.

lama   A Buddhist monk of Tibet or Mongolia. **The Dalai Lama** is the exiled spiritual and political leader of Tibet. He is thought of as the fourteenth incarnation of the Buddha of compassion. In 1989, he won the Nobel Peace Prize for his efforts to peacefully resolve differences between Tibet and China.

make amends   In Alcoholics Anonymous, means to fix or improve something. Amending a wrong usually means saying "I'm sorry." Apologies are nice, but often meaningless. Another way to make amends is to change or amend yourself. Resolve that you will never bring harm that way again.

301

mantra   A sound or combination of sounds in Sanskrit that are believed to have a specific, soothing effect on the nervous system when used as an object of concentration. The word derives from *man* meaning "to think" and *trai* meaning "to protect or free from the bondage of the phenomenal world."

meditation   Derives from the Indian Sanskrit word *medha,* which roughly means "doing the wisdom." At its core, meditation is any form of concentration or technique whose purpose is to quiet the mind, open the heart, and connect with a source bigger than one's normal sense of ego.

mindfulness   *See* inner presence.

monotheism   A doctrine or belief that there is only one God. Back in the time of the ancient Hebrews, there was no other group of people in the world who believed in only one God. The Egyptians, Babylonians, Syrians, Greeks, Indians, Chinese, Africans, Native Americans, Anglo-Saxons, Indonesians—all believed in and prayed to many gods and idols.

needs   Can be defined for the spiritual seeker as those conditions that support his spiritual development. These may include food, clothing, shelter, some friends, some money, some leisure time. Desired possessions or involvements that retard, rather than accelerate, his spiritual growth, would be considered "wants."

obstacles   In the context of spiritual growth, a person's intellectual, emotional, or physical manifestations that keep him from evolving to a higher state of consciousness.

pilgrimage   A journey to a holy place made with spiritual intent.

prayer   Devout petition, addressed to a god or deity. It can also be a sincere attempt to remove the obstacles that keep us from recognizing our dependence on each other and on God.

prostration   Lying face down on one's stomach as an attempt to give up one's pride and arrogance, and to submit to a being in adoration.

puja   A ritual offering, usually to a specific deity, in order to purify oneself and receive the deity's blessing. In puja one offers sweets, waves incense, bows before a picture of the chosen deity, or performs other such rituals.

religion   A personal or institutionalized system grounded in the belief of a supernatural power or creator of the universe.

remorse   Deep anguish and regret for past misdeeds. Although it is sometimes defined as guilt, guilt often has the connotation of being imposed on one from others. On the other hand, remorse occurs when a person clearly sees and feels the painful ramifications of their actions on themselves and others.

retreat   A quiet, private place; a refuge from ordinary demands of life in order to pray, study, or meditate. It's interesting that the word retreat also has the connotation of withdrawing from an enemy.

salat   A formal prayer Muslims are required to perform five times daily—early morning, noon, mid-afternoon, sunset, and evening.

self-consciousness   A term that refers to the tendency to feel concerned with how one appears to others, or even oneself. Losing self-consciousness feels good because you can become so absorbed in an activity that you no longer are concerned with how you look.

self-remembering   The ability to be aware of one's own body, thoughts and emotions while simultaneously being fully aware of one's environment.

service   An action or gesture offered with the intent of helping the person or organization receiving the service.

Shema   The most basic prayer in Judaism. It is recited twice a day, morning and night. It starts, "Hear, O Israel, the Lord our God, the Lord is One." (Deuteronomy 6:4)

sin   As translated from ancient Aramaic, originally was an archery term that meant "to miss the bulls-eye or mark." At one time it simply helped spiritual seekers identify when they were doing something that was steering them away from their spiritual goals. Unfortunately, in recent times, the word has taken on a more condemning tone.

spiritual group   Consists of students and teachers who share the common goal of wanting to know God, love, or peace within. They acknowledge their interdependence and work together in their quest for higher possibilities.

spirituality   Any practice that helps a person to quiet their mind, open their heart, and connect with a Being greater than their normal sense of self.

student   One who understands that spiritual growth is directly dependent upon one's sincere desire to learn. He or she understands the importance of the qualities of hope, curiosity, and openness to learning, and actively cultivates these qualities. He or she seeks out opportunities to learn, and the invaluable input of teachers.

suffering   The tendency to dwell on or resist a specific situation that is causing pain in one's life. Unlike pain, which is inevitable, suffering is optional since it is primarily a function of one's mind resisting the pain or unpleasantness of life.

Tantra   Derives from the Sanskrit root word *Tan,* which loosely translated means "to extend, expand, weave, or manifest." Tantra is a spiritual approach that emphasizes the use of the senses and sexual energy to aid in one's spiritual evolution.

Tao Te Ching   A book supposedly written by Lao Tzu. Roughly translated, the book title can be interpreted as "The Way and Its Power." The word *Tao* can be roughly translated as "the way," or in other contexts, as "the supreme formless, or God."

teachers   Teachers are of two types: those who are not necessarily aware that a student is learning from them, and those who are. Both types of teachers can help others to learn about themselves and the world. Animals and other creatures may also serve as teachers to students who are willing to regard them in that manner.

Ten Commandments   Contain the ethical prescriptions for most of the world today, certainly the Western world. Jews, Christians, and Moslems all abide by them, and ascribe them to Moses.

tool   Any technique or idea that has a practical application in learning about oneself, or practical use in bringing a person closer to a higher state of consciousness.

Torah   The Torah consists of the first five books of the Old Testament. To the Jew, there is no "Old Testament" because the books that Christians call the New Testament are not part of Jewish scripture. The Torah contains the whole body of Jewish law and teachings.

vipassana   Means "insight." It refers to a meditation technique that the Buddha himself taught. In this method, a person briefly labels his or her thoughts, feelings, and sensations as they are observed.

waking up   Refers to the process of being able to see the emotions, motivations, thoughts, and selves that literally run our lives. As a person wakes up, they realize their ego, or multitude of selves, filters their worldview and determines their experience of life.

WET, or way of the easiest thing   A force in the universe that gets people to do what's easiest for them and what pleases them. It is also an approach to life that, if not veered from occasionally, leads to a lack of growth, boredom, and an avoidance of activities that could rekindle a person's spiritual longings.

yoga   Means "union." The end of all these paths is Union. Union with what? Hindus believe that man is capable of a state of consciousness in which the individual self is merged with the infinite Being. This state, called self-realization, is the ultimate knowing of God. The Hindu word for God is Brahman.

Surfing to Enlightenment

The following Web addresses, with brief descriptions of their contents, are meant to help you find information, resources, and groups that may help you on your spiritual path. While I've categorized them into different subheadings, many of these sites have a plethora of information that transcends one simple category. An asterisk (*) beside an address denotes spiritual teachers and groups that teach meditations requiring a special initiation process (see Chapter 11, "The Art of Meditation").

In addition to these sites, I highly recommend the site www.ask.com. Here you can simply type a question, in standard English, of exactly what you're looking for. For example, if you want to know more about the Holy Spirit, you can simply type in "Where can I find out about the Holy Spirit?" Then press "Enter." You will be given a list of choices. Simply click on whatever seems most appropriate, and see if it takes you to the information you desire.

Good luck, and may the Force be with you!

Buddhism

www.tibet.com

The official site of Tibetan government in exile includes links to the Dalai Lama's schedule.

www.tricycle.com

Online site for Tricycle Magazine (a Buddhist review) includes links to Zen centers. Simple and straightforward information on Buddhism.

Christian

alapadre.net

Catholic site based in Alabama with links of Catholic interest, including the Archdiocese of Mobile, Alabama.

www.bible.com

Christian site including Bible references, book and audiocassette offers, and online ministry.

www.faithseekers.com/mission

Christian focus of mission and ministry work.

people.morehead-st.edu/fs/t.pitts/christn.htm

This site gives a wide overview of different denominations of Christianity and various teachings. Lots of links.

Hinduism

www.hinduismtoday.kauai.hi.us

Web site for *Hinduism Today* magazine based on the teachings of Satguru Sivay Subramuniy Asisam.

www.geocities.com/athens/oracle/2178-

Useful information on Hinduism; history, book recommendations, articles, and links established to inspire Hindus.

www.hindu.org

Excellent resource center on Hinduism. Includes glossary and links to tons of information on teachers, retreat centers, and so on.

Islam

www.islam.com

Site currently under construction dedicated to promoting awareness and education of the Islamic religion and Muslim peoples.

www.religioustolerance.org/islam.htm

This site provides an excellent overview of Islam and the teachings of Mohammed.

Judaism

www.digiserve.com/mystic/Jewish/

Interesting site on Jewish mysticism, includes links.

shamash.org/lists/scj-faq/HTML/faq/hl-index.html

Provides answers to any question about Judaism that you can imagine.

Pagan/Occult

www.amystickalgrove.com

Site for pagans, witches, shamans, or anyone with a connection to "Nature and/or SpellCasting."

Taoism

www.clas.ufl.edu/users/gthursby/taoism/

A smorgasbord of anything you ever wanted to know about Taoism and its many related ideas, philosophies, and methods.

Spiritual, General

www.alcoholics-anonymous.org/econtent.html

The home page of A.A., with lots of good links and information.

www.breath.org/alchemyc

Online magazine; a look at modern society from a standpoint of how it helps or hinders spiritual growth.

www.geocities.com/Athens/Parthenon/4735/index.html

A fun Web site; nondenominational, nonsectarian, independent commentary on issues of interest and importance to seekers in search of the truth about themselves.

www.Innerself.com/magazine/spirituality

Middle-of-the-road New Age, books, nutrition, astrology, humor. Innerself magazine includes link to swamibeyondananda (a man posing as a swami who makes good fun of the New Age).

www.spiritualityhealth.com

Site includes theologians, philosophers, researchers from diverse disciplines, teachers, and writers offering resources for growth and self-knowledge.

www.spiritwalk.org, previously **www.geocities.com**

"Resources for awakening"; new Web site still in construction, currently being transferred from www.geocities.com. Daily meditations, quotes, readings.

Spiritual Masters/Teachers/Teachings

www.adidam.org/

Web site of Adi da Samraj (Da Free John).

www.alltm.org/
www.maharishi.org/

Sites relating to Maharishi Mahesh Yogi and Transcendental Meditation; courses, programs.

www.ammachi.org/

The official Web site for Ammachi includes linking pages, schedule.

www.artofliving.org

Devoted to the teachings of Sri Sri Ravi Shankar, teacher of traditional Vedic format Sudarshon Kriya (breathing); centers worldwide.

www.buddhanet.net/psymed1.htm

Jack Kornfield, author of "a Path with Heart" simple text, no links.

cleargreen.com

Official site of the Carlos Castaneda teachings in their current form.

www.ex-cult.org/Groups/Rama/dalilama.txt

Text by Kate Wheeler, a former Buddhist nun. Very good essay on finding a teacher. Some commentary from the Dalai Lama.

www.facim.org/

Web site for "A Course in Miracles," teaching the path of forgiveness as the way to inner peace.

www.gurdieff.org

Gurdieff International Review with essays, commentaries, and book and music references related to the extraordinary late teacher George Ivonovitch Gurdieff.

*home.att.net/~h.kight/index/htm

"Spiritual Freedom Satsang" site listing links to Sant Mat/Surat Shabd Yoga by a teacher influenced by Master Kirpal Singh among others. Multiple-language site.

www.ozemail.com.au/~vsivasup/sai/index.html

Resources relating to Sri Satya Sai Baba; links all sites relating to Sai Baba.

ramdasstapes.org/

The "official site" for Ram Dass, lecturer and Author of *Be Here Now.*

www.siddhayoga.org/

Siddha yoga under the current teaching of Gurumayi from the lineage of Muktananda.

www.sun-angel.com/emporium/sow/malidoma.html

Site of teacher Malidoma Patrice Some, a tribal-born African. With a foot in both worlds he comes to teach tribal wisdom and the importance of remembering our purpose.

*www.Unity-of-Man.org

Site of Sant Kripal Singh, a deceased master of the Surat shabd yoga, considered by some to be the indirect and deepest of practices if under the guidance of a living master.

www.wideopenwin.com/dynamic.html

Lists previous and current "awakened teachers."

*yogananda.com

Site of Self-Realization Fellowship, founded by Paramahansa Yogananda, dedicated to spiritual unfoldment.

Yoga Related

www.gurmukh.com

Kundalini yoga teacher Gurmukh Kaur Khalsa's site with yoga information for pre- and postnatal care, Kundalini yoga, and meditation.

www.yoga directory.com

Search engine for yoga resource, retreats, and centers.

www.yogasite.com

An eclectic linking site for yoga-related subjects.

Everything Explained in 800 Words

The Universe has about a billion galaxies, with about a billion stars in each galaxy. That means that planet Earth is a tiny speck in an infinite ocean of space and energy. Earth is like a small airport for souls, with thousands of arrivals and departures every hour. In the short time between when a soul arrives and departs on airport Earth, there is a game they play. They call the game "Life," and it has various rules and goals like any other game.

Based on the millions of people who have had near-death experiences and have come back to report what happened, certain assumptions can be made. First, there is a Higher Power of some kind who truly cares about the souls that visit planet Earth. Second, this Higher Power seems to ask everyone who is dying the same basic two questions. The first question is, "What did you learn about being a kind and loving person?" followed by, "How well did you use your gifts to contribute to the good of the world?" Since people from all different cultures report they get asked the same two questions at death, we can safely assume that the Higher Power is interested in our spiritual and personal development.

The first rule in the game of Life is to find out what rules will lead to winning. Winning is defined as the ability to consistently feel deep levels of peace, happiness, and love in one's life. The second aspect of winning is to take the peace, love, and happiness one feels, and live in such a way that you contribute to other people's lives. With such a clearly defined goal, it would seem easy for these souls to learn the "rules" that lead to the destination they desire. This is not the case.

There are many obstacles on the way toward each soul's desired destination. To begin with, each person is brought up in a unique family and cultural situation. One's family and culture effectively "hypnotize" young souls to strongly believe many things that are not true, thereby putting them at odds with reality. For example, in Western culture, we're taught to believe that more money or the right relationship will lead us to lasting happiness. Such cultural conditioning leads us to spend a lot of energy looking for love and happiness in areas outside of our ourselves and our control.

Another obstacle to winning in Life (finding lasting peace, love, and happiness) is the fact that our minds are almost totally out of control and they never shut up. Most people don't even know this, and will get defensive if you inform them about their obvious condition. But since people have almost no control over their own minds, they end up primarily focusing on worries, problems, and what's wrong with themselves and their life. Furthermore, they have no training in how to control their own minds, so they can do little or nothing about it. What they are told and believe will "cure" their lack of peace is one simple lie. They are told that *"If you could simply control more of the events and people in your life to be the way you want them to be, you'd achieve lasting happiness."*

In fact, when things go the way we want, we do feel good for a brief period of time. That's why we become addicted to the process. But people who have the most control, such as Donald Trump or the President of the United States, are not one iota happier than other people. Control simply doesn't lead to lasting happiness. But people don't see this obvious situation because they get lost in blame, denial, or distraction. With blame, people see the problem as being in the world or with someone else. They become helpless victims. With denial, people refuse even to see that they have a problem (i.e., they aren't winning), and therefore do nothing to move closer to their goal. And with distractions (TV, drugs, etc.), people are too busy to attend to the overall underlying problem.

The most efficient means to winning (finding lasting peace, love, and happiness) is to tune into the peace, love, and happiness within. Our minds are like radio receivers. An infinite number of stations are being broadcast. Some are playing beautiful music, whereas others are playing noise. Our mission, should we decide to accept it, is to learn ways of tuning into the stations that play the type of music that feels good to us. There are many methods for doing this, such as prayer, meditation, being in nature, feeling grateful, and various spiritual practices. Once a person learns how to tap into the "stations" that feel great, from their own personal abundance they can more easily contribute their goodness to the rest of the world.

Index

A

AA (Alcoholics
Anonymous), 70
history, 70-71
making amends, 73
twelve steps, 72
acting without attach-
ment, 197
active meditations,
120-122
contemplating the
answer to a simple
question,
120-121
acts of reverence
(Buddhism), 81-82
acupuncture, Qigong,
127-129
addiction, twelve-step
programs, 76-77
admitting condition,
twelve-step programs,
75
agnostics, 214
Airport Vortex
(Sedona), 243
alchemy, 181
Alcoholics
Anonymous. See AA

aligning with the
Divine
appreciating beauty
in people and the
world, 203-204
"everything's per-
fect" mentality,
204-206
gratitude, 200
Thank-You prayer,
201-202
thanking versus
asking, 200
human displays of
divinity, 202
Allah (Islamic God),
54
ally (spiritual being of
energy), 288
altars, 237
assembling your
own, 238
community, 239
altered states of con-
sciousness
dance, 284-285
ecstatic, 285
free-form, 285
rhythm, 285
drugs, 281
entheogens, 282

guidelines,
282-283
psychedelic drugs,
282
secret potions,
281
music, 283-284
drumming, 284
singing, 284
alternate road to
wealth, money, 184
amends (AA), 73
Andrews, Lynn, 288
anecdotes for money
traps, 183-184
animal treatment,
Judaism, 48
answers to simple
questions, active
meditations, 120-121
Anxious Stimulation
Filler (selves), 160
appreciating beauty in
people and the
world, 203-204
arrogance (money
trap), 182
art, healing, 273
extraordinary forces,
274-275
shadow side, 275

art of conversation, 212
  asking big questions, 212-213
  exploring the depths of conversation, 213-214
artistic calling, creativity, 268-269
ascetics, 62
asking questions, prayer, 91-93
assembling altars, 238
Assisi (pilgrimage), 245
atman (soul), Hinduism, 60
attachment (money trap), 182
attitude of service, 111
Autobiography of a Yogi, 57
avoiding learning from life situations (negativity), 138
  blame, 139
  denial, 138
  distracting self from feeling pain, 138
awareness of partner's needs, relationships, 153-154

B

bar mitzvah, Judaism, 49

beauty appreciation (people and the world), 203-204
Bell Rock Vortex (Sedona), 243
beneficial remorse, 151
Bhagavad-Gita (Hindu text), 80
Bhakti-yoga (Hindu devotion), 58, 80, 127
  deities, 80-81
"Big Raft" (Mahayana), Buddhism sect, 64
blame
  avoiding learning from life situations, 139
  letting go in relationships, 150-151
Blaming Excuse Maker (selves), 159
bodhisattvas (Buddhism), 82
Bodidharma, 129
body-centered practices, 125
  breath, pranayama exercises, 131
  martial arts, 129-130
    empty self, 130
    T'ai Chi, 130-131
  Qigong, 127-129
  whirling, 133
  yoga, 126-127
    hatha, 126

Book of Changes, The, 127
Book of the Way and Its Power (*Tao Te Ching*), Taoism, 66
books, 264-266
Boone, Pat, 289
Borysenko, Joan, 289
Boynton Canyon Vortex (Sedona), 243
Brahman, 59
breath
  body-centered practices, pranayama exercises, 131
  meditation, 117-118
Buddha, 61
Buddhism, 61-62
  devotion, acts of reverence, 81-82
  Eightfold Path, 63
  expansion, 64-65
    Hinayana sect, 64-65
    Mahayana sect, 64
  Four Noble Truths, 62-63
  karma, 62
  labeling moment-to-moment thoughts (mindfulness), 24
  nirvana, 31, 58
  philosophy versus religion, 64
  satori, 31
  Tantra, 278-280
    circular breathing, 280-281

making love in
slow motion, 281
Web sites, 305
Burton, Levar, 290

C

caring for others,
twelve-step programs,
74-75
Cathedral Rock Vortex
(Sedona), 243
chanting, increasing
and maintaining
devotion, 87-88
charity (zakat), pillar
of Islam, 54
Chia, Mantak, 290
Chopra, Deepak,
M.D., 291
Christianity, 49
devotion, 84-86
forms of prayer, 97
inseparability of
love and pain, 51
judgments of Jesus,
50-51
Paul's teachings,
51-52
Web sites, 306
Chungliang Al Huang,
131
circular breathing
(Tantric technique),
280-281

cleansing rituals,
increasing and main-
taining devotion,
86-87
Cohen, Allen, 291
comedy movies,
258-260
*Communication
Miracles for Couples*,
150
community altars, 239
connecting to the
sacred in daily life
appreciating beauty
in people and the
world, 203-204
"everything's per-
fect" mentality,
204-206
gratitude, 200
Thank-You prayer,
201-202
thanking versus
asking, 200
human displays of
divinity, 202
consciousness
altering with dance,
284-285
ecstatic, 285
free-form, 285
rhythm, 285
altering with drugs,
281
entheogens, 282
guidelines,
282-283

psychedelic drugs,
282
secret potions,
281
altering with music,
283-284
drumming, 284
singing, 284
growth, internal
tools, 36
consistency, TM (tran-
scendental medita-
tion), 117
conversation, 212
asking big ques-
tions, 212-213
exploring the
depths of conversa-
tion, 213-214
courage, 17
creativity, 268
artistic calling,
268-269
creating our lives,
271
healing art, 273
extraordinary
forces, 274-275
shadow side, 275
inviting creativity
into your life,
272-273
opening up to
creation, 270
inner critic,
270-271
liberation, 271

overcoming resistance, 273
product versus process, 269
Csikszentmihalyi, Mihaly (psychologist), *Flow*, 29
curiosity, 20-21

D

Dalai Lama, 14, 293-294
dance, 284-285
   ecstatic, 285
   free-form, 285
   rhythm, 285
darshan (viewing of the deity), Hinduism, 95
Dass, Ram, 291-292
Davis, Bruce, 292
death, 247
   as an active part of life, 248-249
   awareness of the miracle of life, 248
   eradicating pain, 253-254
   experiencing growth through pain, 251-253
   five stages, 249-250
   hospice, 250-251
   "little deaths," 251
defining spirituality, 4
   experimental attitude, 11-12

highs and lows in feelings, 10-11
knowing your target, 4
motivations to seek spirituality, 8-9
questions and answers, 4-6
sense of separation, 9-10
versus rituals, 6-7
wayward hope, 7-8
deities, Hindu devotees, 80-81
denial, avoiding learning from life situations, 138
dependence versus independence, 229
dependentitis, 228
depths of conversation, 213-214
Dersu Uzala, 104
detractors, twelve-step programs, 76
devotees, 95
devotion, 79
   Buddhism, acts of reverence, 81-82
   Christianity, 84-86
   gurus (spiritual teachers)
      gurukripa, 82
      shaktipat, 83-84
   Hinduism, 80
      deities, 80-81

methods for increasing and maintaining, 86
      chanting, 87-88
      cleansing rituals, 86-87
disidentification (selves), 168-169
distracting self from feeling pain, avoiding learning from life situations, 138
divinity, human displays, 202
dowsing, 242
drama movies, 260-262
drugs, 281
   entheogens, 282
   guidelines, 282-283
   psychedelic drugs, 282
   secret potions, 281
drumming, 284
Dukka (Noble Truth of Suffering), 62
Dyer, Wayne, 292-293

E

Eastern religions
   Buddhism, 61-62
      Eightfold Path, 63
      expansion, 64-65
      Four Noble Truths, 62-63

karma, 62
philosophy versus religion, 64
Hinduism, 58
choice of personal God, 59
liberation, 60-61
Taoism
Chuang Tzu, 66
Lao Tzu, 65-66
yin-yang symbol, 67-68
ecstatic dancing, 285
ego, transcending, 38-39
escaping the thought/selves prison, 40-42
waking up, 39-40
Eightfold Path (Buddhism), 63
El Santuario de Chimayo (pilgrimage), 244
Elk, Agnes Whistling (teacher), 288
empty self (state of consciousness), 130
energy vortexes (Sedona), 242-243
Airport Vortex, 243
Bell Rock Vortex, 243
Boynton Canyon Vortex, 243
Cathedral Rock Vortex, 243

enlightenment, 31-33, 61
gurus (spiritual teachers), 60
entheogens, altering states of consciousness, 282
equanimity, 191
eradicating pain, 2 53-254
"everything's perfect" mentality, aligning with the Divine, 204-206
Experience of God, The, 13, 287
experience of presence, watching a self until it disappears, 170-171
experiencing the sacred in daily life
appreciating beauty in people and the world, 203-204
"everything's perfect" mentality, 204-206
gratitude, 200
Thank-You prayer, 201-202
thanking versus asking, 200
human displays of divinity, 202

experimental attitude, seeking spirituality, 11-12
exploring the depths of conversation, 213-214
extraordinary forces, art and healing, 274-275

F

facing fears, 209
faith (shahada), pillar of Islam, 54
fakirs, 126
false gurus, 60
Farrell, Wayne, 293
the fast (Ramadan), pillar of Islam, 54
feeding selves deliberately, "I Want" exercise, 173
feng shui, 203
filtering view of the world, selves, 37-38
Five Pillars of Islam, 54
charity (zakat), 54
faith (shahada), 54
the fast (Ramadan), 54
pilgrimage (Mecca), 54
prayer (salat), 54
five stages of death, 249-250

Flow (Csikszentmihalyi), 29

flow, outer presence, 29
  feel of flow, 31
  turning any situation into a flow activity, 29
forms of prayer, 94-97
  Christianity, 97
  Hinduism, 94-95
  Judaism, 95-96
  Muslim, 96
formula for prayer, 99-100
Four Noble Truths (Buddhism), 62-63
free energy transformation, dealing with resistance from friends and family, 172-173
free-form dancing, 285

G

gaining strength through growth, 209-210
Gandhi, 16
Ganesha, 94
God
  defined, 92
  Hinduism, choice of personal God, 59

grace through service, prayer, 93-94
gratitude, connecting to the sacred in daily life, 200
  Thank-You prayer, 201-202
  thanking versus asking, 200
growth
  consciousness, internal tools, 36
  experiencing through pain of sickness, accidents, and dying, 251-253
  gaining strength, 209-210
guidelines, altering states of consciousness with substances, 282-283
Gurdjieff, G. I. (Russian mystic), 31
gurukripa, 82
gurus, devotional, 60
  gurukripa, 82
  shaktipat, 83-84

H

Handbook to Higher Consciousness, The, 253
hatha yoga, 126
Hay, Louise, 293

healing art, 273
  extraordinary forces, 274-275
  shadow side, 275
highs and lows in feelings, seeking spirituality, 10-11
Hinayana ("Little Raft"), Buddhism sect, 65
Hinduism, 58
  choice of personal God, 59
  darshan (viewing of the deity), 95
  devotion, 80
    deities, 80-81
  forms of prayer, 94-95
  gurus, 60
    gurukripa, 82
    shaktipat, 83-84
  liberation, 60-61
  samadhi, 31
  Web sites, 306
history, pilgrimages, 243-244
Holy Spirit, 86
honesty, 14
  relationships, 149-150
hope, 7-8
  movies, 262-263
hospice care, 250-251
hot-and-cold game, making your vocation your vacation, 194

human displays of divinity, 202
humility, 15-16
humor, 16-17
Hurried Task Completer (selves), 158-159

I

I Ching, 127
"I Want" exercise, feeding selves deliberately, 173
Idle Worrier (selves), 162-163
imprisonment (selves)
  escaping the thought/selves prison, 40-42
  waking up, 39-40
increasing devotion, methods, 86
  chanting, 87-88
  cleansing rituals, 86-87
independence versus dependence, 229
India (pilgrimage), 246
initiation meditations, 122
inner critic, creativity, 270-271
inner presence, 24-25

experiencing simultaneously with outer presence, enlightenment, 31-33
intuition, 25
  listening to your thoughts and feelings, 26-28
insight meditation (Vipassana), 117
intentional teachers, 231
internal microscopes, 36
internal tools, consciousness growth, 36
interpreting your negative emotions, 142-144
Intimacy and Sexual Ecstasy, 279
intuition, inner presence, 25
  listening to your thoughts and feelings, 26-28
inviting creativity into your life, 272-273
Islam, 52
  Allah, 54
  Koran, 53
  masters, Shaykh, 55
  pillars, 54
    charity (zakat), 54
    faith (shahada), 54

the fast (Ramadan), 54
pilgrimage (Mecca), 54
prayer (salat), 54
Sufism, 55
Web sites, 306

J

Jerusalem (pilgrimage), 246
Jesus, Christianity, 50-51
Jnana yoga (Hinduism), 58, 127
jobs. *See* livelihoods
joy movies, 262-263
Judaism, 47
  bar mitzvah, 49
  forms of prayer, 95-96
  laws, 47-48
    mitzvoth, 48
    social censure, 49
    treatment of animals, 48
    tzedeakah, 48
  love and brotherhood, 48-49
  Web sites, 307
judgment, overcoming in relationships, 154-155
  practicing forgiveness, 154

K

Kali, 94
karate, 129
karma, 62
karma yoga, 127, 195-196
　acting without attachment, 197
　surrendering to God, 196
Kataripayit, 129
kindness, 18
Know-It-All Judger (selves), 164-166
Koran, Islam, 53
kosher (Judaism), 48
Kübler-Ross, Elisabeth (five stages of death), 249

L

Lama, 14
laws of Judaism, 47-48
　mitzvoth, 48
　social censure, 49
　treatment of animals, 48
　tzedeakah, 48
laziness (money trap), 183
"let thy will be done" prayer, 97
Levine, Stephen (pain and death), 253

ley lines, 241
　Alfred Watkins, 241-242
　dowsing and mapping, 242
liberation
　creativity, 271
　moksha, Hinduism, 60-61
life
　as a creation, 271
　inviting creativity into, 272-273
　students, 230
listening to your thoughts and feelings, intuition, 26-28
Little Book of Big Questions, The, 4, 92
"little deaths," 251
"Little Raft" (Hinayana), Buddhism sect, 65
livelihoods
　choosing the right occupation, 190
　facing fears, 192-193
　karma, 195-196
　　acting without attachment, 197
　　surrendering to God, 196
　learning about yourself on the job, 191-192

making your vocation your vacation, 194
　hot-and-cold game, 194
　Moses model, 194-195
quality of caring and consciousness you bring to your job, 191
living your dreams, 210-211
locating teachers, 231
Loggins, Kenny, 294
Looking Stupid Avoider (selves), 161-162
love and brotherhood, Judaism, 48-49
LSD, 282

M

Magga (Noble Truth of the Path), 63
Maharishi Mahesh Yogi, 117
Mahatma Gandhi, 16
Mahayana ("Big Raft"), Buddhism sect, 64
maintaining devotion, methods, 86
　chanting, 87-88
　cleansing rituals, 86-87

making amends (AA), 73

making love in slow motion (Tantric technique), 281

mantra
    meditation, 115-116
    yoga, 127

mapping, 242

martial arts, 129-130
    empty self, 130
    Qigong, 128
    T'ai Chi, 130-131

Master Zhou (Qigong), 128

masters
    Islam, Shaykh, 55
    Web sites, 308-309

Mecca (pilgrimage), pillar of Islam, 54

medicine wheels, 240

meditation, 113
    active, contemplating the answer to a simple question, 120-121
    breath, 117-118
    initiation, 122
    quieting the mind, 114-115
    transcendental (TM), 115
        consistency, 117
        mantra, 115-116
    visualization, 118
        Pure Love, 119-120

megalithic monuments, 240

methods
    increasing and maintaining devotion, 86
        chanting, 87-88
        cleansing rituals, 86-87
    service, 109-111
    teachers, 233-234

Mevlana Jalaluddin Rumi (Sufi teacher and poet), 133

Millman, Dan, 294

mind, quieting through meditation, 114-115

mindfulness, 24-25
    intuition, listening to your thoughts and feelings, 25-28

miracle of life, 248

mission of money, 180-181

mitzvoth, Judaism, 48

MMDA (drug), 282

moksha (liberation), Hinduism, 60

money, 179-181
    alternate road to wealth, 184
    anecdotes for money traps, 183-184
    mission statement, 181
    tithing, 185-187
    traps, 181
        arrogance, 182
        attachment, 182
        laziness, 183
        not having enough, 182
        selfishness, 182

monotheism, 46

monuments, 240

Moses model, making your vocation your vacation, 194-195

Mother Teresa, 296

motivations, seeking spirituality, 8-9

movies, 258
    comedy, 258-260
    dramas, 260-262
    hope and joy, 262-263

music, 283-284
    drumming, 284
    singing, 284

Muslims, forms of prayer, 96

N

naturalness of service, 105-107

need to be right, letting go in relationships, 150-151

needs
    awareness of partner's needs in relationships, 153-154
    versus wants, 108

negativity, 137-138
  avoiding learning
    from life situations,
    138
    blame, 139
    denial, 138
    distracting self
      from feeling
      pain, 138
  interpreting your
    negative emotions,
    142-144
  resistance, 139-140
    effect of single
      shortcomings,
      140
    signposts, 141
  serving as a catalyst
    to turn to a spiri-
    tual technique,
    144-146
Nirodha (Noble Truth
  of the End of
  Suffering), 63
nirvana, 31, 58
Noble Truth of
  Suffering (Dukka), 62
Noble Truth of the
  Cause of Suffering
  (Samudaya), 62
Noble Truth of the
  End of Suffering
  (Nirodha), 63
Noble Truth of the
  Path (Magga), 63
"not enough" money
  trap, 182

O

obstacles to service,
  107-109
Occult Web sites, 307
occupations. *See* livelihoods
opening up to cre-
  ation, 270
  inner critic, 270-271
  liberation, 271
outdoor sacred spaces,
  239-240
outer presence, 28
  awareness of activi-
    ties, 28-29
  experiencing simul-
    taneously with
    inner presence,
    enlightenment,
    31-33
  flow, 29
    feel of flow, 31
    turning any situa-
      tion into a flow
      activity, 29
  lost in thoughts, 29
overcoming
  judgment in rela-
    tionships, 154-155
    practicing forgive-
      ness, 154
  resistance, creativity,
    273

separateness in rela-
  tionships, 151
  answering ques-
    tions that reveal
    something about
    yourself, 152
Oxford Group, teach-
  ing personal relation-
  ship with God, 70-71

P

Pagan Web sites, 307
pain, eradication,
  253-254
Paul (disciple), teach-
  ings, 51-52
Peele, Dr. Stanton
  (addiction profes-
  sional), 76
philosophy versus reli-
  gion, Buddhism, 64
pilgrimage (Mecca),
  pillar of Islam, 54
pilgrimages, 243
  Assisi, 245
  El Santuario de
    Chimayo, 244
  history, 243-244
  India, 246
  Jerusalem, 246
  Santiago de
    Compostela, 245
pillars (Islam), 54
  charity (zakat), 54

faith (shahada), 54
the fast (Ramadan), 54
pilgrimage (Mecca), 54
prayer (salat), 54
power spots, 241
    Alfred Watkins, 241-242
    dowsing and mapping, 242
powerlessness, 71
practicing forgiveness, overcoming judgment in relationships, 154
pranayama yoga, 131
prayer, 91
    asking questions, 91-93
    forms of, 94-97
        Christianity, 97
        Hinduism, 94-95
        Judaism, 95-96
        Muslim, 96
    formula, 99-100
    grace through service, 93-94
    "let thy will be done," 97
    quiet time, 98-99
    salat, pillar of Islam, 54
    Thank-You prayer, 201-202

thanking versus asking, 200
presence, watching a self until it disappears, 170-171
present moment, 23
    inner presence, 24-25
        intuition, 25-28
    outer presence, 28
        awareness of activities, 28-29
        flow, 29-31
        lost in thoughts, 29
present-time awareness, 37-38
    transcending the ego, 38-39
prey (what you are looking for), 288
process versus product, creativity, 269
psychedelic drugs, altering states of consciousness, 282
pujas (cleansing ritual), 87
pure awareness, 37-38
Pure Love meditation, 119
    variations, 119-120

Q

Qigong, 127-129
qualities (spirituality)
    courage, 17
    curiosity, 20-21
    honesty, 14
    humility, 15-16
    humor, 16-17
    kindness, 18
    sense of urgency, 19
questions
    art of conversation, 212-213
    contemplating answers, active meditations, 120-121
    prayer, 91-93
quiet time prayer, 98-99

R

radical honesty, relationships, 149-150
Raja yoga, 127
Ram, 94
Ramadan (fast), pillar of Islam, 54
reacting machines, 168
readings, 264-266
recognizing teachers, questions to ask yourself, 232-233

relationships
    awareness of partner's needs,
        153-154
    letting go of blame
        and need to be
        right,
        150-151
    making shadows
        visible, 148
    overcoming judgment, 154-155
        practicing forgiveness, 154
    overcoming separateness, 151
        answering questions that reveal
            something about
            yourself, 152
    radical honesty,
        149-150
religions, 6-7, 46-47
    Buddhism
        devotion, acts of
            reverence, 81-82
        Eightfold Path, 63
        expansion, 64-65
        Four Noble
            Truths, 62-63
        karma, 62
        labeling moment-
            to-moment
            thoughts (mind-
            fulness), 24
        nirvana, 31, 58

philosophy versus
    religion, 64
    satori, 31
    Tantra, 278-280
    Web sites, 305
Christianity, 49
    devotion, 84-86
    forms of prayer,
        97
    inseparability of
        love and pain, 51
    judgments of
        Jesus, 50-51
    Paul's teachings,
        51-52
    Web sites, 306
Eastern
    Buddhism, 61-65
    Hinduism, 58-61
    Taoism, 65-68
Islam, 52
    Allah, 54
    Koran, 53
    masters, Shaykh,
        55
    pillars, 54
    Sufism, 55
    Web sites, 306
Judaism, 47
    bar mitzvah, 49
    forms of prayer,
        95-96
    laws, 47-48
    love and brother-
        hood, 48-49
    Web sites, 307

Western
    Christianity, 49
    Islam, 52
    Judaism, 47
remorse, 150
repetition of stories,
    selves recognition,
    169
resistance
    family and friends,
        172-173
    negativity, 139-140
        effect of single
            shortcomings,
            140
        signposts, 141
    overcoming (creativ-
        ity), 273
resources
    books and other
        readings, 264-266
    movies, 258
        comedy, 258-260
        dramas, 260-262
        hope and joy,
            262-263
    Web sites, 305
        Buddhism, 305
        Christianity, 306
        general spiritual-
            ity, 307-308
        Hinduism, 306
        Islam, 306
        Judaism, 307
        masters, 308-309
        Occult, 307
        Pagan, 307
        Taoism, 307

teachers, 308-309
teachings,
  308-309
yoga, 309
rhythm dancing, 285
Right Action
  (Eightfold Path), 63
Right Concentration
  (Eightfold Path), 63
Right Effort (Eightfold
  Path), 63
Right Mindfulness
  (Eightfold Path), 63
Right Speech
  (Eightfold Path), 63
Right Thought
  (Eightfold Path), 63
Right Understanding
  (Eightfold Path), 63
Right Work (Eightfold
  Path), 63
Righteous Winner
  (selves), 163-164
risking your way into
  life, avoiding the
  WET force, 209
    facing fears, 209
    gaining strength
      through growth,
      209-210
Robinson, Jonathan,
  297
Roth, Gabrielle (dance
  teacher and author),
  285
Rumi (mystic), 100

S

sacred spaces, 237
  altars, 237
    assembling your
      own, 238
    community, 239
  energy vortexes,
    242-243
  ley lines, 241
    Alfred Watkins,
      241-242
    dowsing and map-
      ping, 242
  monuments, 240
  outdoor, 239-240
  pilgrimages, 243
    Assisi, 245
    El Santuario de
      Chimayo, 244
    history, 243-244
    India, 246
    Jerusalem, 246
    Santiago de
      Compostela, 245
  power spots, 241
    Alfred Watkins,
      241-242
    dowsing and map-
      ping, 242
Sai Baba (guru), 83
Saint Francis of Assisi,
  15
salat (prayer), pillar of
  Islam, 54, 96
samadhi, 31

Samudaya (Noble
  Truth of the Cause of
  Suffering), 62
Santiago de
  Compostela (pilgrim-
  age), 245
Santos, Daniel
  (healer), 251
Saraswati, 94
satori, 31
secret potions, altering
  states of conscious-
  ness, 281
Sedona energy vor-
  texes, 242-243
    Airport Vortex, 243
    Bell Rock Vortex,
      243
    Boynton Canyon
      Vortex, 243
    Cathedral Rock
      Vortex, 243
seeking spirituality
  experimental atti-
    tude, 11-12
  highs and lows in
    feelings, 10-11
  motivations, 8-9
  sense of separation,
    9-10
self-consciousness, los-
  ing through outer
  presence, 28
    awareness of activi-
      ties, 28-29
    flow, 29-31
    lost in thoughts, 29
self-honesty, 14

self-importance, 41, 155
self-remembering, 32
selfishness (money trap), 182
selves, 158
  Anxious Stimulation Filler, 160
  Blaming Excuse Maker, 159
  disidentification, 168-169
  feeding deliberately, "I Want" exercise, 173
  Hurried Task Completer, 158-159
  Idle Worrier, 162-163
  imprisonment
    escaping the thought/selves prison, 40-42
    waking up, 39-40
  Know-It-All Judger, 164-166
  Looking Stupid Avoider, 161-162
  recognizing the repetition of our stories, 169
  Righteous Winner, 163-164
  seeing things without filtering or judgment, 37-38
  Selves Diagram, 36-37
  Task Completer Scanner, 158
  watching a self until it disappears, 170-171
Selves Diagram, 36
  subpersonalities, 37
sense of separation, seeking spirituality, 9-10
sense of urgency, 19
Sense of Wonder, A, 240
separateness, overcoming in relationships, 151
  answering questions that reveal something about yourself, 152
service, 103-105
  attitude, 111
  available needs, 109-111
  naturalness, 105-107
  obstacles, 107-109
  receiving grace through prayer, 93-94
sexuality, Tantra, 278-280
  circular breathing, 280-281
  making love in slow motion, 281
shadow side, art and healing, 275
shahada (faith), pillar of Islam, 54
shaktipat, 83-84
Shaykh, 55
sheikh (whirling master teacher), 133
shortcomings, effect on happiness, 140
Siddhartha, science of Buddhism, 57-62
  Eightfold Path, 63
  Four Noble Truths, 62-63
  karma, 62
Siegel, Bernie, M.D., 294
signposts, recognizing negative emotions, 141
sin, 158
sincerity, 19
Sinetar, Marsha, 295
singing, 284
Sobriety Demystified, 76
social censure, Judaism, 49
soft styles (Qigong martial arts), 128
softening around the pain, 253-254
soul, atman (Hinduism), 60
space, sacred. *See* sacred spaces
spiritual groups, 234-235
spirituality, 4

defining what you seek, 4
experimental attitude, 11-12
highs and lows in feelings, 10-11
motivations for seeking, 8-9
questions and answers, 4-6
sense of separation, 9-10
versus rituals, 6-7
wayward hope, 7-8
Web sites, 307-308
spontaneity, 211-212
Stonehenge, 240
Straight Track Club, 242
students of spirituality, 228
being a student of life, 230
dependence versus in-dependence, 229
dependentitis, 228
subpersonalities, Selves Diagram, 37
suffering, 144
Sufism, 55
Supreme Self, Hinduism, 60-61
surrendering to God, 196
Sweat Your Prayers: Movement as Spiritual Practice, 285

T

T'ai Chi, 130-131
Chungliang Al Huang's videos, 131
Tantra, 278-280
circular breathing, 280-281
making love in slow motion, 281
Tao Te Ching (Book of the Way and Its Power), Taoism, 66
Taoism
Chuang Tzu, 66
Lao Tzu, 65-66
Web sites, 307
yin-yang symbol, 67-68
Tart, Charles, 295-296
Task Completer Scanner (selves), 158
teachers, 230
Hinduism gurus, 60, 82-84
locating, 231
methods, 233-234
recognizing, 232
sheikhs (whirling), 133
spiritual groups, 234-235
Web sites, 308-309
teachings
Paul (disciple), 51-52

Web sites, 308-309
Ten Commandments, 48
Thank-You prayer, 201-202
thanking versus asking (gratitude), 200
Tibetan Book of the Dead, The, 248
tithing, 185-187
TM (transcendental meditation), 115
consistency, 117
mantra, 115-116
tools, consciousness growth, 36
Torah, 47
transcendental meditation. *See* TM
transcending the ego, 38-39
escaping the thought/selves prison, 40-42
waking up, 39-40
transformation, free energy, 172
dealing with resistance from friends and family, 172-173
traps of money, 181
arrogance, 182
attachment, 182
laziness, 183

not having enough, 182
selfishness, 182
treatment of animals, Judaism, 48
Twelve-Step approach
AA (Alcoholics Anonymous)
history, 70-71
steps, 72
addiction, 76-77
admitting condition, 75
assessing the condition of your spiritual life, 73
caring for others, 74-75
detractors, 76
Oxford Group teachings, 71
tzedeakah, Judaism, 48
Tzu, Chuang (mystic writer), 66
Tzu, Lao (originator of Taoism), 65-66

U-V

unintentional teachers, 231
urgency, 19

variations, Pure Love meditation, 119-120
Vipassana meditation (insight), 117
visualization meditation, 118
Pure Love, variations, 119-120
voluntary simplicity, 185
vortexes of energy, 242-243

W

wake-up calls, negative emotions, 144-146
wakefulness, 32
waking up (transcending the ego), 39-40
wants versus needs, 108
watching a self until it disappears, 170-171
Watkins, Alfred, 241-242
Wave, The, 285
way of the easiest thing. *See* WET force
Web sites, 305
Buddhism, 305
Christianity, 306
general spirituality, 307-308
Hinduism, 306
Islam, 306
Judaism, 307
masters, 308-309
Occult, 307
Pagan, 307
Taoism, 307
teachers and teachings, 308-309
yoga, 309
WET force (way of the easiest thing), 208
living your dreams, 210-211
risking your way into life, 209
facing fears, 209
gaining strength through growth, 209-210
whirling, 133
whirling dervishes, 285
Who Dies?, 253
Williamson, Marianne, 296-297
work. *See* livelihoods

X-Z

XTC (drug), 282

Yantra yoga, 127
yin-yang symbol, Taoism, 67-68
yoga, 59, 126-127
Bhakti-yoga (Hindu devotion), 58, 80, 127
deities, 80-81
hatha, 126
Jnana yoga, 58, 127
karma, 127, 195-196

acting without
attachment, 197
surrendering to
God, 196
mantra, 127
pranayama, 131
Raja, 127
Web sites, 309
Yantra, 127

zakat (charity), pillar
of Islam, 54

Quality Tapes and Books

by Jonathan Robinson

Special Offer for Readers of
The Complete Idiot's Guide to
Awakening Your Spirituality

AUDIO TAPES ($10 each or three tapes for $25):

1. *The Ten Minute Pure Love Meditation.* On side one, the art of meditation is described. On side two, a 10-minute guided meditation is provided that moves many people to tears of joy in a very short period of time.

2. *Seven Secrets to Greater Happiness.* Learn the seven key behaviors that truly lead to a life of inner fulfillment and long-term satisfaction.

3. *Playful and Passionate Relationships.* Describes several simple actions for creating long-term satisfying relationships. Includes practical suggestions for keeping love and romance alive.

4. *A Spiritual Approach to Money and Work* **(four tapes plus workbook for $30).** In this full-day seminar, Jonathan Robinson provides a step-by-step approach for making more money doing what you love, making work more meaningful and enjoyable, marketing yourself more effectively, and staying consistently motivated.

VIDEOS ($19.95 each):

1. *Intimacy and Sexual Ecstasy.* Learn the best ways to increase pleasure, romance, and communication. Includes attractive couples demonstrating advanced sexual techniques known as Tantra. For adults only.

2. *Sixty Minutes to a Smoke-Free Life.* Learn how to finally quit cigarettes for good. Includes methods for overcoming cravings, staying consistently motivated over a long period of time, and avoiding weight gain.

BOOKS:

1. *Real Wealth: A Spiritual Approach to Money and Work* ($12.95)

2. *Communication Miracles: Creating More Love and Less Conflict* ($10.95)

3. *The Experience of God: How Well-Known Seekers Encounter the Sacred* ($12.95)

4. *Instant Insight: 200 Ways to Create the Life You Really Want* ($8.95)

5. *The Little Book of Big Questions* ($8.95)

6. *Shortcuts to Bliss: The 50 Best Ways to Enhance Your Life* ($11.95)

7. *Shortcuts to Success: Master Your Money, Time, Health and Relationships* ($12.95)

Learn more about these books and other offerings of Jonathan Robinson by visiting his Web site at **www.howtotools.com.**

YOU CAN ORDER THESE BOOKS DIRECTLY FROM HIS WEB SITE AND AVOID SHIPPING CHARGES!

Order form on NEXT PAGE

Yes, send me my copies of Jonathan's wonderful tapes and books.

AUDIO TAPES:

❏ *The Ten Minute Pure Love Meditation* $10

❏ *Seven Secrets to Greater Happiness* $10

❏ *Playful and Passionate Relationships* $10

❏ All three of the above tapes $25

❏ *A Spiritual Approach to Money and Work* (four tapes) $30

VIDEOS:

❏ *Intimacy and Sexual Ecstasy* $19.95

❏ *Sixty Minutes to a Smoke-Free Life* $19.95

BOOKS:

❏ *Real Wealth: A Spiritual Approach to Money ...* $12.95

❏ *Communication Miracles: Creating More Love ...* $10.95

❏ *The Experience of God ...* $12.95

❏ *Instant Insight ...* $8.95

❏ *The Little Book of Big Questions* $8.95

❏ *Shortcuts to Bliss ...* $11.95

❏ *Shortcuts to Success ...* $12.95

Shipping/handling charges:

Audio/Video/Book: Add $3.00 for one or two items;
add $.50 for each additional item.   _____

Subtotal: _____

California residents add 7% sales tax: _____

TOTAL: _____

Payment to be made in U.S. funds

❏ Check or money order enclosed

❏ I'd like to charge to (for $20 or more):
     ❏ MasterCard   ❏ Visa

Account #: _____

Exp. Date: _____ Signature: _____

Send this order form with your check, money order, or charge information to:

Jonathan Robinson
278 Via El Encantador
Santa Barbara, CA 93111

OR fax to: 805-967-4128

Allow up to four to six weeks for delivery.

Ship to:

Name: _____

Address: _____

City, State, Zip: _____

E-mail: _____ Telephone: _____